GIRL GENIUS

AGATHA HETERODYNE
&
THE CLOCKWORK PRINCESS

A Gaslamp Fantasy
with
ADVENTURE, ROMANCE & MAD SCIENCE

Story by Kaja & Phil
Pencils by Phil Fog
Colors by Cheyenne Wright

AIRSHIP
ENTERTAINMENT

OTHER BOOKS FROM AIRSHIP ENTERTAINMENT
AND STUDIO FOGLIO

Girl Genius® Graphic Novels

Girl Genius Volume One:
Agatha Heterodyne and the Beetleburg Clank

Girl Genius Volume Two:
Agatha Heterodyne and the Airship City

Girl Genius Volume Three:
Agatha Heterodyne and the Monster Engine

Girl Genius Volume Four:
Agatha Heterodyne and the Circus of Dreams

Girl Genius Volume Five:
Agatha Heterodyne and the Clockwork Princess

Girl Genius Volume Six:
Agatha Heterodyne and the Golden Trilobite

Girl Genius Volume Seven:
Agatha Heterodyne and the Voice of the Castle

Girl Genius Volume Eight:
Agatha Heterodyne and the Chapel of Bones

Girl Genius Volume Nine:
Agatha Heterodyne and the Heirs of the Storm

Girl Genius Volume Ten:
Agatha Heterodyne and the Guardian Muse

Girl Genius Volume Eleven:
Agatha Heterodyne and the Hammerless Bell

Girl Genius Volume Twelve:
Agatha Heterodyne and the Siege of Mechanicsburg

Girl Genius® Novels

Girl Genius: Agatha H. and the Airship City

Girl Genius: Agatha H. and the Clockwork Princess

Girl Genius® is published by:
Airship Entertainment™: a happy part of Studio Foglio, LLC
2400 NW 80th St #129 Seattle WA 98117-4449, USA

Please visit our Web sites at www.airshipbooks.com and www.girlgenius.net

Story by Phil & Kaja Foglio. Pencils by Phil Foglio. Main story colors by Cheyenne Wright. Selected spot illustrations colored by Kaja Foglio and/or Cheyenne Wright. Logos, Lettering, Artist Bullying & Book Design by Kaja. Fonts mostly by Comicraft– www.comicbookfonts.com.

The material in this collection originally appeared from June 2005-March 2006 at www.girlgenius.net.

Fourth Printing: September 2013 • ISBN 978-1-890856-39-7
PRINTED IN THE USA

This book is dedicated to Phil's Mother, Ottilie Dorothea Millson, maker of monster-makers.

KAJA FOGLIO

Professor Foglio was, late last fall, informed that she had been selected to participate in a mandatory academic exchange program with the University of Pu'lukka Ranga, located on a rather small island somewhere in the Pacific. Realizing that she would no longer need her winter ensemble, she graciously presented her famously distinctive lab-grown "über-chinchilla" coat to her academic rival, the head of the Department of Socioeconomic Storytelling. By some odd coincidence, the head of the Department of Socioeconomic Storytelling was mysteriously abducted the next day, never to be heard from again save for a hastily scrawled note-in-a-bottle found washed up on the beach several months later. This note, although mostly incoherent, appeared to be mainly an analysis of the economic costs of being marooned upon a volcanic island populated exclusively by a type of giant saurian as yet unknown to Science. Professor Foglio has heard nothing further about the academic exchange program, and hopes that the proceeds from the sale of this textbook will allow her to buy a new coat.

PHIL FOGLIO

Continues his field research into the early life of Agatha Heterodyne, a task until recently made ever more difficult by the proliferation of sensationalist novels purporting to chronicle the life of lady Heterodyne, only without so many clothes. Professor Foglio has labored mightily to explain to these fabricators that they are spreading misinformation, unduly influencing the reading public's perception of the Lady Heterodyne, and stealing the Professor's ideas without sufficient remuneration. Surprisingly few of these publishers burned to the ground in unexpected ways before word got around, and such faux chronicles are quite rare of late. He is, however, quite fond of the series of music-hall songs currently making the rounds in the larger towns, and has been known to belt out all twenty-five verses of "Whoops Now, My Lady, Your Monster's Loose Again" if no one manages to stop him in time.

CHEYENNE WRIGHT

Recently, Professor Wright has taken up residence within the ruins of the late Professor Voltavia's "Thunder Tower'" which, despite the craters, continues to dominate the skyline of T.P.U.'s eastern campus; even after the recent interdepartmental fracas between the (ultimately triumphant) Department of Meteorology and the Department of Falling Sky Rocks (formerly Meteoritics). It is there that he continues his experiments with "Artificial Color." You can view the latest results of his research at www.arcanetimes.com.

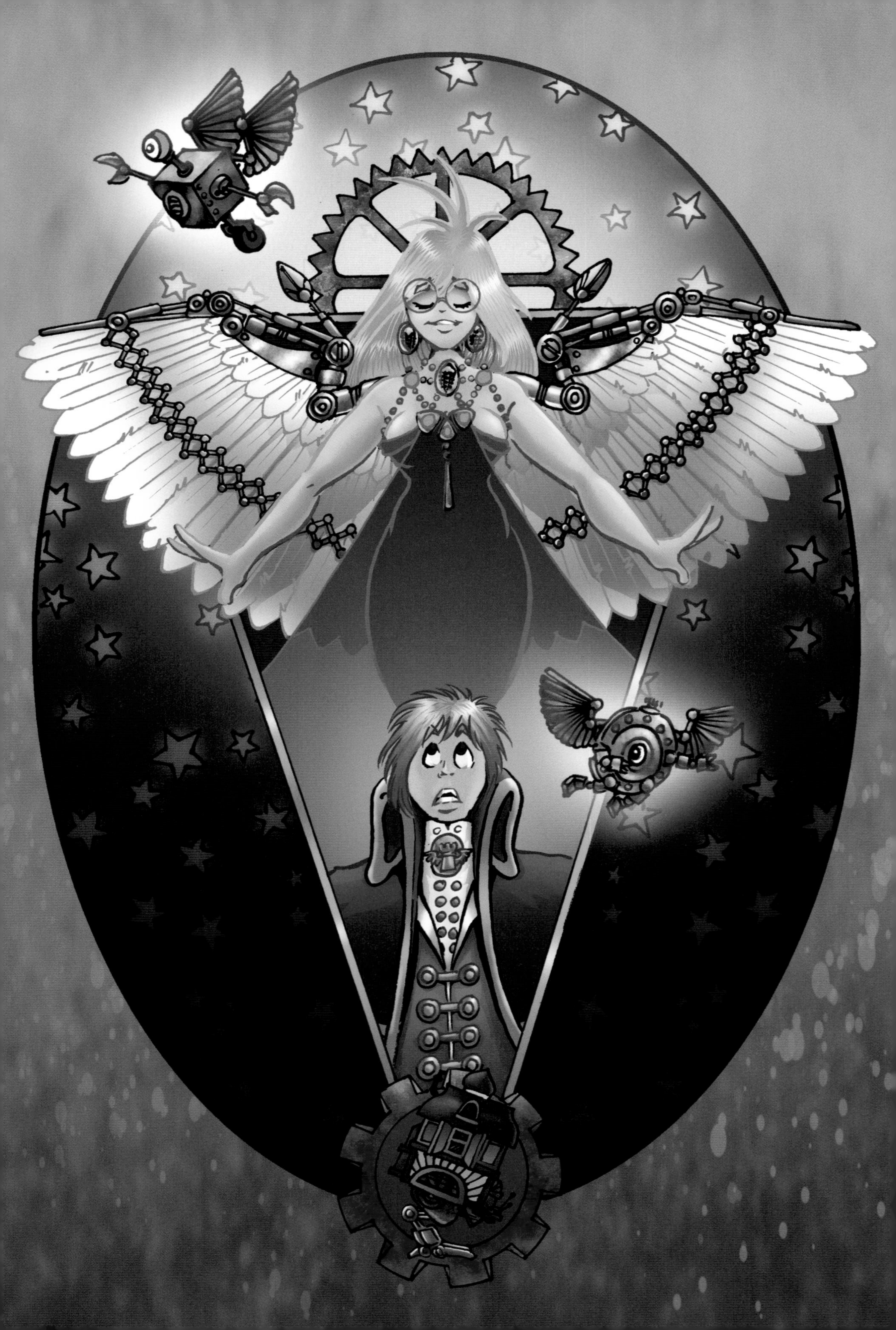

• THE STORY SO FAR •

Agatha Clay is a young Mad Scientist (or "Spark" to be polite.) Traveling with her is Krosp I, a failed experiment created to be the "Emperor of all Cats."

Agatha is also the last of the famous Heterodyne family—beloved heroes who disappeared under mysterious circumstances many years ago. Folk legend claims that they will someday return, but so far they haven't managed it.

Agatha and Krosp have just escaped from Baron Klaus Wulfenbach—a powerful Spark who rules most of Europe. After crashing their small dirigible, they met Master Payne's Circus of Adventure—a traveling show specializing in popular melodramas about the Heterodynes. Now, thanks to a ruse concocted by the Circus, the Baron believes that Agatha is dead. Unfortunately, so does the Baron's son Gilgamesh, who became very attached to Agatha while she was staying on board the giant airship *Castle Wulfenbach*.

The circus players are happy with the success of their trick, and although Agatha now feels safe, her new friend Zeetha is not so sure. Zeetha is the lost princess of a lost city, and a fearsome swordmistress. She has decided to teach Agatha to defend herself—whether she likes it or not.

Although everyone in the Circus knows that Agatha is a Spark, they do not know that she is a member of the real-life Heterodyne family. In the Heterodyne plays Agatha is given the role of Lucrezia Mongfish, the "villain's beautiful daughter" who later married Bill Heterodyne and became Agatha's mother. She finds this very odd, but plays her part well. Agatha can be a lot like her mother, especially when she is angry…or really into a part.

Recently, the Circus encountered three live Jägermonsters who had been hung on a gallows and left to die. The Jägermonsters are a group of monstrous soldiers created by the not-so-heroic ancestors of the Heterodynes, and they have never been popular. Most of them now work for the Baron. Agatha set the hanging Jägers free and they disappeared into the night, but they may still be out there somewhere…

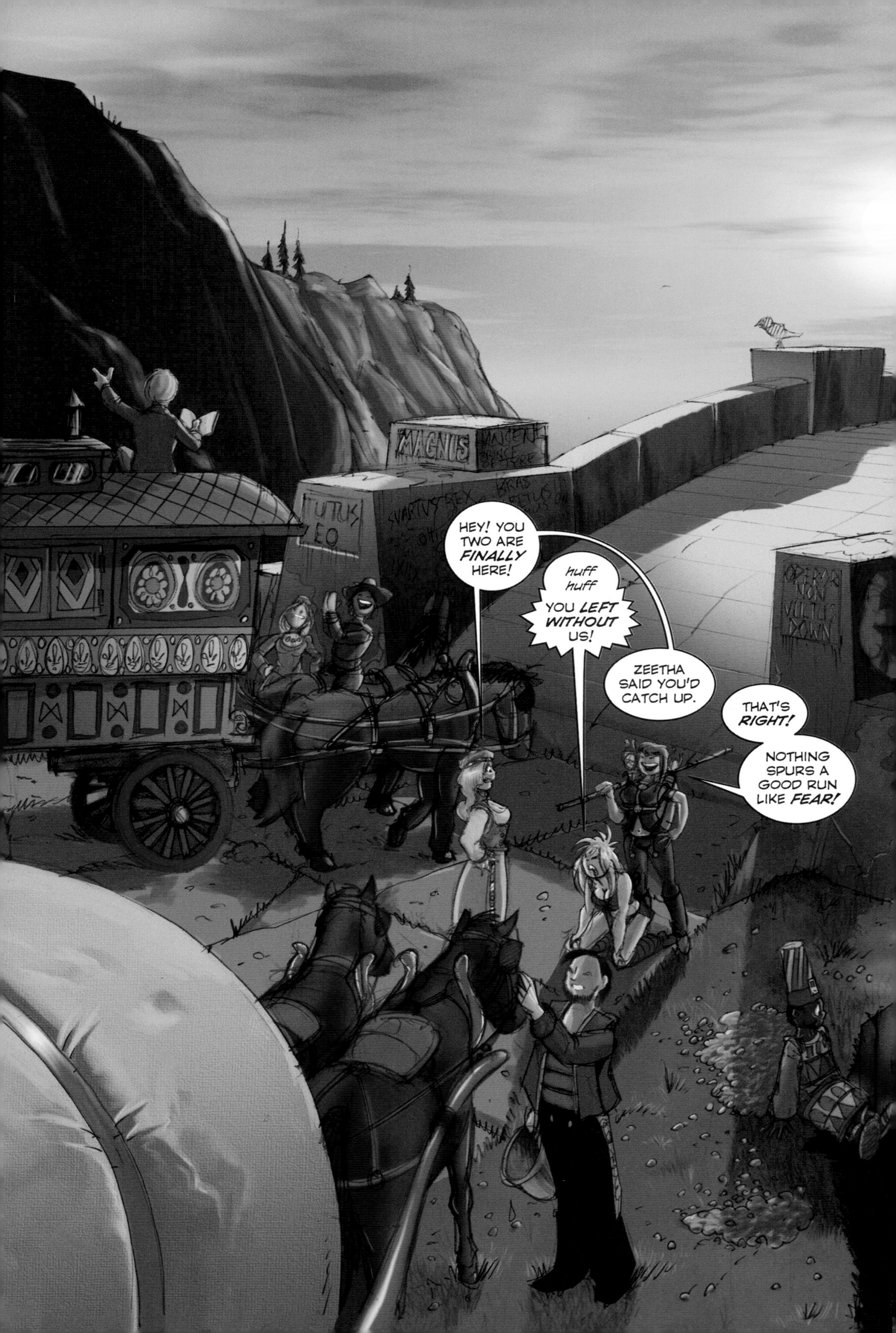
HEY! YOU TWO ARE *FINALLY* HERE!
huff huff
YOU *LEFT WITHOUT* US!
ZEETHA SAID YOU'D CATCH UP.
THAT'S *RIGHT!*
NOTHING SPURS A GOOD RUN LIKE *FEAR!*

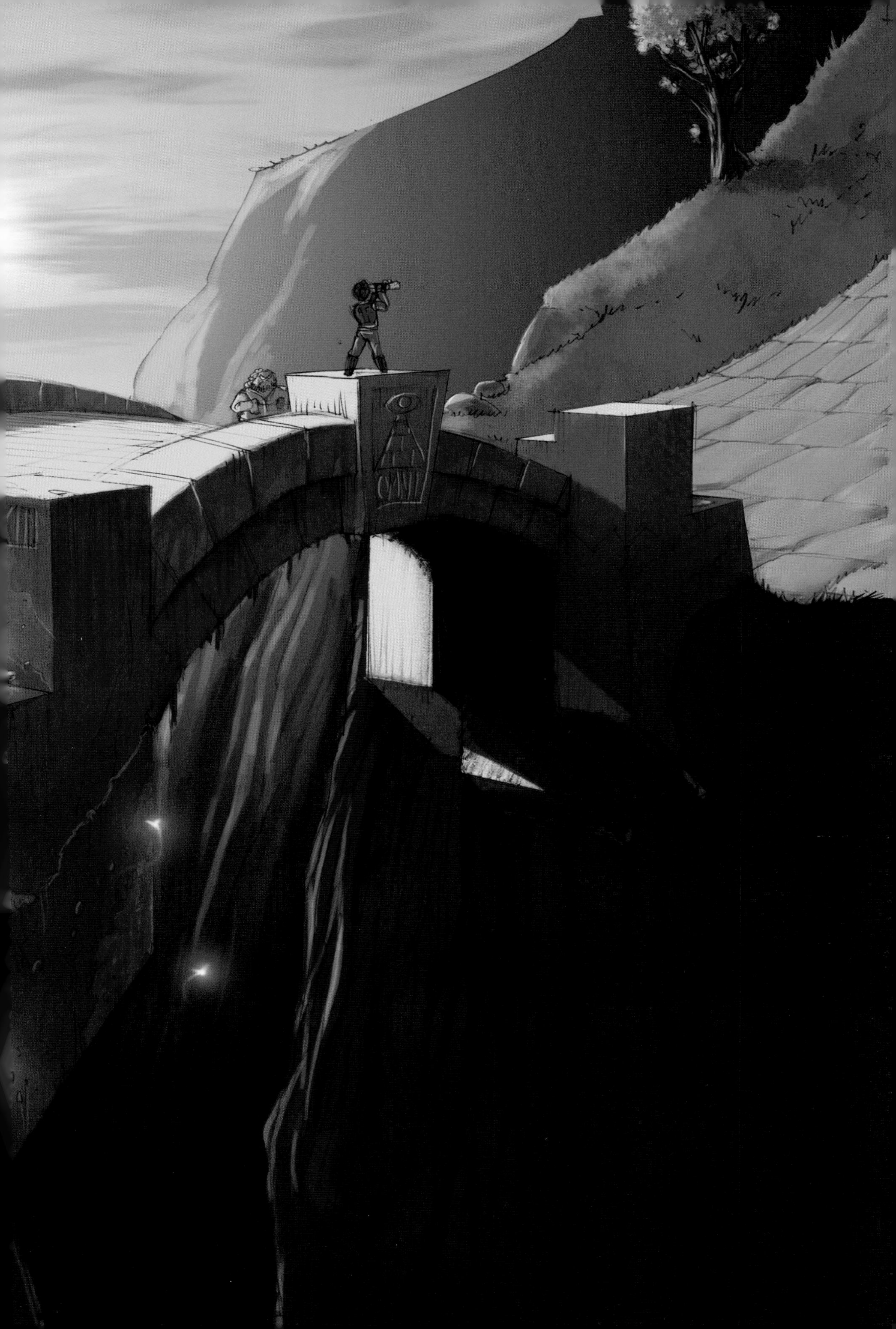
OMNI

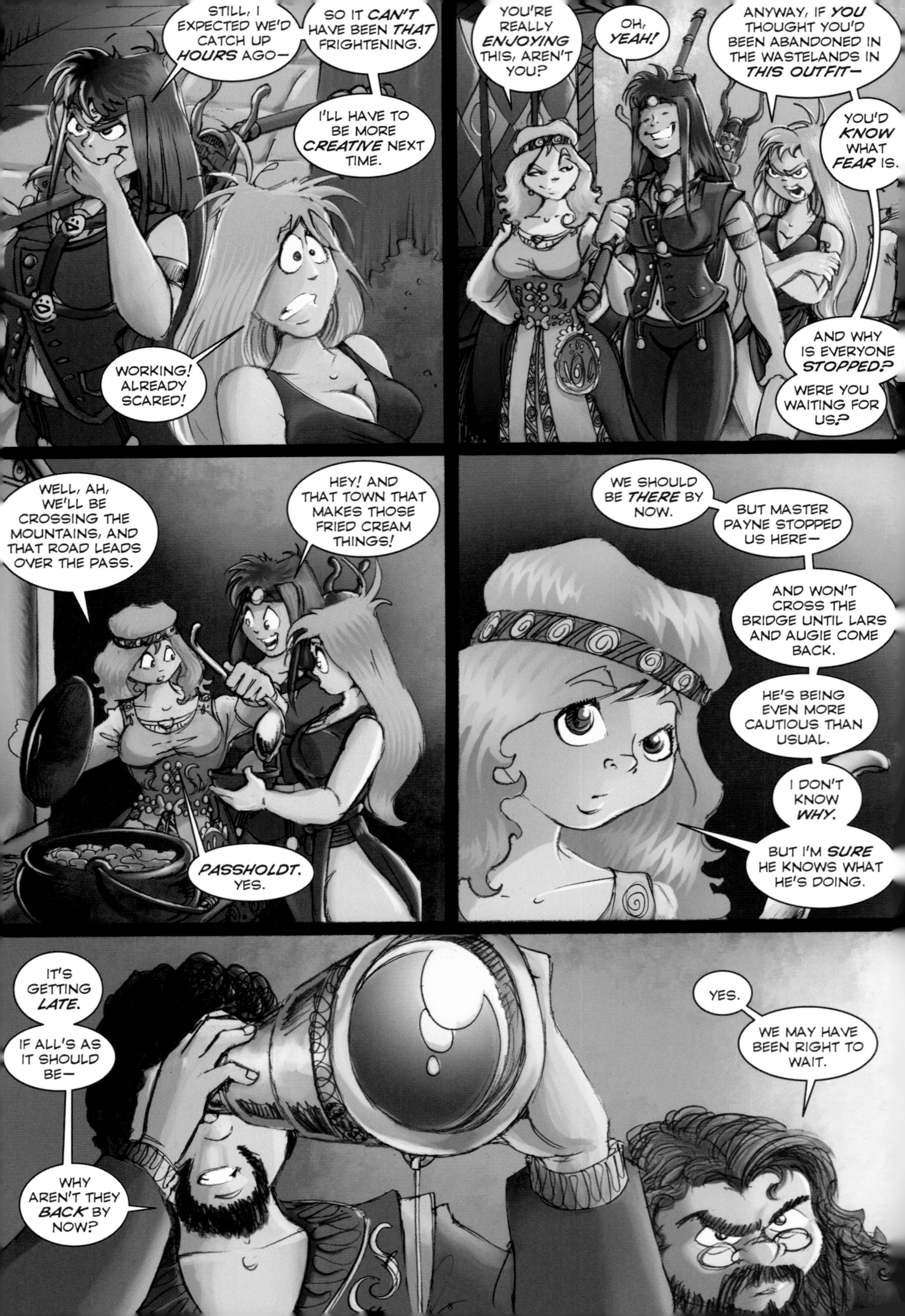
STILL, I EXPECTED WE'D CATCH UP HOURS AGO—
SO IT CAN'T HAVE BEEN THAT FRIGHTENING.
I'LL HAVE TO BE MORE CREATIVE NEXT TIME.
WORKING! ALREADY SCARED!
YOU'RE REALLY ENJOYING THIS, AREN'T YOU?
OH, YEAH!
ANYWAY, IF YOU THOUGHT YOU'D BEEN ABANDONED IN THE WASTELANDS IN THIS OUTFIT—
YOU'D KNOW WHAT FEAR IS.
AND WHY IS EVERYONE STOPPED?
WERE YOU WAITING FOR US?
WELL, AH, WE'LL BE CROSSING THE MOUNTAINS, AND THAT ROAD LEADS OVER THE PASS.
HEY! AND THAT TOWN THAT MAKES THOSE FRIED CREAM THINGS!
PASSHOLDT. YES.
WE SHOULD BE THERE BY NOW.
BUT MASTER PAYNE STOPPED US HERE—
AND WON'T CROSS THE BRIDGE UNTIL LARS AND AUGIE COME BACK.
HE'S BEING EVEN MORE CAUTIOUS THAN USUAL.
I DON'T KNOW WHY.
BUT I'M SURE HE KNOWS WHAT HE'S DOING.
IT'S GETTING LATE.
IF ALL'S AS IT SHOULD BE—
WHY AREN'T THEY BACK BY NOW?
YES.
WE MAY HAVE BEEN RIGHT TO WAIT.

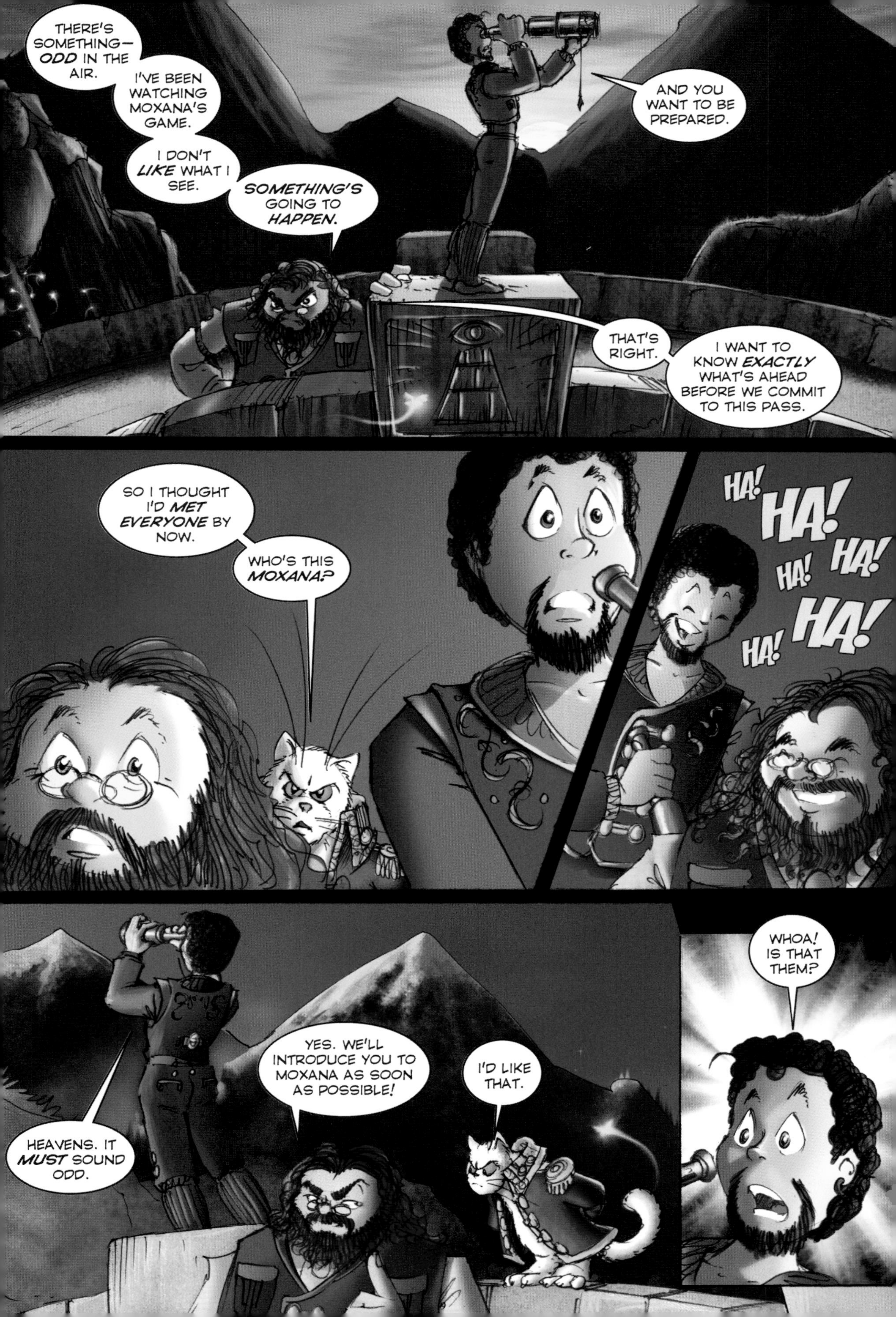
THERE'S SOMETHING— *ODD* IN THE AIR.
I'VE BEEN WATCHING MOXANA'S GAME.
I DON'T *LIKE* WHAT I SEE.
SOMETHING'S GOING TO *HAPPEN.*
AND YOU WANT TO BE PREPARED.
THAT'S RIGHT.
I WANT TO KNOW *EXACTLY* WHAT'S AHEAD BEFORE WE COMMIT TO THIS PASS.
SO I THOUGHT I'D *MET EVERYONE* BY NOW.
WHO'S THIS *MOXANA?*
HA! HA! HA! HA! HA! HA!
HEAVENS. IT *MUST* SOUND ODD.
YES. WE'LL INTRODUCE YOU TO MOXANA AS SOON AS POSSIBLE!
I'D LIKE THAT.
WHOA! IS THAT THEM?

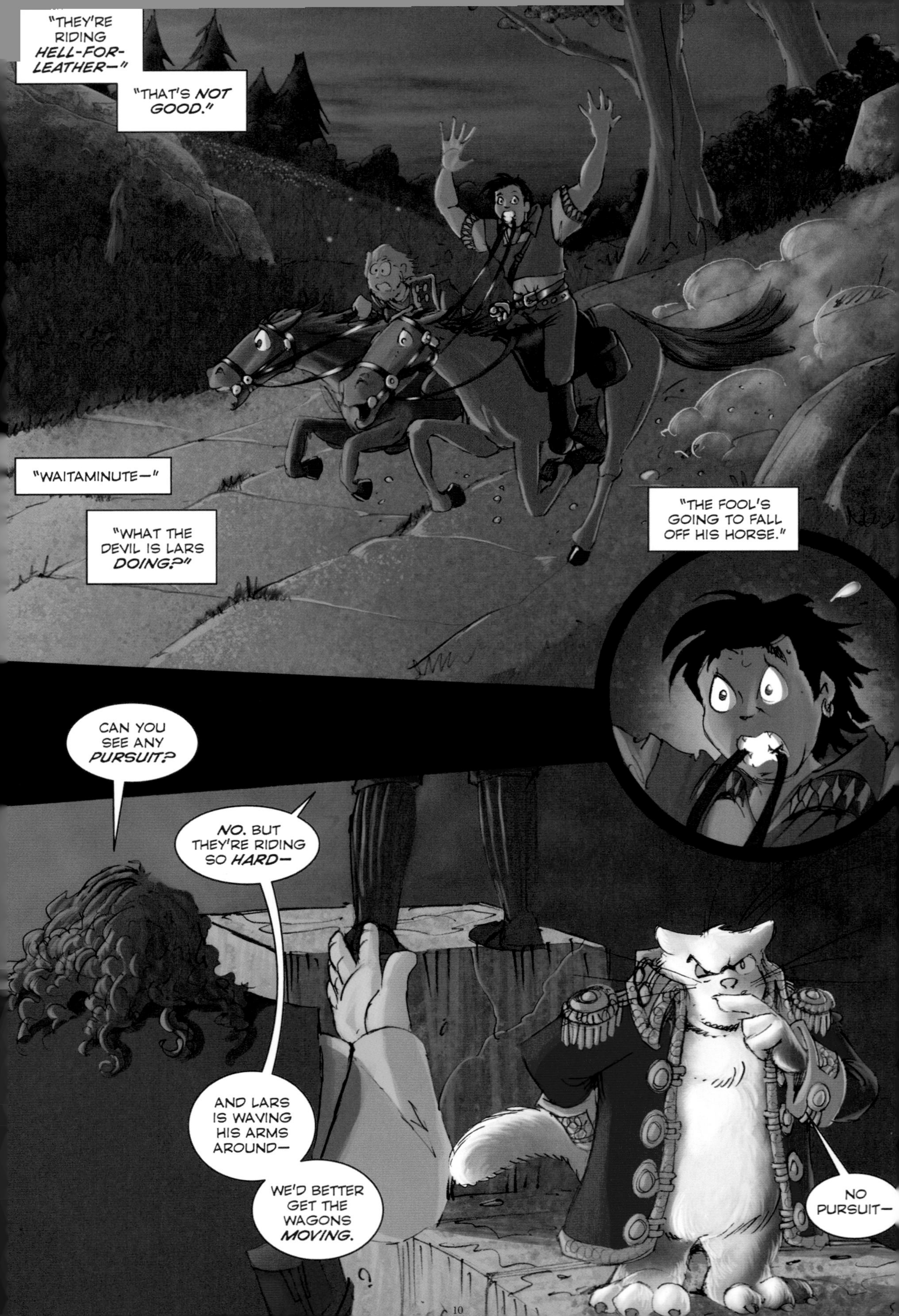
"THEY'RE RIDING HELL-FOR-LEATHER—"
"THAT'S NOT GOOD."
"WAITAMINUTE—"
"WHAT THE DEVIL IS LARS DOING?"
"THE FOOL'S GOING TO FALL OFF HIS HORSE."
CAN YOU SEE ANY PURSUIT?
NO. BUT THEY'RE RIDING SO HARD—
AND LARS IS WAVING HIS ARMS AROUND—
WE'D BETTER GET THE WAGONS MOVING.
NO PURSUIT—

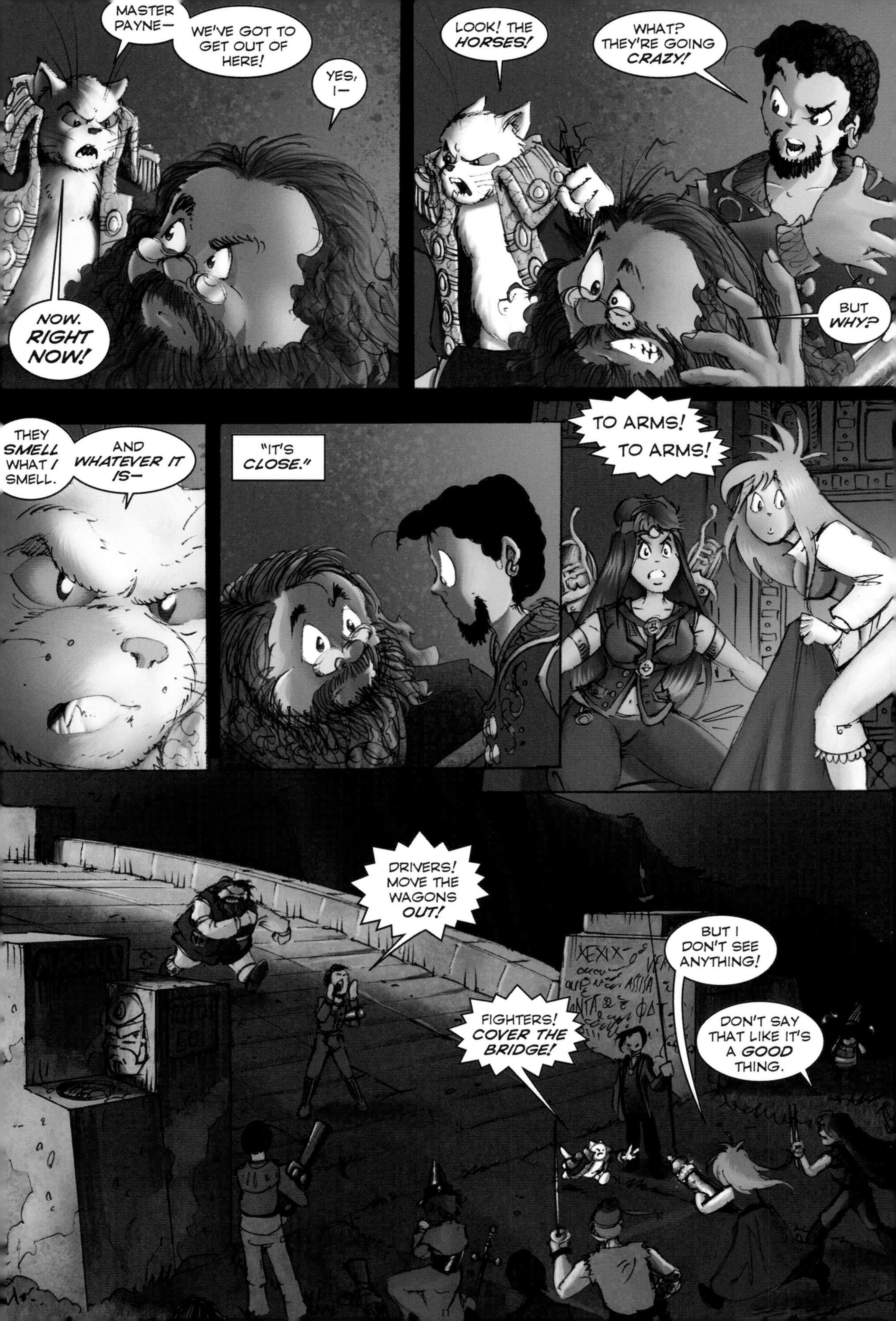
MASTER PAYNE—
WE'VE GOT TO GET OUT OF HERE!
YES, I—
NOW. RIGHT NOW!
LOOK! THE HORSES!
WHAT? THEY'RE GOING CRAZY!
BUT WHY?
THEY SMELL WHAT I SMELL.
AND WHATEVER IT IS—
"IT'S CLOSE."
TO ARMS! TO ARMS!
DRIVERS! MOVE THE WAGONS OUT!
FIGHTERS! COVER THE BRIDGE!
BUT I DON'T SEE ANYTHING!
DON'T SAY THAT LIKE IT'S A GOOD THING.

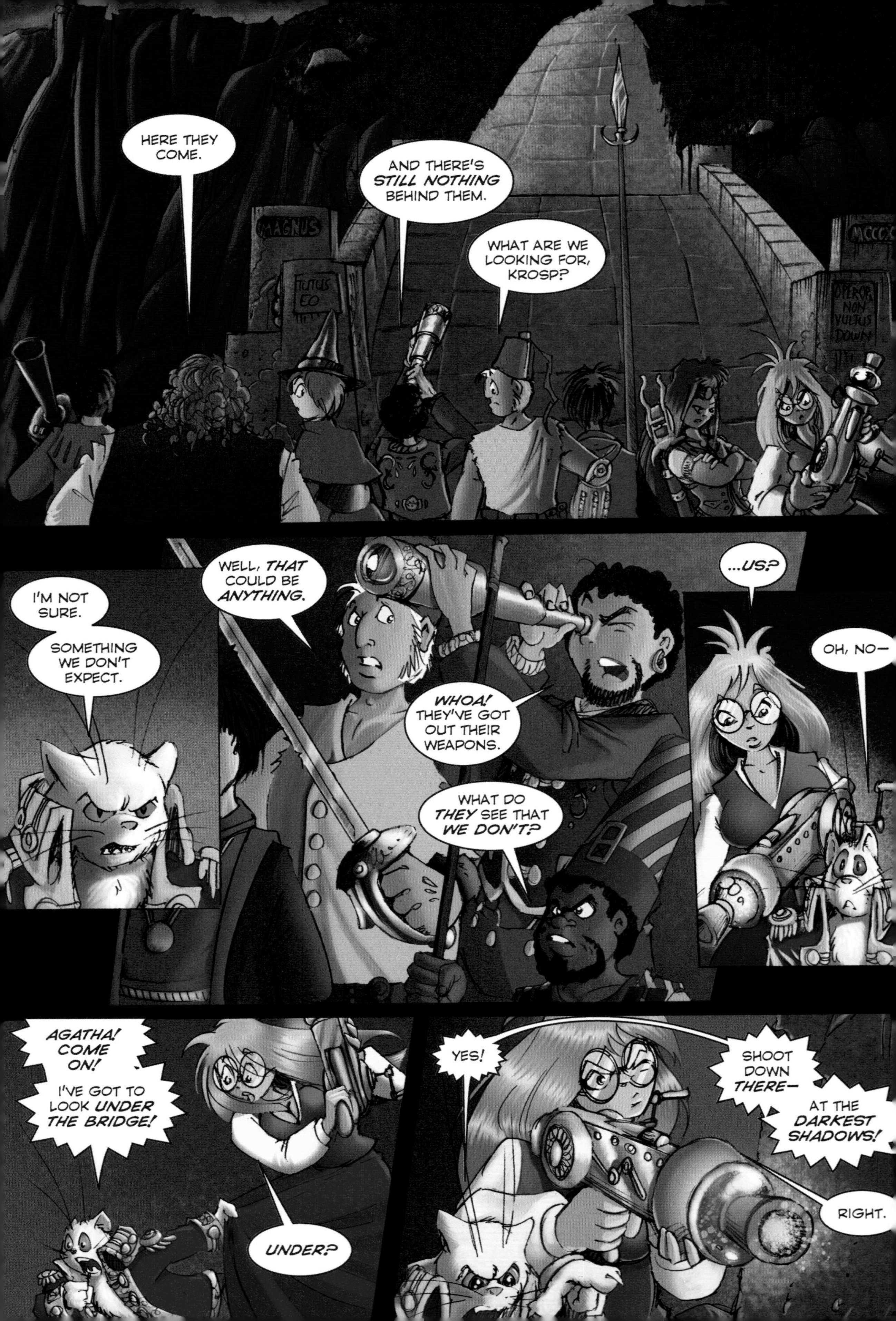

HERE THEY COME.
AND THERE'S STILL NOTHING BEHIND THEM.
WHAT ARE WE LOOKING FOR, KROSP?
MAGNUS
TUTUS EO
OPEROR NON VULTUS DOWN
I'M NOT SURE.
SOMETHING WE DON'T EXPECT.
WELL, THAT COULD BE ANYTHING.
WHOA! THEY'VE GOT OUT THEIR WEAPONS.
WHAT DO THEY SEE THAT WE DON'T?
...US?
OH, NO—
AGATHA! COME ON!
I'VE GOT TO LOOK UNDER THE BRIDGE!
UNDER?
YES!
SHOOT DOWN THERE—
AT THE DARKEST SHADOWS!
RIGHT.

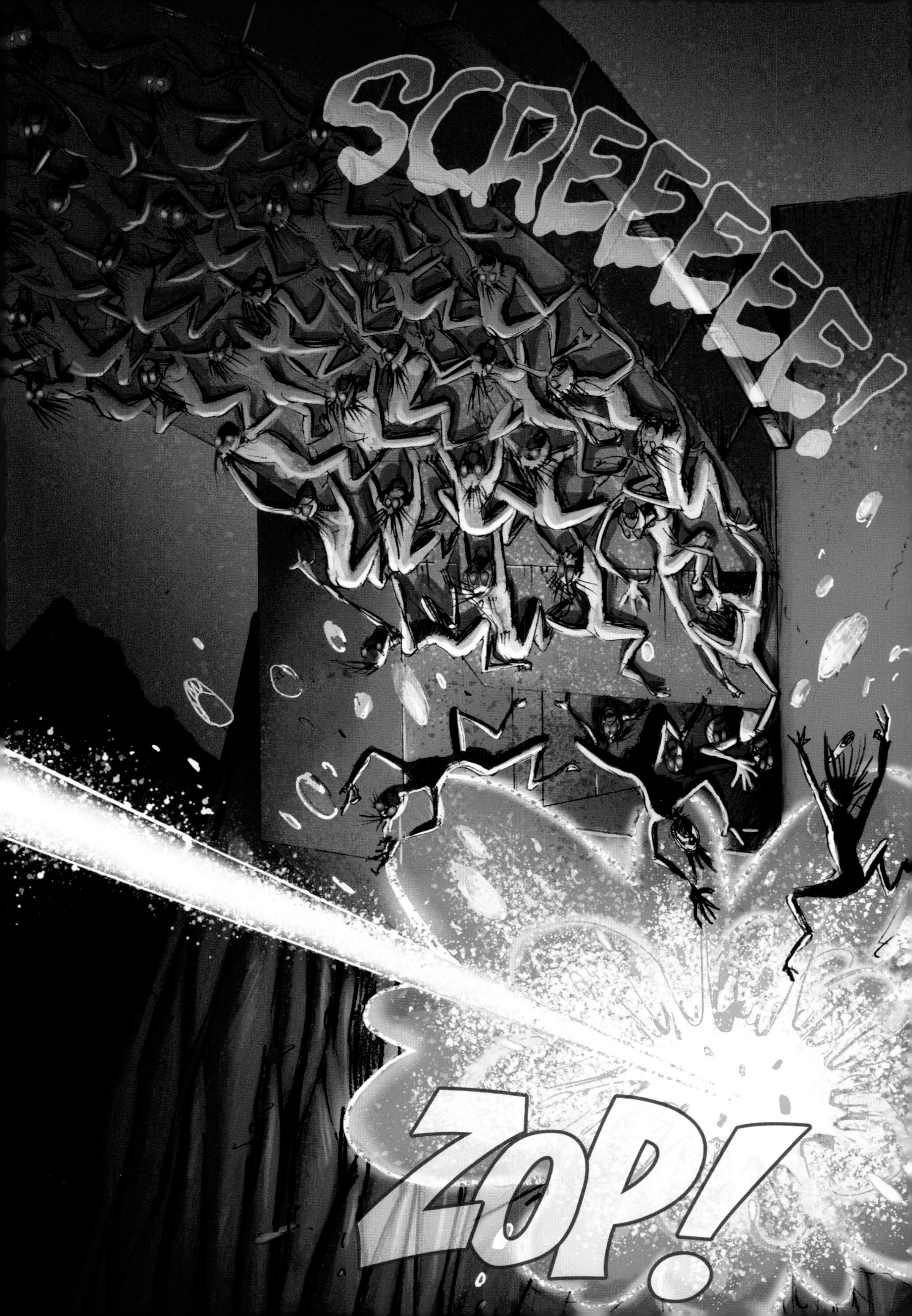
SCREEEEE!
ZOP!

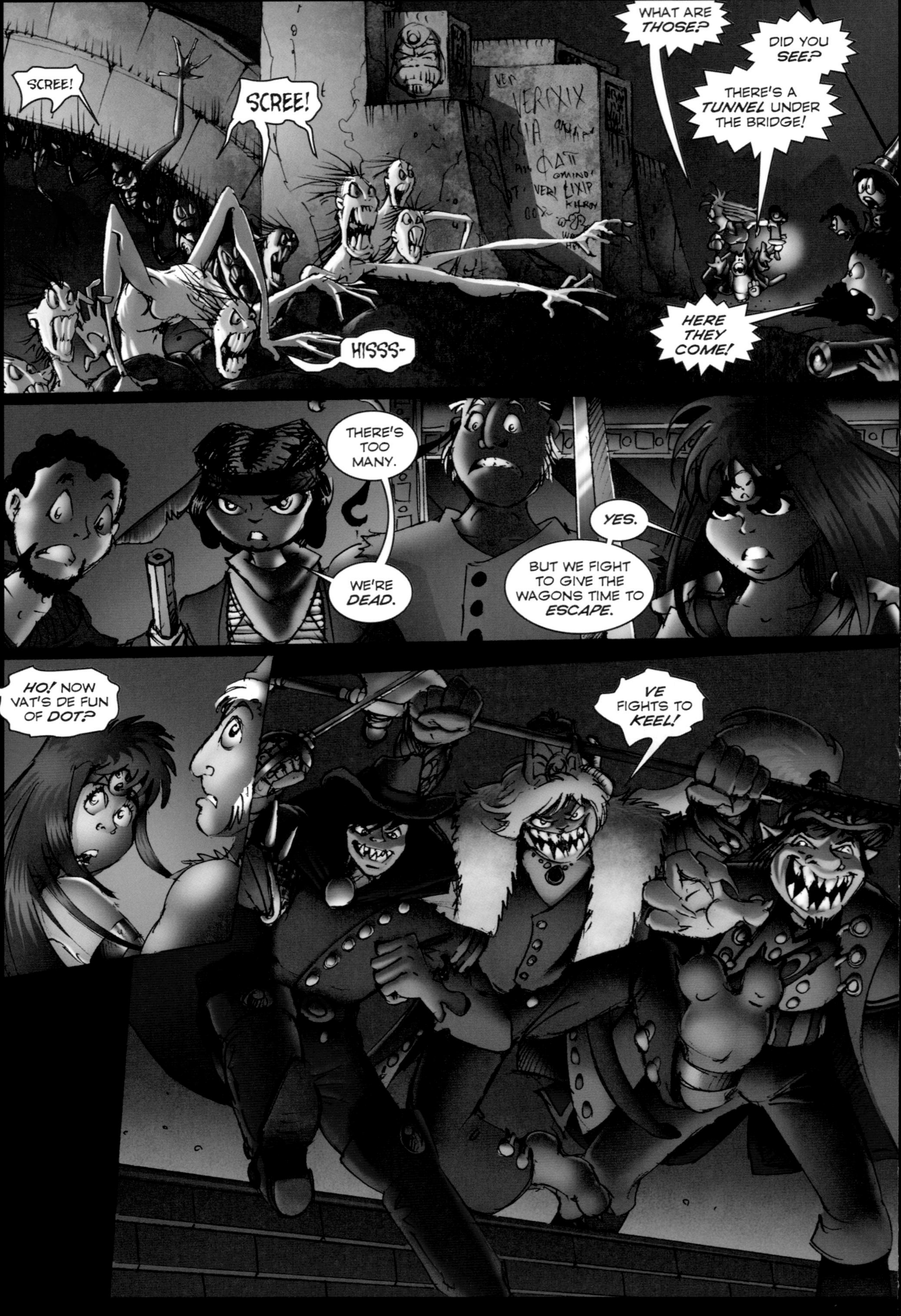
SCREE!
SCREE!
HISSS-
WHAT ARE THOSE?
DID YOU SEE?
THERE'S A TUNNEL UNDER THE BRIDGE!
HERE THEY COME!
THERE'S TOO MANY.
WE'RE DEAD.
YES.
BUT WE FIGHT TO GIVE THE WAGONS TIME TO ESCAPE.
HO! NOW VAT'S DE FUN OF DOT?
VE FIGHTS TO KEEL!

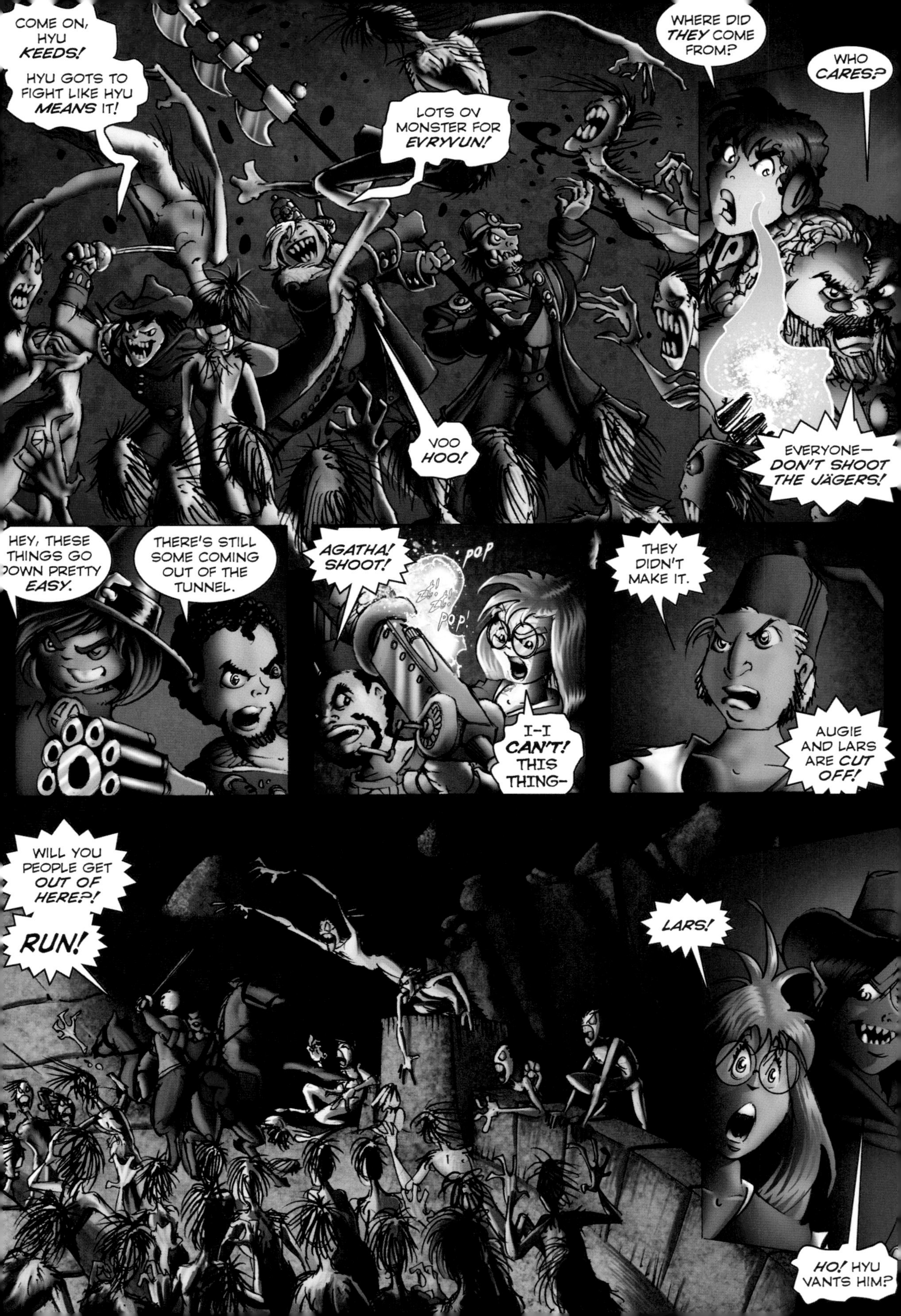
COME ON, HYU KEEDS!
HYU GOTS TO FIGHT LIKE HYU MEANS IT!
LOTS OV MONSTER FOR EVRYVUN!
WHERE DID THEY COME FROM?
WHO CARES?
VOO HOO!
EVERYONE— DON'T SHOOT THE JÄGERS!
HEY, THESE THINGS GO DOWN PRETTY EASY.
THERE'S STILL SOME COMING OUT OF THE TUNNEL.
AGATHA! SHOOT!
POP
ZT! ZT!
POP!
I-I CAN'T! THIS THING-
THEY DIDN'T MAKE IT.
AUGIE AND LARS ARE CUT OFF!
WILL YOU PEOPLE GET OUT OF HERE?!
RUN!
LARS!
HO! HYU VANTS HIM?

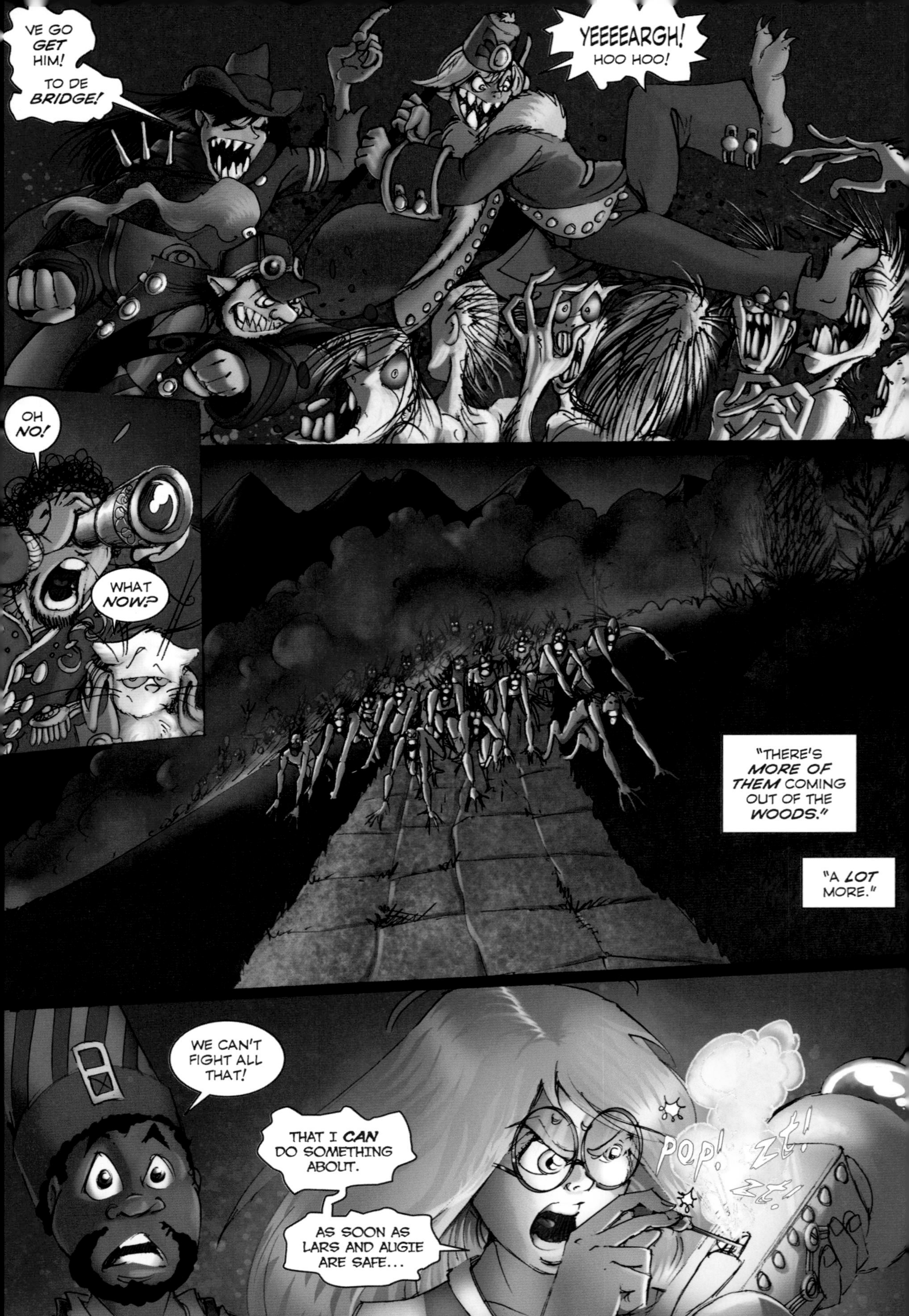

VE GO *GET* HIM!
TO DE *BRIDGE!*
YEEEEARGH! HOO HOO!
OH *NO!*
WHAT *NOW?*
"THERE'S *MORE OF THEM* COMING OUT OF THE *WOODS.*"
"A *LOT* MORE."
WE CAN'T FIGHT ALL THAT!
THAT I *CAN* DO SOMETHING ABOUT.
AS SOON AS LARS AND AUGIE ARE SAFE...
POP! ZT! ZZT!

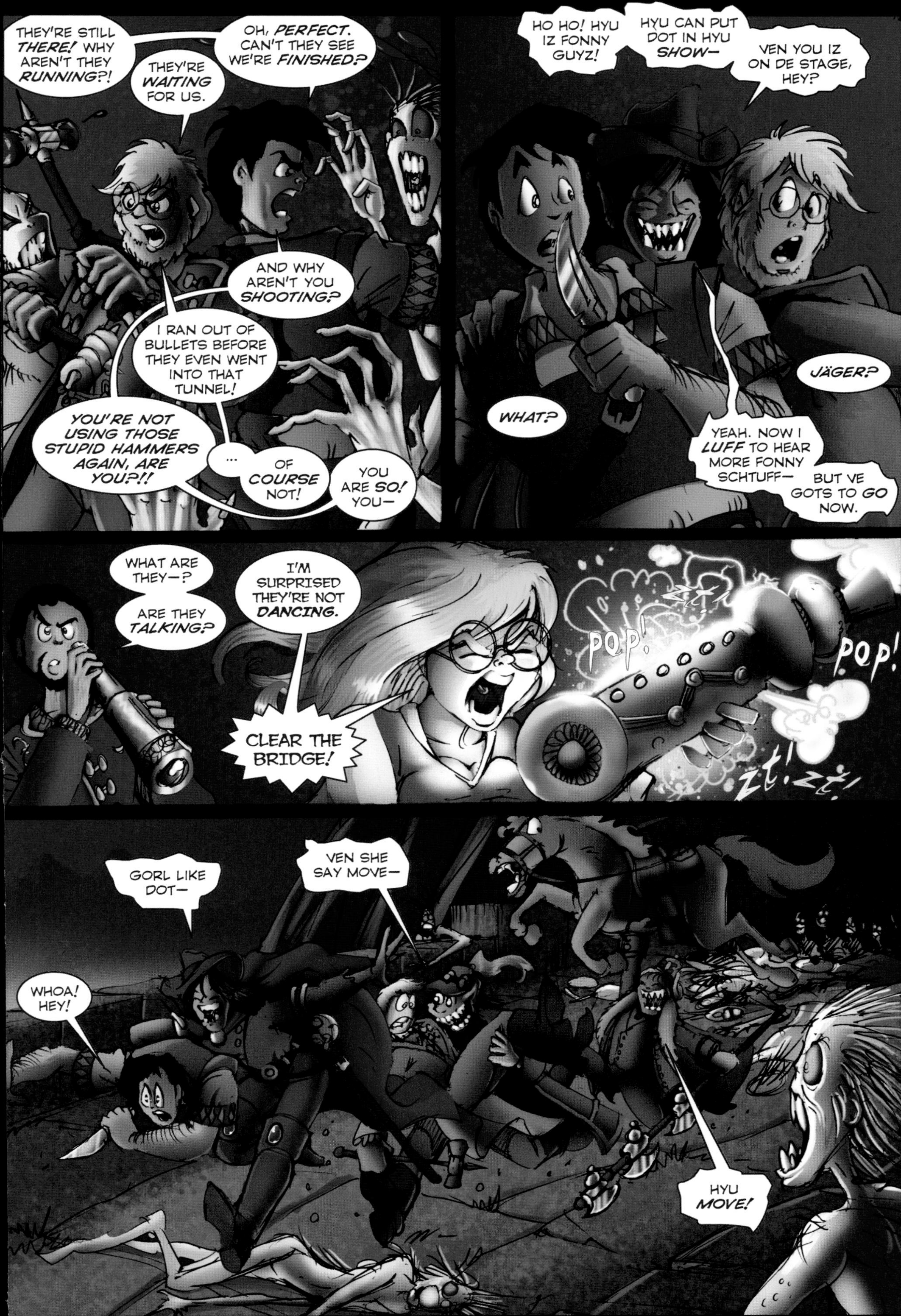
THEY'RE STILL THERE! WHY AREN'T THEY RUNNING?!
OH, PERFECT. CAN'T THEY SEE WE'RE FINISHED?
THEY'RE WAITING FOR US.
AND WHY AREN'T YOU SHOOTING?
I RAN OUT OF BULLETS BEFORE THEY EVEN WENT INTO THAT TUNNEL!
YOU'RE NOT USING THOSE STUPID HAMMERS AGAIN, ARE YOU?!!
...
OF COURSE NOT!
YOU ARE SO! YOU—
HO HO! HYU IZ FONNY GUYZ!
HYU CAN PUT DOT IN HYU SHOW—
VEN YOU IZ ON DE STAGE, HEY?
WHAT?
JÄGER?
YEAH. NOW I LUFF TO HEAR MORE FONNY SCHTUFF—
BUT VE GOTS TO GO NOW.
WHAT ARE THEY—?
ARE THEY TALKING?
I'M SURPRISED THEY'RE NOT DANCING.
CLEAR THE BRIDGE!
POP!
ZT!
POP!
ZT! ZT!
GORL LIKE DOT—
VEN SHE SAY MOVE—
WHOA! HEY!
HYU MOVE!

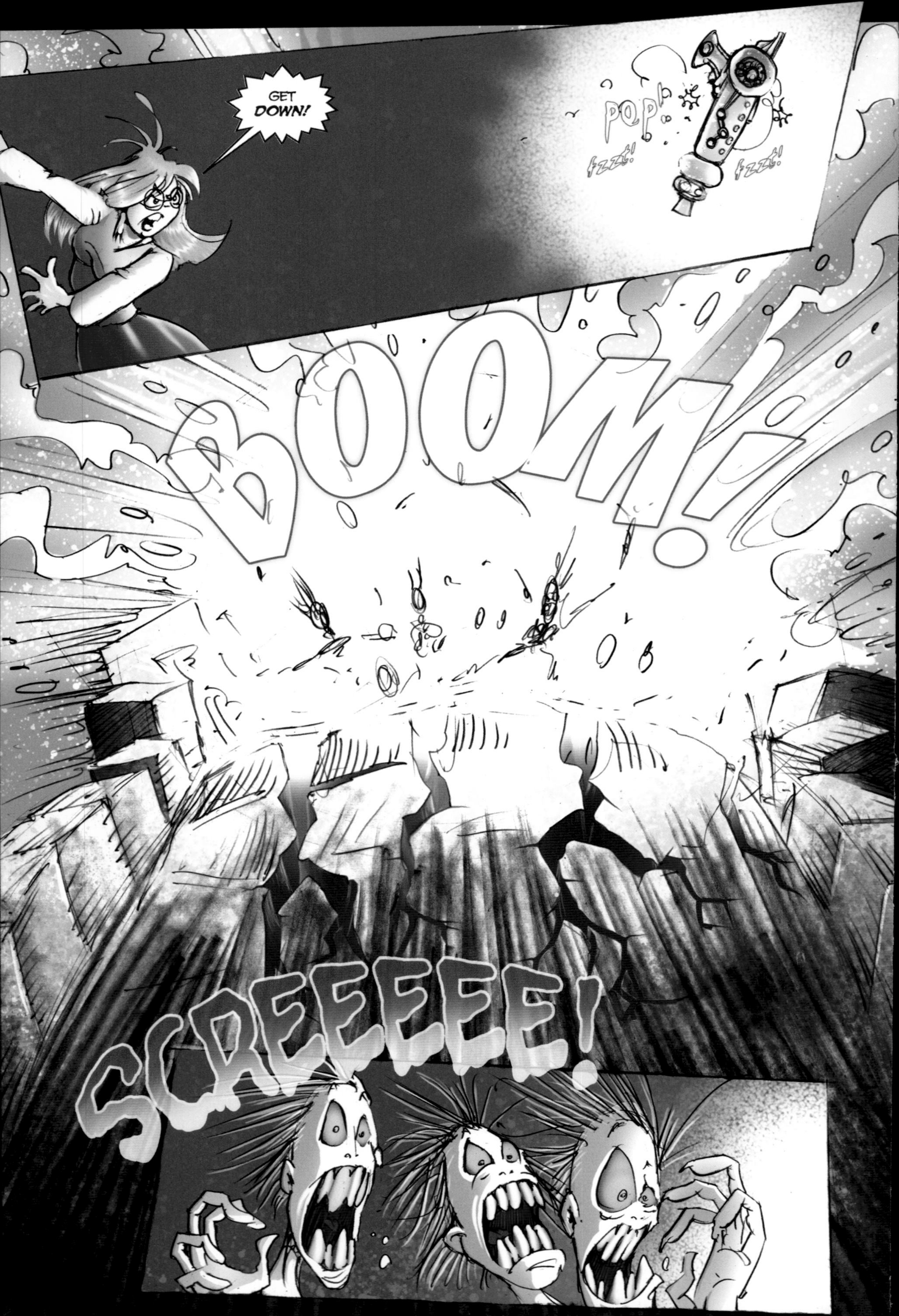
GET DOWN!
POP
fzzt!
fzzt!
BOOM!
SCREEEEE!

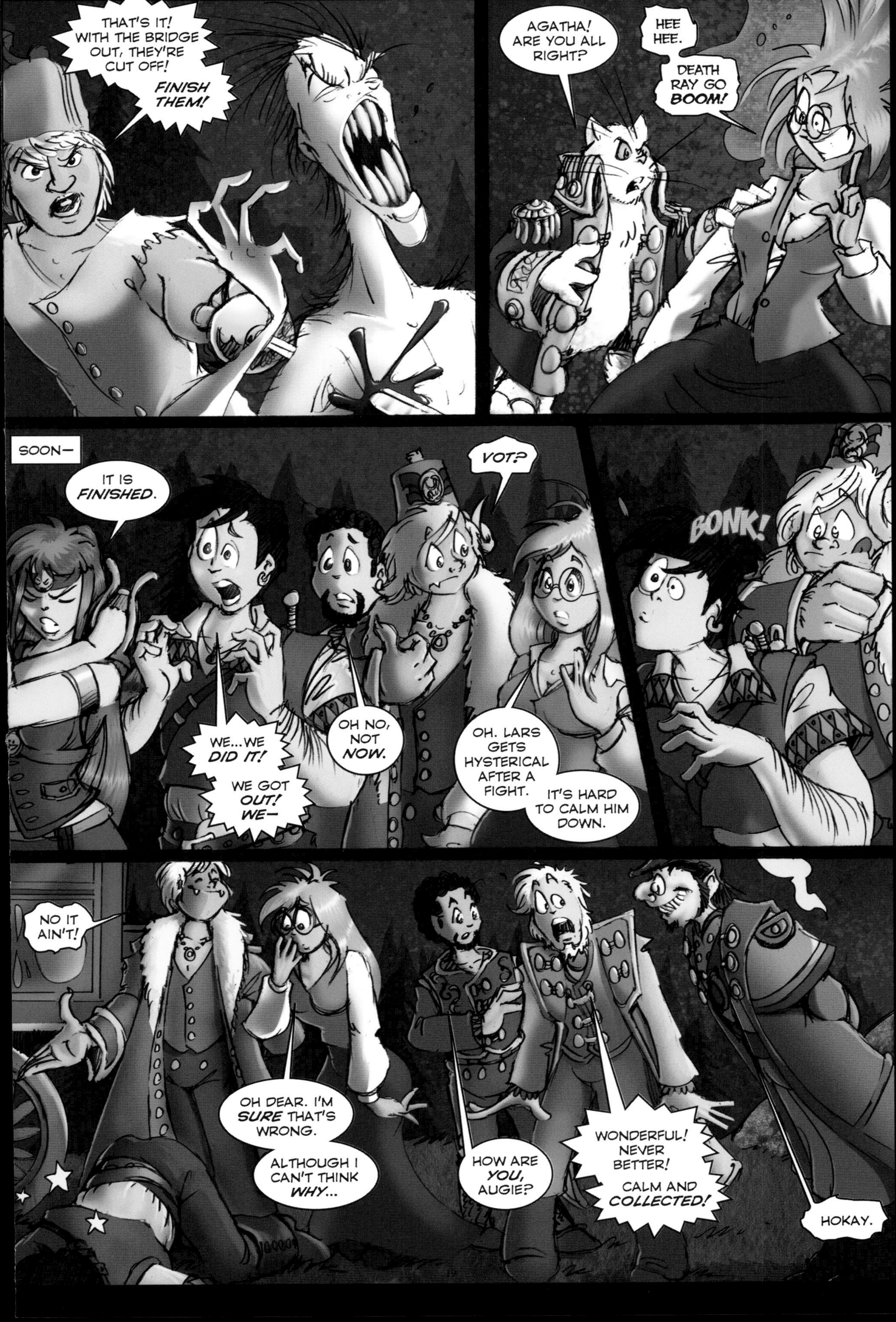
THAT'S IT! WITH THE BRIDGE OUT, THEY'RE CUT OFF! FINISH THEM!
AGATHA! ARE YOU ALL RIGHT?
HEE HEE.
DEATH RAY GO BOOM!
SOON—
IT IS FINISHED.
WE...WE DID IT!
WE GOT OUT! WE—
OH NO, NOT NOW.
VOT?
OH. LARS GETS HYSTERICAL AFTER A FIGHT.
IT'S HARD TO CALM HIM DOWN.
BONK!
NO IT AIN'T!
OH DEAR. I'M SURE THAT'S WRONG.
ALTHOUGH I CAN'T THINK WHY...
HOW ARE YOU, AUGIE?
WONDERFUL! NEVER BETTER!
CALM AND COLLECTED!
HOKAY.

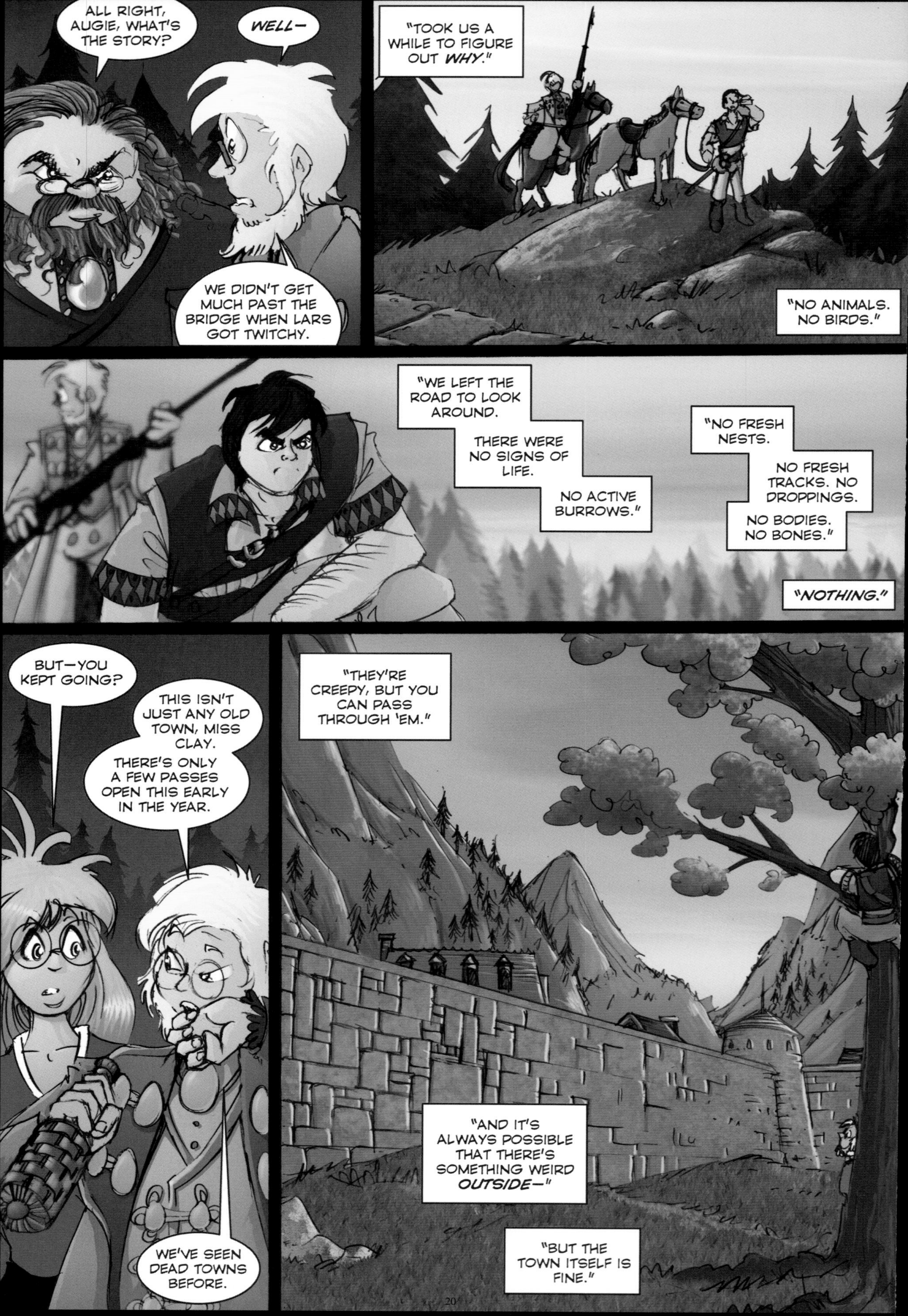
ALL RIGHT, AUGIE, WHAT'S THE STORY?
WELL—
WE DIDN'T GET MUCH PAST THE BRIDGE WHEN LARS GOT TWITCHY.
"TOOK US A WHILE TO FIGURE OUT WHY."
"NO ANIMALS. NO BIRDS."
"WE LEFT THE ROAD TO LOOK AROUND.
THERE WERE NO SIGNS OF LIFE.
NO ACTIVE BURROWS."
"NO FRESH NESTS.
NO FRESH TRACKS. NO DROPPINGS.
NO BODIES. NO BONES."
"NOTHING."
BUT—YOU KEPT GOING?
THIS ISN'T JUST ANY OLD TOWN, MISS CLAY.
THERE'S ONLY A FEW PASSES OPEN THIS EARLY IN THE YEAR.
WE'VE SEEN DEAD TOWNS BEFORE.
"THEY'RE CREEPY, BUT YOU CAN PASS THROUGH 'EM."
"AND IT'S ALWAYS POSSIBLE THAT THERE'S SOMETHING WEIRD OUTSIDE—"
"BUT THE TOWN ITSELF IS FINE."

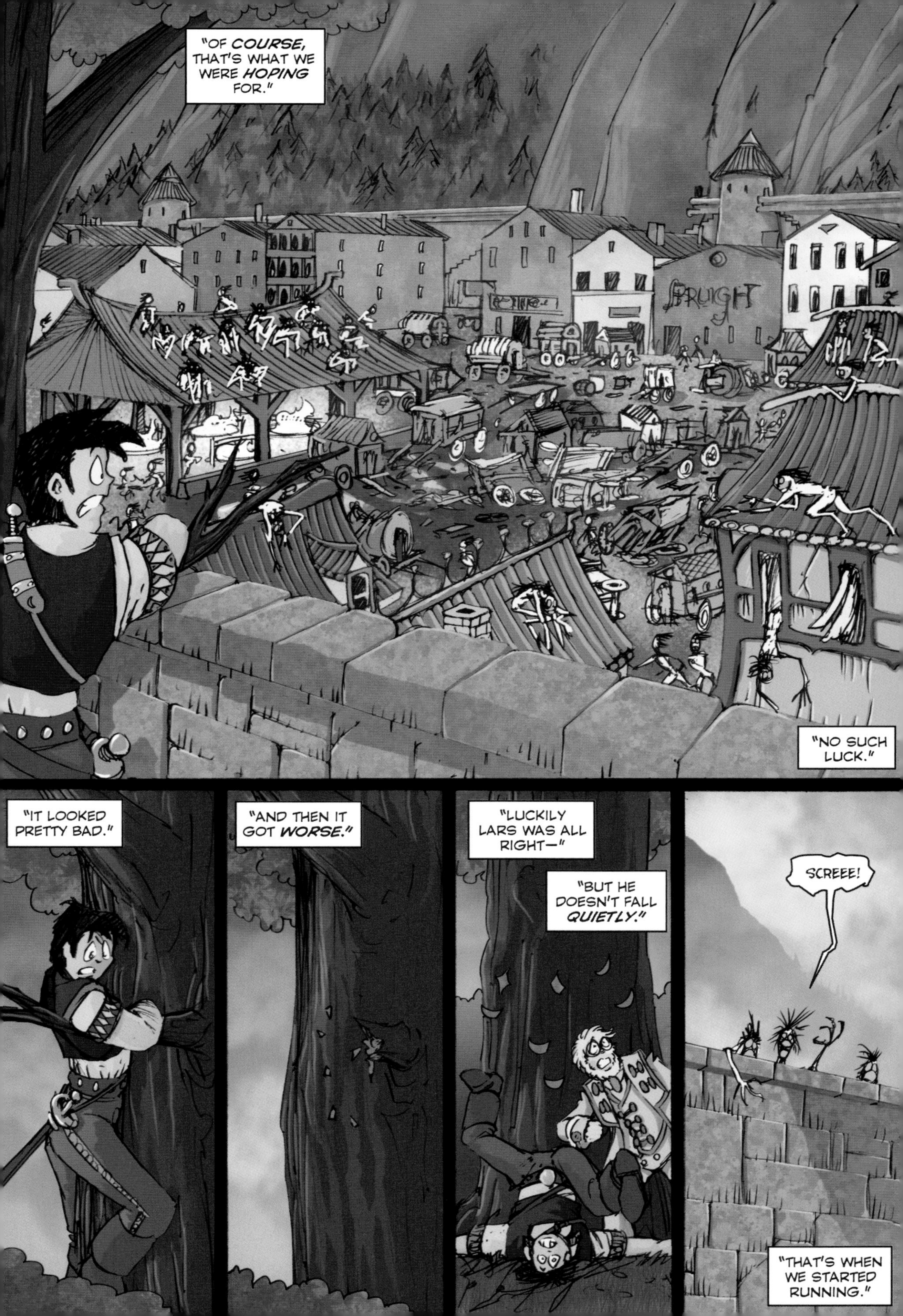
"OF COURSE, THAT'S WHAT WE WERE HOPING FOR."
SPRUIGHT
"NO SUCH LUCK."
"IT LOOKED PRETTY BAD."
"AND THEN IT GOT WORSE."
"LUCKILY LARS WAS ALL RIGHT—"
"BUT HE DOESN'T FALL QUIETLY."
SCREEE!
"THAT'S WHEN WE STARTED RUNNING."

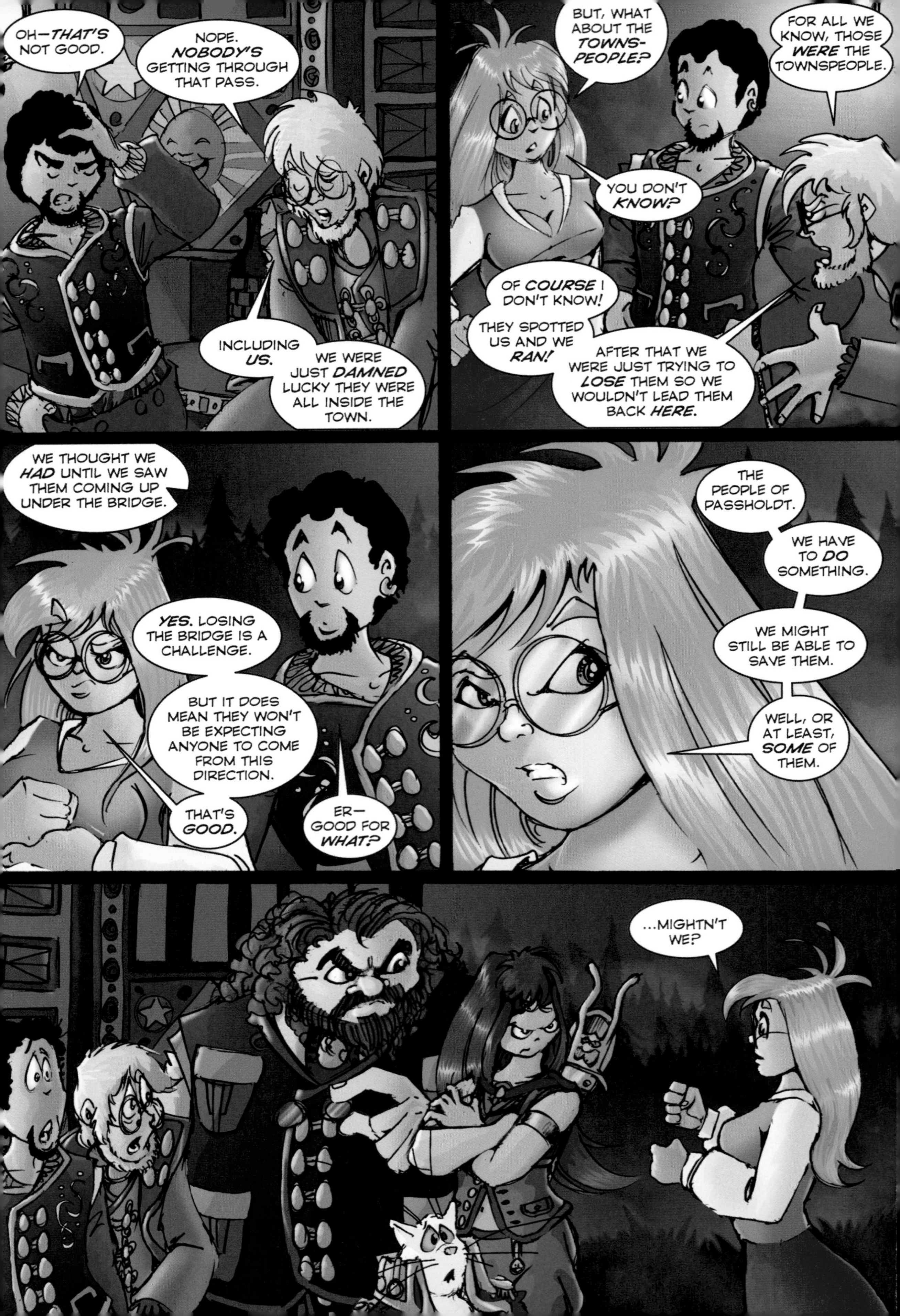
OH—THAT'S NOT GOOD.
NOPE. NOBODY'S GETTING THROUGH THAT PASS.
INCLUDING US.
WE WERE JUST DAMNED LUCKY THEY WERE ALL INSIDE THE TOWN.
BUT, WHAT ABOUT THE TOWNS-PEOPLE?
FOR ALL WE KNOW, THOSE WERE THE TOWNSPEOPLE.
YOU DON'T KNOW?
OF COURSE I DON'T KNOW!
THEY SPOTTED US AND WE RAN!
AFTER THAT WE WERE JUST TRYING TO LOSE THEM SO WE WOULDN'T LEAD THEM BACK HERE.
WE THOUGHT WE HAD UNTIL WE SAW THEM COMING UP UNDER THE BRIDGE.
YES. LOSING THE BRIDGE IS A CHALLENGE.
BUT IT DOES MEAN THEY WON'T BE EXPECTING ANYONE TO COME FROM THIS DIRECTION.
THAT'S GOOD.
ER—GOOD FOR WHAT?
THE PEOPLE OF PASSHOLDT.
WE HAVE TO DO SOMETHING.
WE MIGHT STILL BE ABLE TO SAVE THEM.
WELL, OR AT LEAST, SOME OF THEM.
...MIGHTN'T WE?

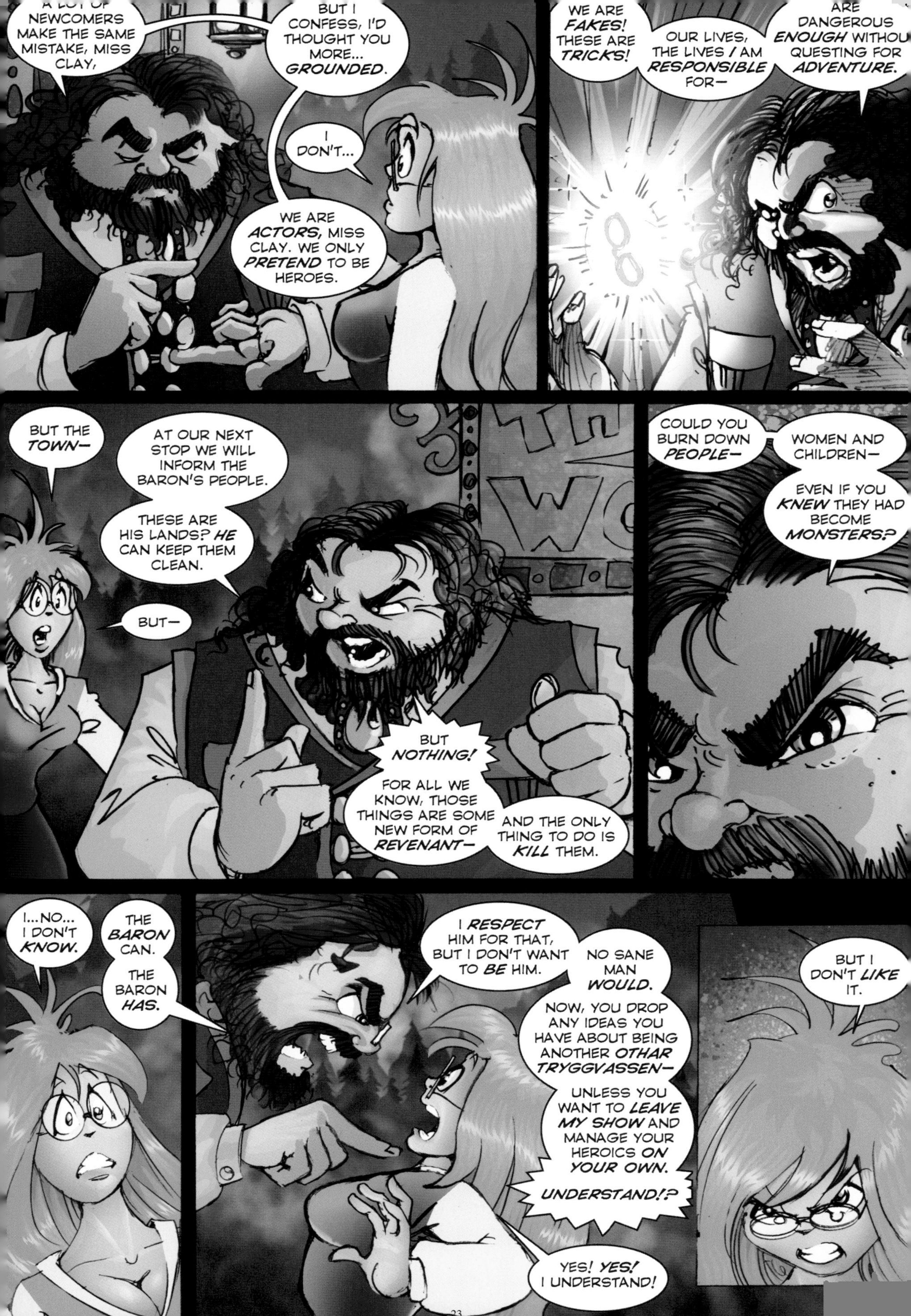

A LOT OF NEWCOMERS MAKE THE SAME MISTAKE, MISS CLAY,
BUT I CONFESS, I'D THOUGHT YOU MORE... GROUNDED.
I DON'T...
WE ARE ACTORS, MISS CLAY. WE ONLY PRETEND TO BE HEROES.
WE ARE FAKES! THESE ARE TRICKS!
OUR LIVES, THE LIVES I AM RESPONSIBLE FOR—
ARE DANGEROUS ENOUGH WITHOU QUESTING FOR ADVENTURE.
BUT THE TOWN—
AT OUR NEXT STOP WE WILL INFORM THE BARON'S PEOPLE.
THESE ARE HIS LANDS? HE CAN KEEP THEM CLEAN.
BUT—
BUT NOTHING!
FOR ALL WE KNOW, THOSE THINGS ARE SOME NEW FORM OF REVENANT—
AND THE ONLY THING TO DO IS KILL THEM.
COULD YOU BURN DOWN PEOPLE—
WOMEN AND CHILDREN—
EVEN IF YOU KNEW THEY HAD BECOME MONSTERS?
I...NO... I DON'T KNOW.
THE BARON CAN.
THE BARON HAS.
I RESPECT HIM FOR THAT, BUT I DON'T WANT TO BE HIM.
NO SANE MAN WOULD.
NOW, YOU DROP ANY IDEAS YOU HAVE ABOUT BEING ANOTHER OTHAR TRYGGVASSEN—
UNLESS YOU WANT TO LEAVE MY SHOW AND MANAGE YOUR HEROICS ON YOUR OWN.
UNDERSTAND!?
YES! YES! I UNDERSTAND!
BUT I DON'T LIKE IT.

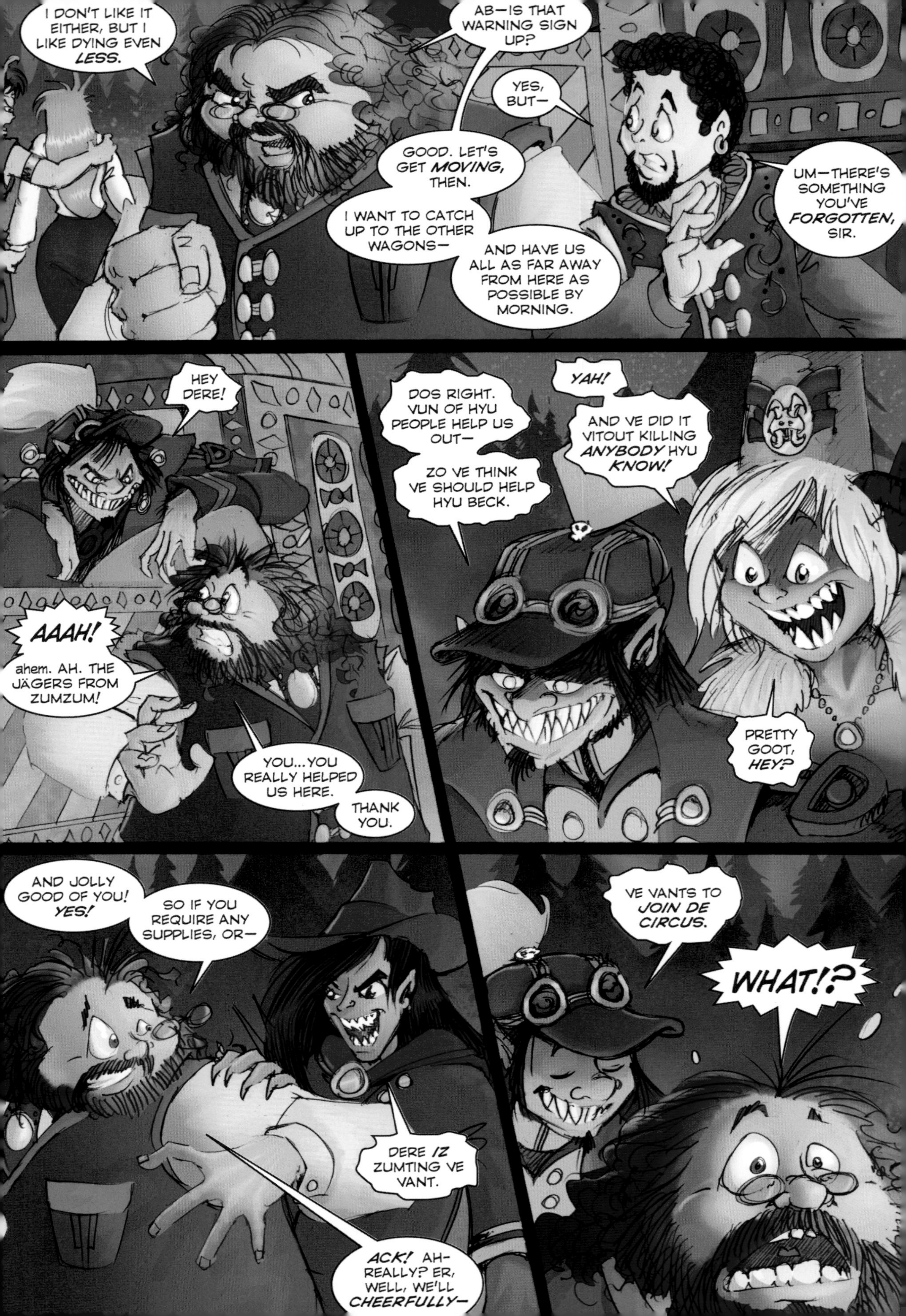
I DON'T LIKE IT EITHER, BUT I LIKE DYING EVEN *LESS.*
AB—IS THAT WARNING SIGN UP?
YES, BUT—
GOOD. LET'S GET *MOVING,* THEN.
I WANT TO CATCH UP TO THE OTHER WAGONS—
AND HAVE US ALL AS FAR AWAY FROM HERE AS POSSIBLE BY MORNING.
UM—THERE'S SOMETHING YOU'VE *FORGOTTEN,* SIR.
HEY DERE!
AAAH!
ahem. AH. THE JÄGERS FROM ZUMZUM!
YOU...YOU REALLY HELPED US HERE.
THANK YOU.
DOS RIGHT. VUN OF HYU PEOPLE HELP US OUT—
ZO VE THINK VE SHOULD HELP HYU BECK.
YAH!
AND VE DID IT VITOUT KILLING *ANYBODY* HYU *KNOW!*
PRETTY GOOT, *HEY?*
AND JOLLY GOOD OF YOU! *YES!*
SO IF YOU REQUIRE ANY SUPPLIES, OR—
DERE *IZ* ZUMTING VE VANT.
ACK! AH-REALLY? ER, WELL, WE'LL *CHEERFULLY—*
VE VANTS TO *JOIN DE CIRCUS.*
WHAT!?

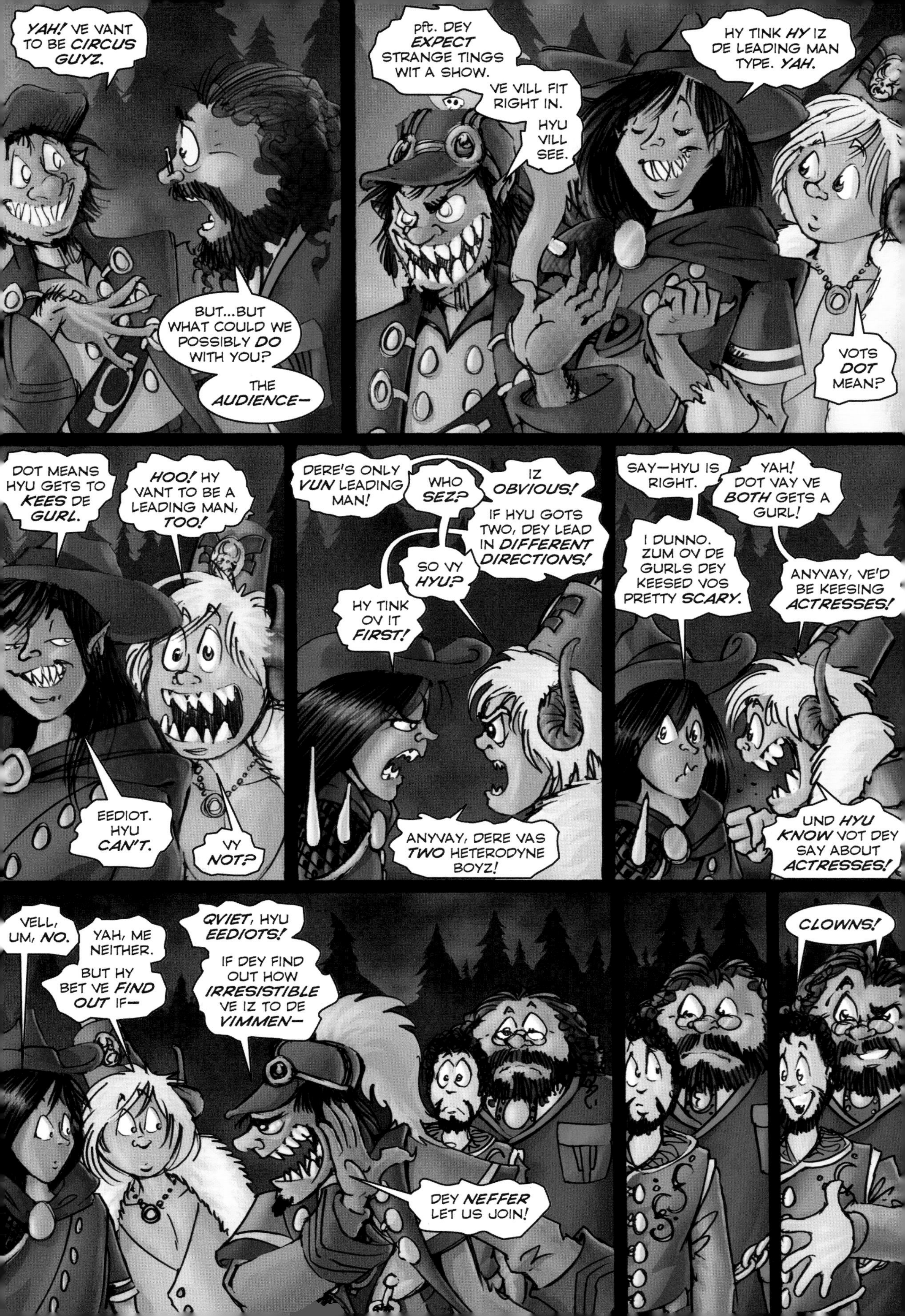

YAH! VE VANT TO BE CIRCUS GUYZ.
BUT...BUT WHAT COULD WE POSSIBLY DO WITH YOU?
THE AUDIENCE—
pft. DEY EXPECT STRANGE TINGS WIT A SHOW.
VE VILL FIT RIGHT IN.
HYU VILL SEE.
HY TINK HY IZ DE LEADING MAN TYPE. YAH.
VOTS DOT MEAN?
DOT MEANS HYU GETS TO KEES DE GURL.
HOO! HY VANT TO BE A LEADING MAN, TOO!
EEDIOT. HYU CAN'T.
VY NOT?
DERE'S ONLY VUN LEADING MAN!
WHO SEZ?
IZ OBVIOUS!
IF HYU GOTS TWO, DEY LEAD IN DIFFERENT DIRECTIONS!
SO VY HYU?
HY TINK OV IT FIRST!
ANYVAY, DERE VAS TWO HETERODYNE BOYZ!
SAY—HYU IS RIGHT.
YAH! DOT VAY VE BOTH GETS A GURL!
I DUNNO. ZUM OV DE GURLS DEY KEESED VOS PRETTY SCARY.
ANYVAY, VE'D BE KEESING ACTRESSES!
UND HYU KNOW VOT DEY SAY ABOUT ACTRESSES!
VELL, UM, NO.
YAH, ME NEITHER.
BUT HY BET VE FIND OUT IF—
QVIET, HYU EEDIOTS!
IF DEY FIND OUT HOW IRRESISTIBLE VE IZ TO DE VIMMEN—
DEY NEFFER LET US JOIN!
CLOWNS!

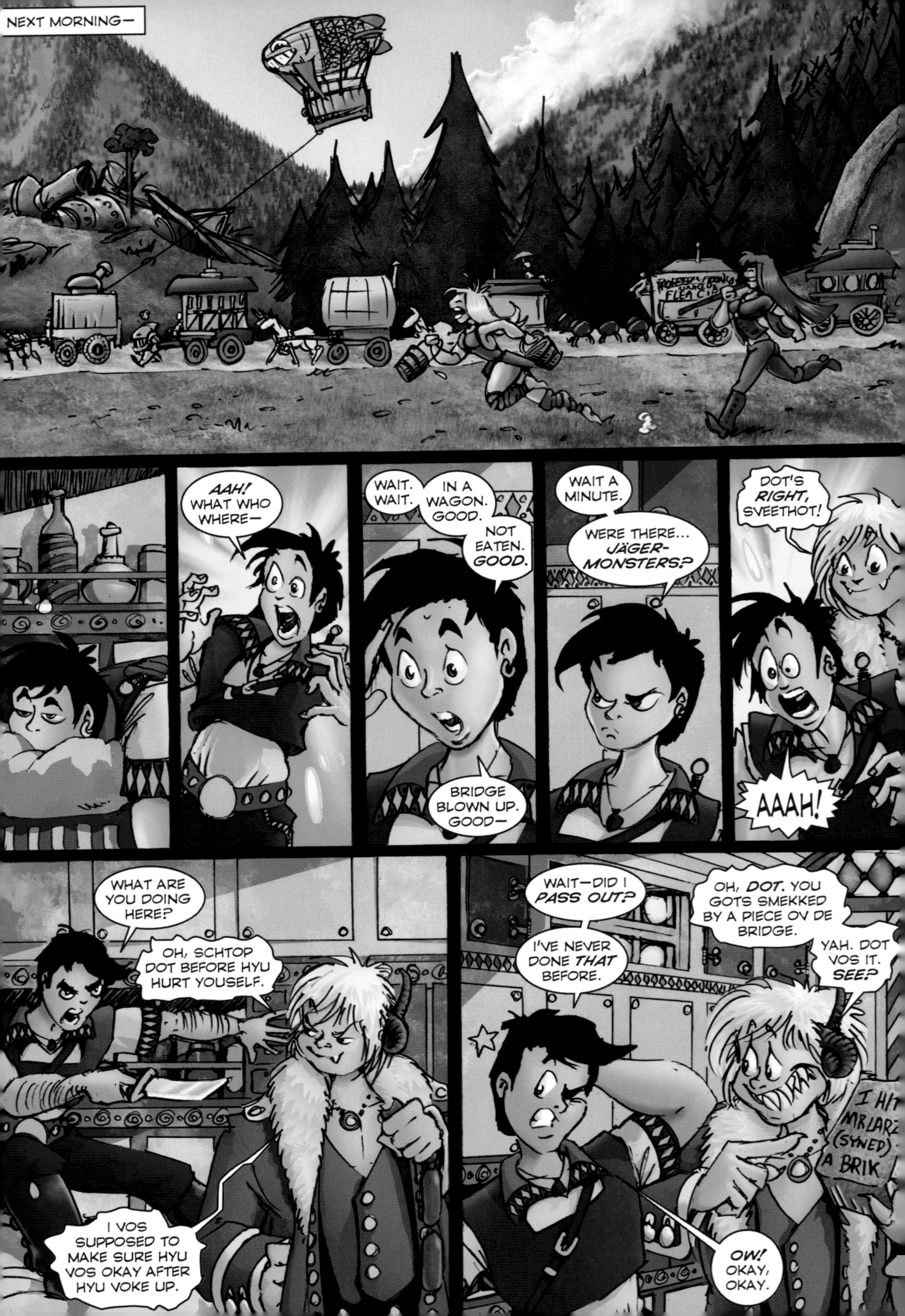
NEXT MORNING—
AAH! WHAT WHO WHERE—
WAIT. WAIT.
IN A WAGON. GOOD.
NOT EATEN. GOOD.
BRIDGE BLOWN UP. GOOD—
WAIT A MINUTE.
WERE THERE... JÄGER-MONSTERS?
DOT'S RIGHT, SVEETHOT!
AAAH!
WHAT ARE YOU DOING HERE?
OH, SCHTOP DOT BEFORE HYU HURT YOUSELF.
I VOS SUPPOSED TO MAKE SURE HYU VOS OKAY AFTER HYU VOKE UP.
WAIT—DID I PASS OUT?
I'VE NEVER DONE THAT BEFORE.
OH, DOT. YOU GOTS SMEKKED BY A PIECE OV DE BRIDGE.
YAH. DOT VOS IT. SEE?
I HIT MR LARZ (SYNED) A BRIK
OW! OKAY, OKAY.

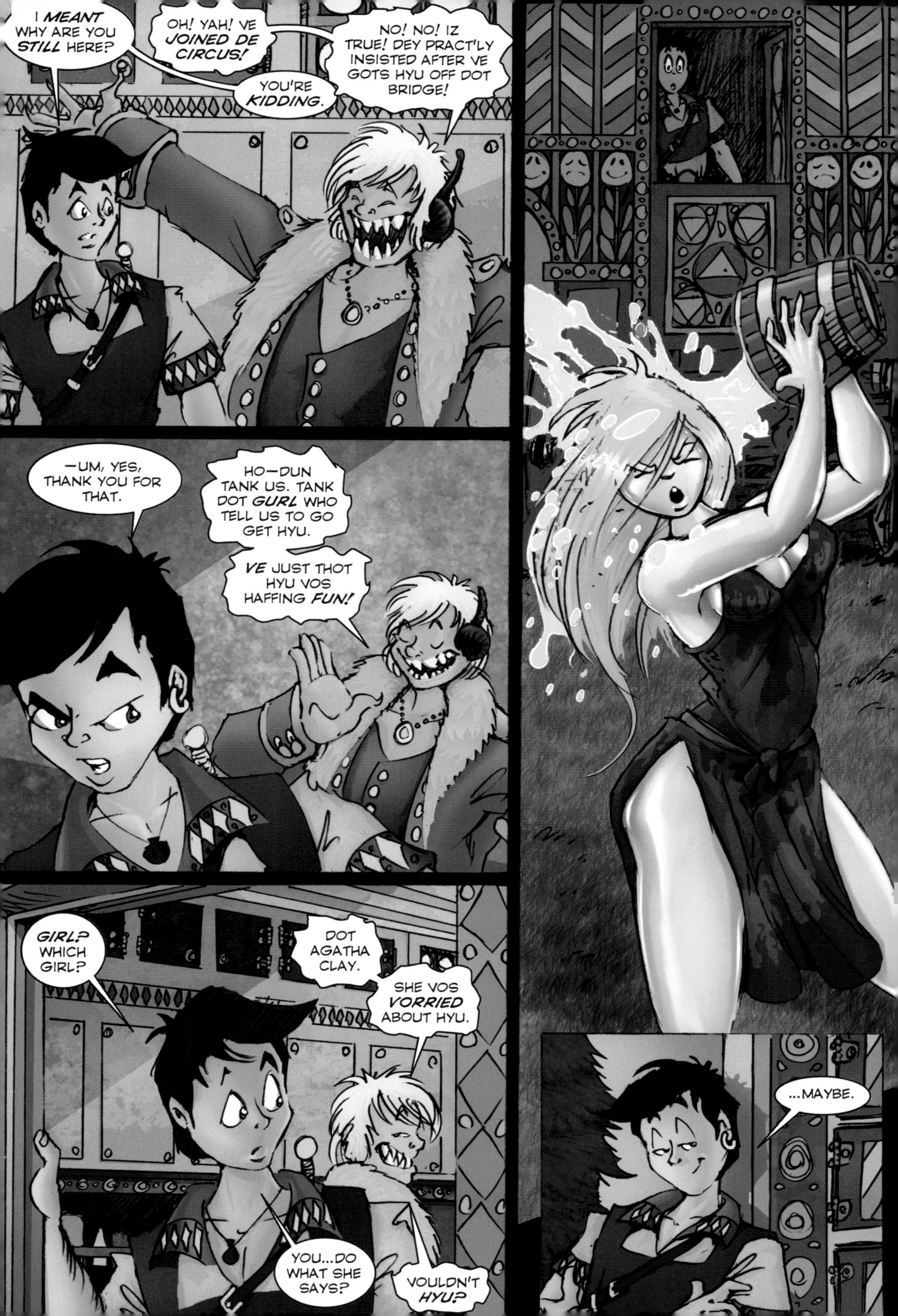

I *MEANT* WHY ARE YOU *STILL* HERE?
OH! YAH! VE *JOINED DE CIRCUS!*
YOU'RE *KIDDING*.
NO! NO! IZ TRUE! DEY PRACT'LY INSISTED AFTER VE GOTS HYU OFF DOT BRIDGE!
—UM, YES, THANK YOU FOR THAT.
HO—DUN TANK US. TANK DOT *GURL* WHO TELL US TO GO GET HYU.
VE JUST THOT HYU VOS HAFFING *FUN!*
GIRL? WHICH GIRL?
DOT AGATHA CLAY.
SHE VOS *VORRIED* ABOUT HYU.
YOU...DO WHAT SHE SAYS?
VOULDN'T *HYU?*
...MAYBE.

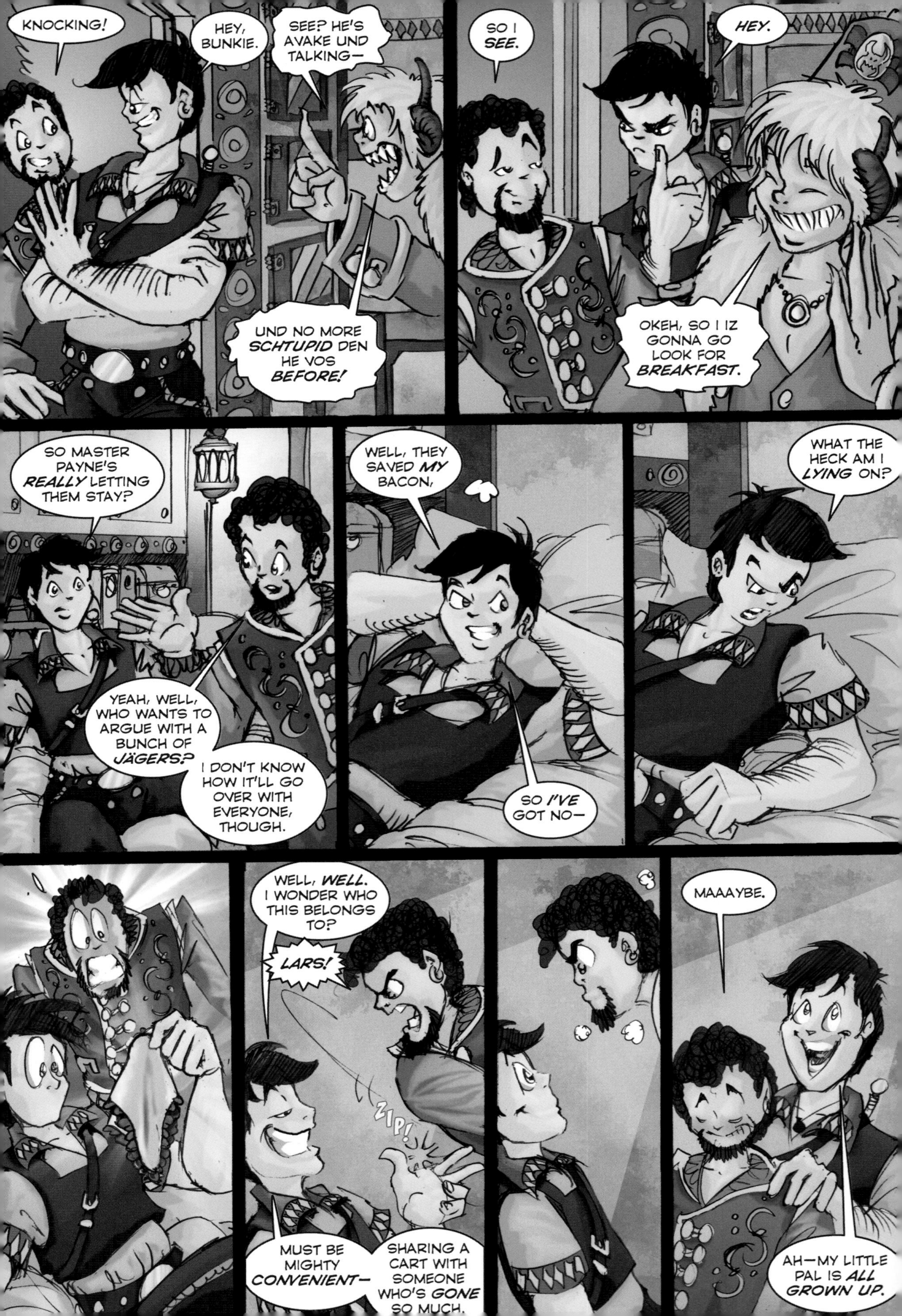
KNOCKING!
HEY, BUNKIE.
SEE? HE'S AVAKE UND TALKING—
UND NO MORE SCHTUPID DEN HE VOS BEFORE!
SO I SEE.
HEY.
OKEH, SO I IZ GONNA GO LOOK FOR BREAKFAST.
SO MASTER PAYNE'S REALLY LETTING THEM STAY?
YEAH, WELL, WHO WANTS TO ARGUE WITH A BUNCH OF JÄGERS?
I DON'T KNOW HOW IT'LL GO OVER WITH EVERYONE, THOUGH.
WELL, THEY SAVED MY BACON,
SO I'VE GOT NO—
WHAT THE HECK AM I LYING ON?
WELL, WELL. I WONDER WHO THIS BELONGS TO?
LARS!
ZIP!
MUST BE MIGHTY CONVENIENT—
SHARING A CART WITH SOMEONE WHO'S GONE SO MUCH.
MAAAYBE.
AH—MY LITTLE PAL IS ALL GROWN UP.

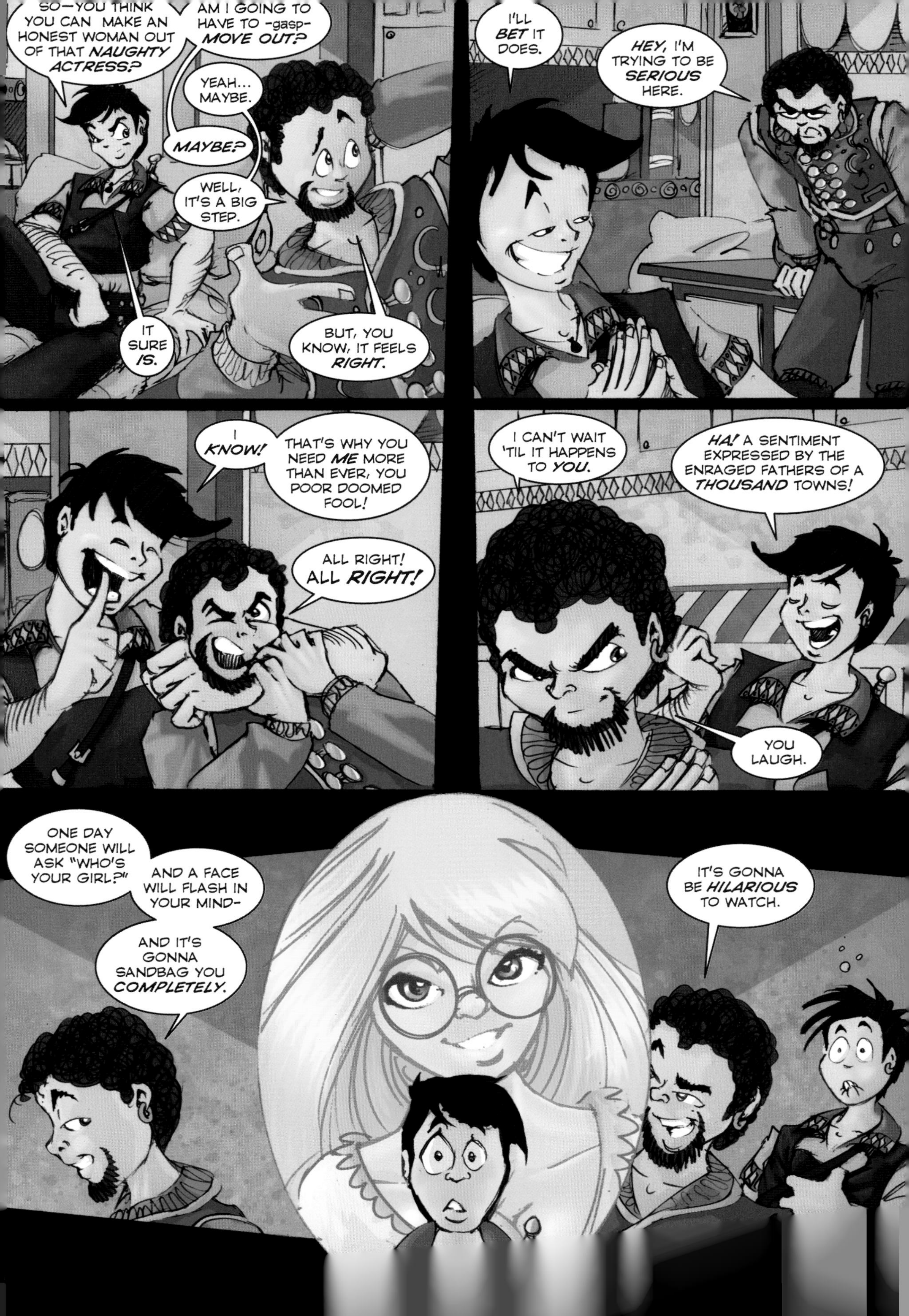

SO—YOU THINK YOU CAN MAKE AN HONEST WOMAN OUT OF THAT NAUGHTY ACTRESS?
AM I GOING TO HAVE TO -gasp- MOVE OUT?
YEAH... MAYBE.
MAYBE?
WELL, IT'S A BIG STEP.
IT SURE IS.
BUT, YOU KNOW, IT FEELS RIGHT.
I'LL BET IT DOES.
HEY, I'M TRYING TO BE SERIOUS HERE.
I KNOW!
THAT'S WHY YOU NEED ME MORE THAN EVER, YOU POOR DOOMED FOOL!
ALL RIGHT! ALL RIGHT!
I CAN'T WAIT 'TIL IT HAPPENS TO YOU.
HA! A SENTIMENT EXPRESSED BY THE ENRAGED FATHERS OF A THOUSAND TOWNS!
YOU LAUGH.
ONE DAY SOMEONE WILL ASK "WHO'S YOUR GIRL?"
AND A FACE WILL FLASH IN YOUR MIND-
AND IT'S GONNA SANDBAG YOU COMPLETELY.
IT'S GONNA BE HILARIOUS TO WATCH.

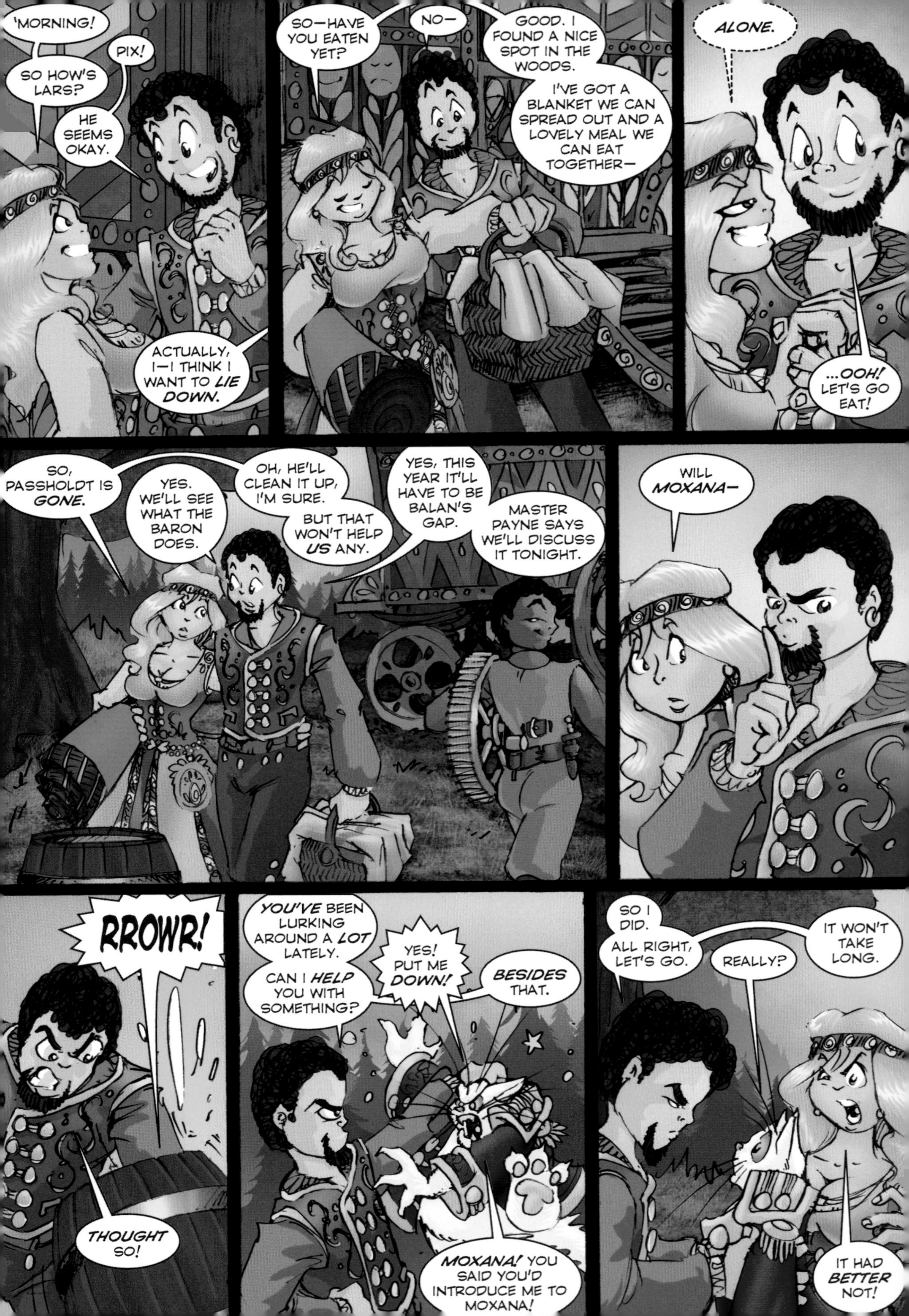
'MORNING!
SO HOW'S LARS?
PIX!
HE SEEMS OKAY.
ACTUALLY, I—I THINK I WANT TO *LIE DOWN.*
SO—HAVE YOU EATEN YET?
NO—
GOOD. I FOUND A NICE SPOT IN THE WOODS.
I'VE GOT A BLANKET WE CAN SPREAD OUT AND A LOVELY MEAL WE CAN EAT TOGETHER—
ALONE.
...OOH! LET'S GO EAT!
SO, PASSHOLDT IS *GONE.*
YES. WE'LL SEE WHAT THE BARON DOES.
OH, HE'LL CLEAN IT UP, I'M SURE.
BUT THAT WON'T HELP *US* ANY.
YES, THIS YEAR IT'LL HAVE TO BE BALAN'S GAP.
MASTER PAYNE SAYS WE'LL DISCUSS IT TONIGHT.
WILL *MOXANA—*
RROWR!
THOUGHT SO!
YOU'VE BEEN LURKING AROUND A *LOT* LATELY.
CAN I *HELP* YOU WITH SOMETHING?
YES! PUT ME *DOWN!*
BESIDES THAT.
MOXANA! YOU SAID YOU'D INTRODUCE ME TO MOXANA!
SO I DID.
ALL RIGHT, LET'S GO.
REALLY?
IT WON'T TAKE LONG.
IT HAD *BETTER* NOT!

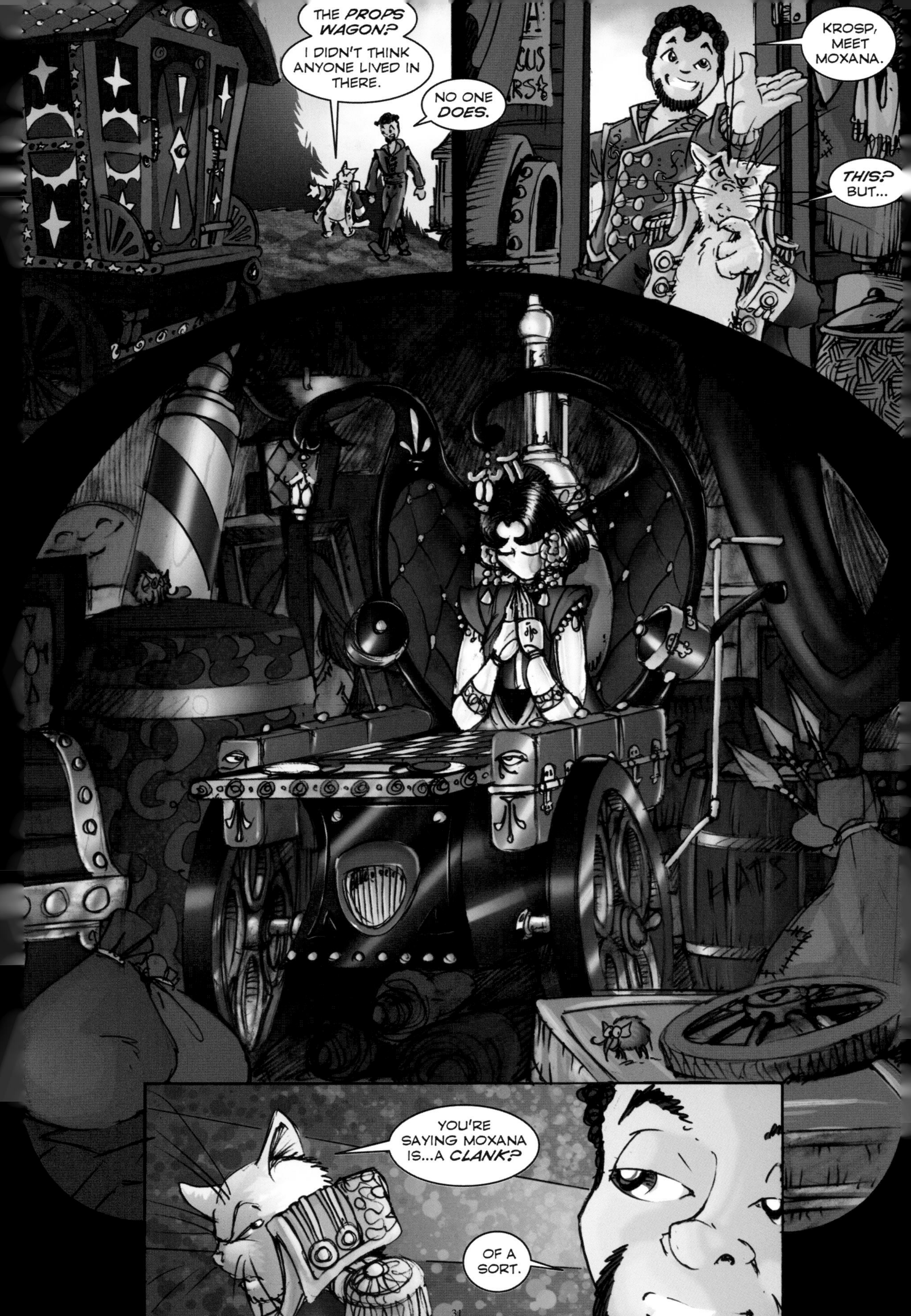
THE PROPS WAGON? I DIDN'T THINK ANYONE LIVED IN THERE.
NO ONE DOES.
KROSP, MEET MOXANA.
THIS? BUT...
HATS
YOU'RE SAYING MOXANA IS...A CLANK?
OF A SORT.

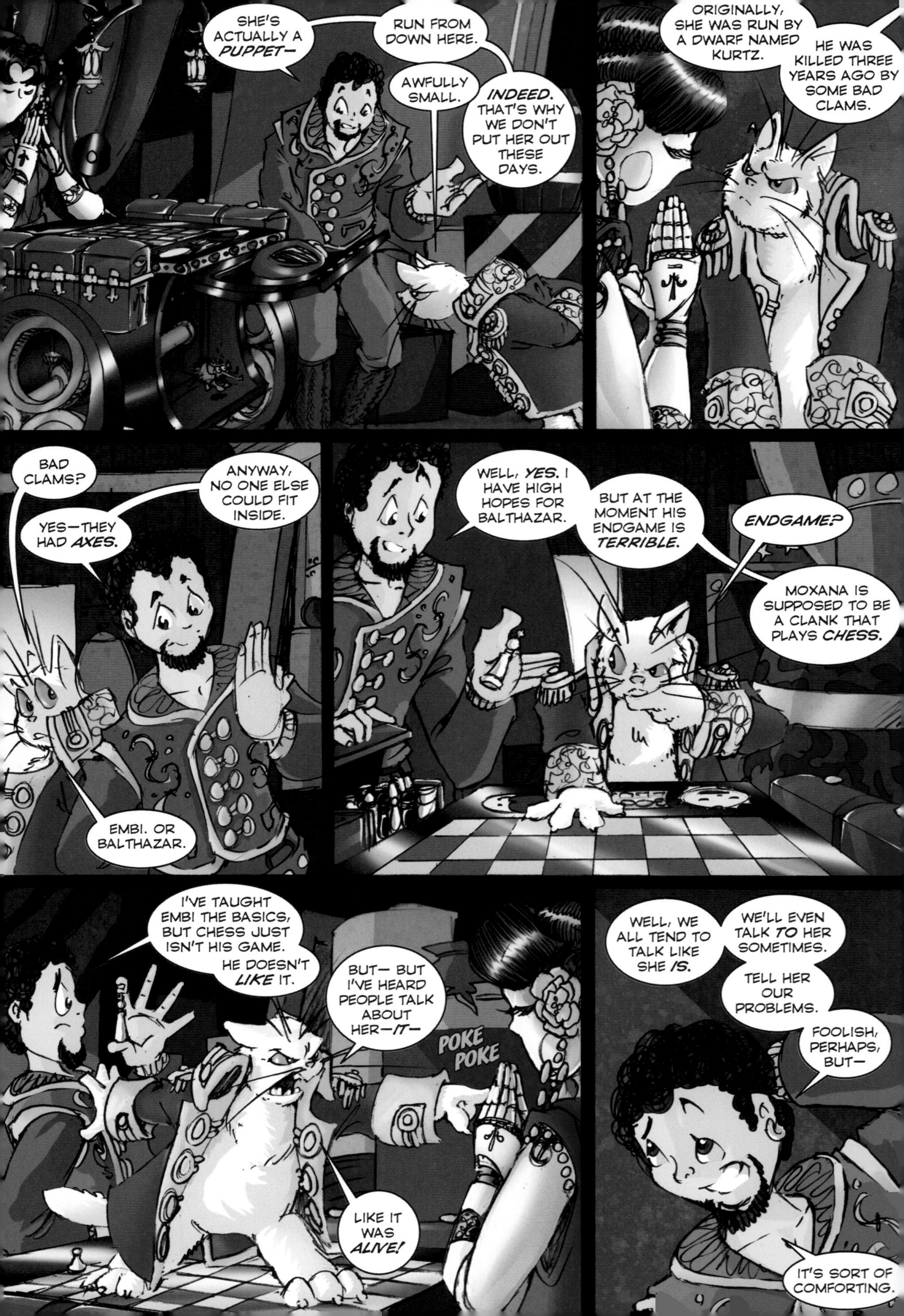
SHE'S ACTUALLY A *PUPPET*—
RUN FROM DOWN HERE.
AWFULLY SMALL.
INDEED. THAT'S WHY WE DON'T PUT HER OUT THESE DAYS.
ORIGINALLY, SHE WAS RUN BY A DWARF NAMED KURTZ.
HE WAS KILLED THREE YEARS AGO BY SOME BAD CLAMS.
BAD CLAMS?
YES—THEY HAD *AXES.*
ANYWAY, NO ONE ELSE COULD FIT INSIDE.
EMBI. OR BALTHAZAR.
WELL, *YES.* I HAVE HIGH HOPES FOR BALTHAZAR.
BUT AT THE MOMENT HIS ENDGAME IS *TERRIBLE.*
ENDGAME?
MOXANA IS SUPPOSED TO BE A CLANK THAT PLAYS *CHESS.*
I'VE TAUGHT EMBI THE BASICS, BUT CHESS JUST ISN'T HIS GAME.
HE DOESN'T *LIKE* IT.
BUT— BUT I'VE HEARD PEOPLE TALK ABOUT HER—*IT*—
POKE POKE
LIKE IT WAS *ALIVE!*
WELL, WE ALL TEND TO TALK LIKE SHE *IS.*
WE'LL EVEN TALK *TO* HER SOMETIMES.
TELL HER OUR PROBLEMS.
FOOLISH, PERHAPS, BUT—
IT'S SORT OF COMFORTING.

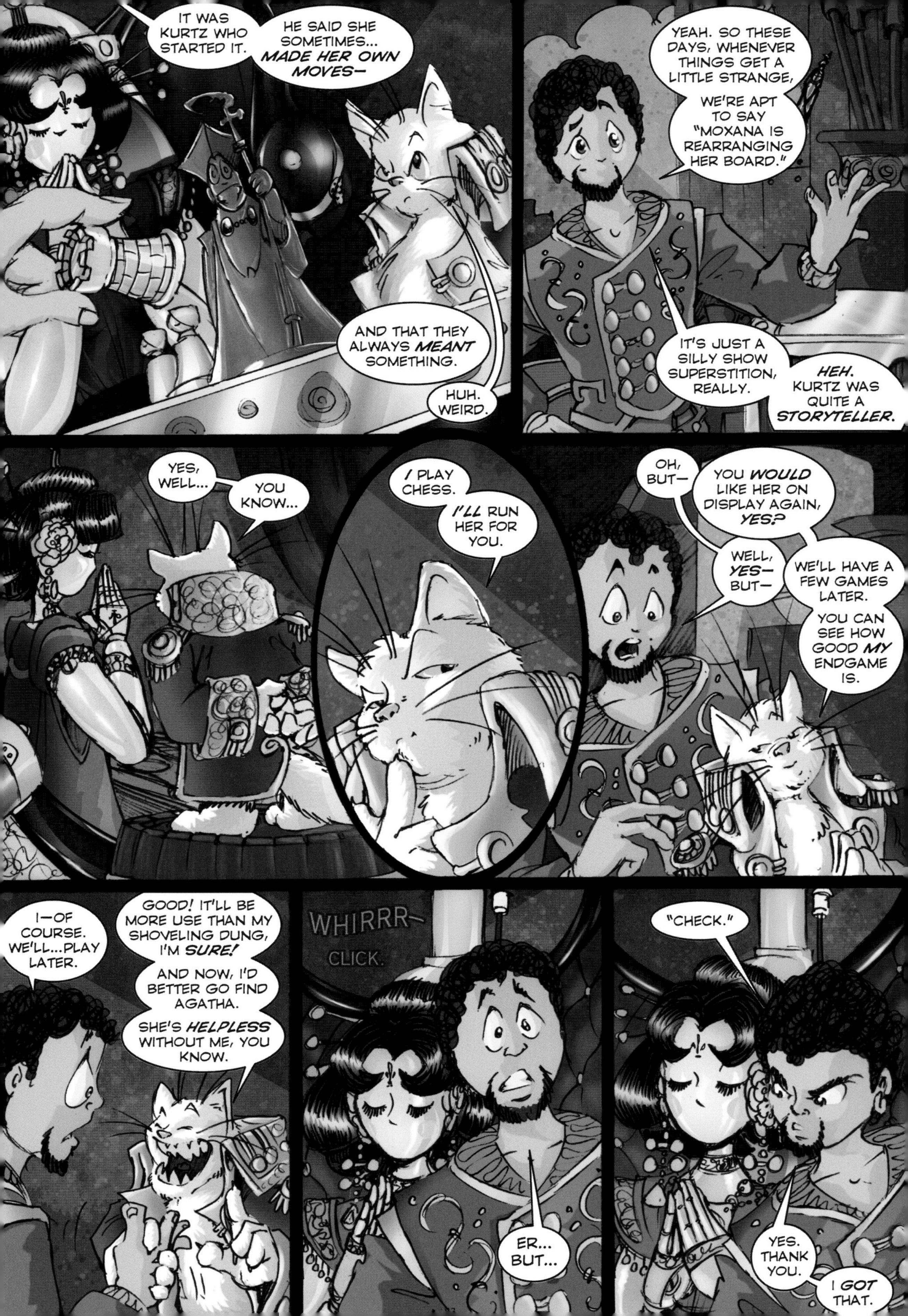

IT WAS KURTZ WHO STARTED IT.
HE SAID SHE SOMETIMES... MADE HER OWN MOVES—
AND THAT THEY ALWAYS MEANT SOMETHING.
HUH. WEIRD.
YEAH. SO THESE DAYS, WHENEVER THINGS GET A LITTLE STRANGE,
WE'RE APT TO SAY "MOXANA IS REARRANGING HER BOARD."
IT'S JUST A SILLY SHOW SUPERSTITION, REALLY.
HEH. KURTZ WAS QUITE A STORYTELLER.
YES, WELL...
YOU KNOW...
I PLAY CHESS.
I'LL RUN HER FOR YOU.
OH, BUT—
YOU WOULD LIKE HER ON DISPLAY AGAIN, YES?
WELL, YES— BUT—
WE'LL HAVE A FEW GAMES LATER.
YOU CAN SEE HOW GOOD MY ENDGAME IS.
I—OF COURSE. WE'LL...PLAY LATER.
GOOD! IT'LL BE MORE USE THAN MY SHOVELING DUNG, I'M SURE!
AND NOW, I'D BETTER GO FIND AGATHA.
SHE'S HELPLESS WITHOUT ME, YOU KNOW.
WHIRRR—
CLICK.
ER... BUT...
"CHECK."
YES. THANK YOU.
I GOT THAT.

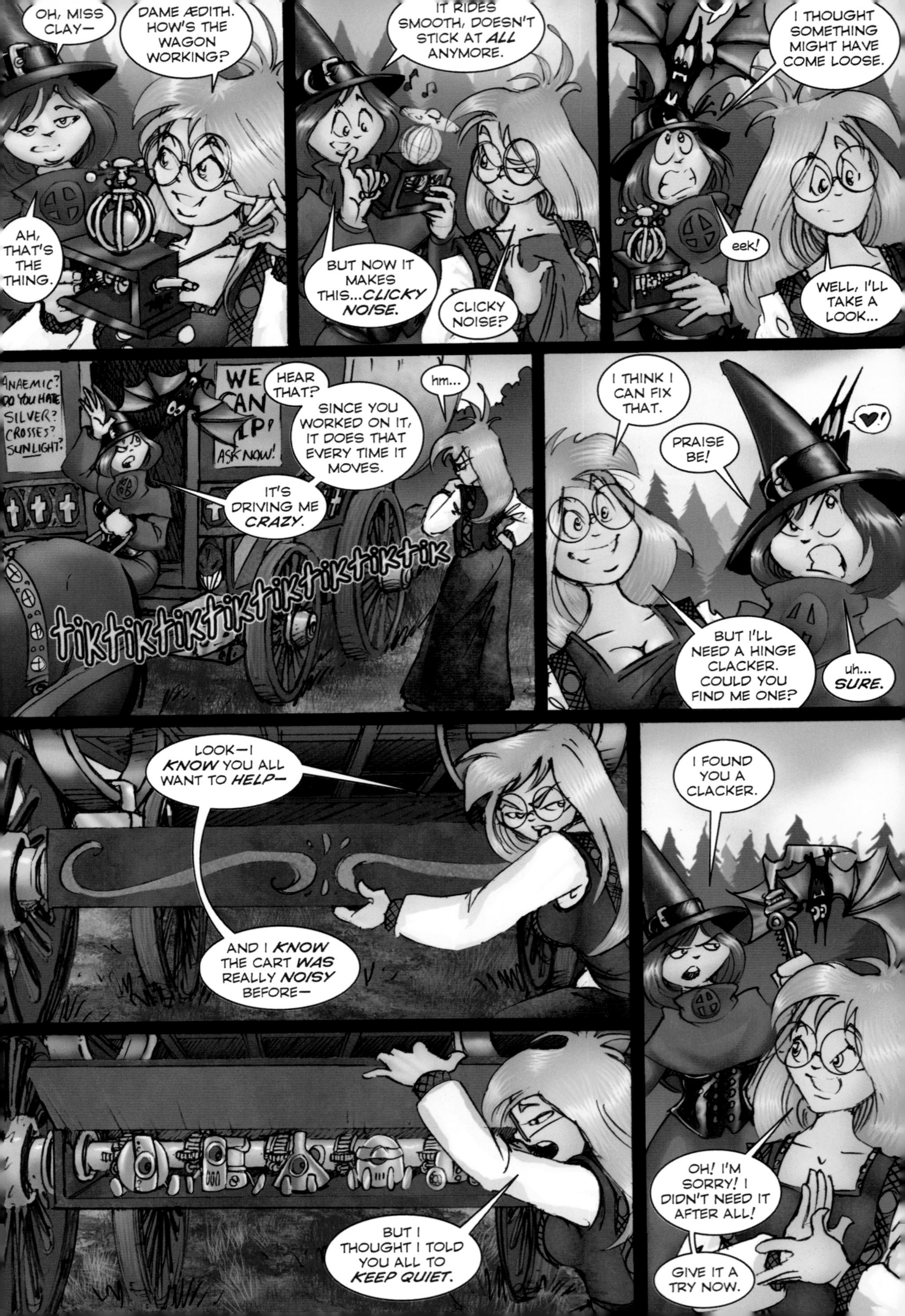
OH, MISS CLAY—
DAME ÆDITH. HOW'S THE WAGON WORKING?
AH, THAT'S THE THING.
IT RIDES SMOOTH, DOESN'T STICK AT ALL ANYMORE.
BUT NOW IT MAKES THIS...CLICKY NOISE.
CLICKY NOISE?
I THOUGHT SOMETHING MIGHT HAVE COME LOOSE.
eek!
WELL, I'LL TAKE A LOOK...
ANAEMIC? DO YOU HATE SILVER? CROSSES? SUNLIGHT?
WE CAN ...LP! ASK NOW!
HEAR THAT?
SINCE YOU WORKED ON IT, IT DOES THAT EVERY TIME IT MOVES.
IT'S DRIVING ME CRAZY.
hm...
tiktiktiktiktiktiktiktiktik
I THINK I CAN FIX THAT.
PRAISE BE!
BUT I'LL NEED A HINGE CLACKER. COULD YOU FIND ME ONE?
uh... SURE.
LOOK—I KNOW YOU ALL WANT TO HELP—
AND I KNOW THE CART WAS REALLY NOISY BEFORE—
BUT I THOUGHT I TOLD YOU ALL TO KEEP QUIET.
I FOUND YOU A CLACKER.
OH! I'M SORRY! I DIDN'T NEED IT AFTER ALL!
GIVE IT A TRY NOW.

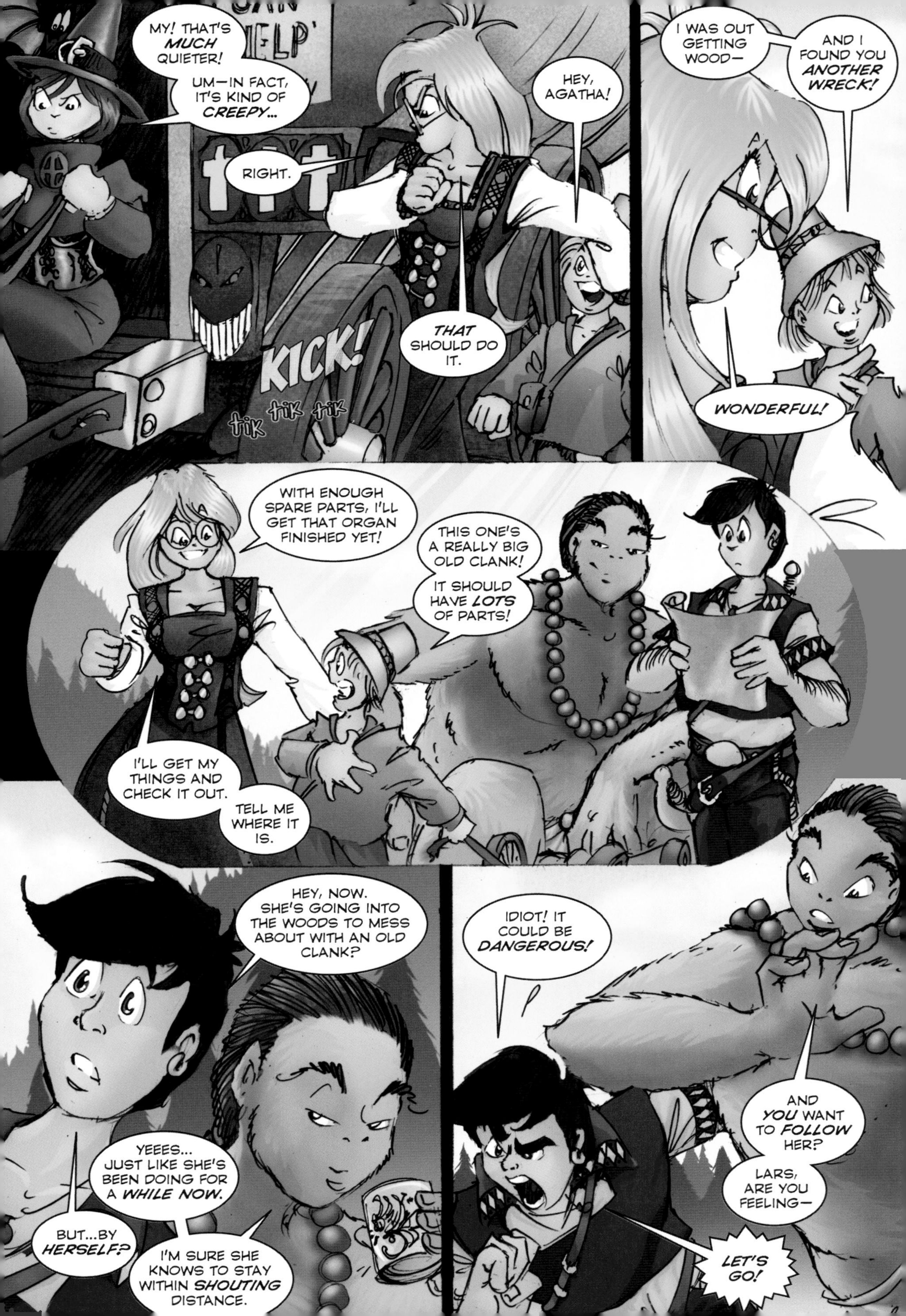

MY! THAT'S *MUCH* QUIETER!
UM—IN FACT, IT'S KIND OF *CREEPY*...
RIGHT.
tik tik tik
KICK!
THAT SHOULD DO IT.
HEY, AGATHA!
I WAS OUT GETTING WOOD—
AND I FOUND YOU *ANOTHER WRECK!*
WONDERFUL!
WITH ENOUGH SPARE PARTS, I'LL GET THAT ORGAN FINISHED YET!
THIS ONE'S A REALLY BIG OLD CLANK!
IT SHOULD HAVE *LOTS* OF PARTS!
I'LL GET MY THINGS AND CHECK IT OUT.
TELL ME WHERE IT IS.
HEY, NOW. SHE'S GOING INTO THE WOODS TO MESS ABOUT WITH AN OLD CLANK?
YEEES... JUST LIKE SHE'S BEEN DOING FOR A *WHILE NOW*.
BUT...BY *HERSELF?*
I'M SURE SHE KNOWS TO STAY WITHIN *SHOUTING* DISTANCE.
IDIOT! IT COULD BE *DANGEROUS!*
AND *YOU* WANT TO *FOLLOW* HER?
LARS, ARE YOU FEELING—
LET'S GO!

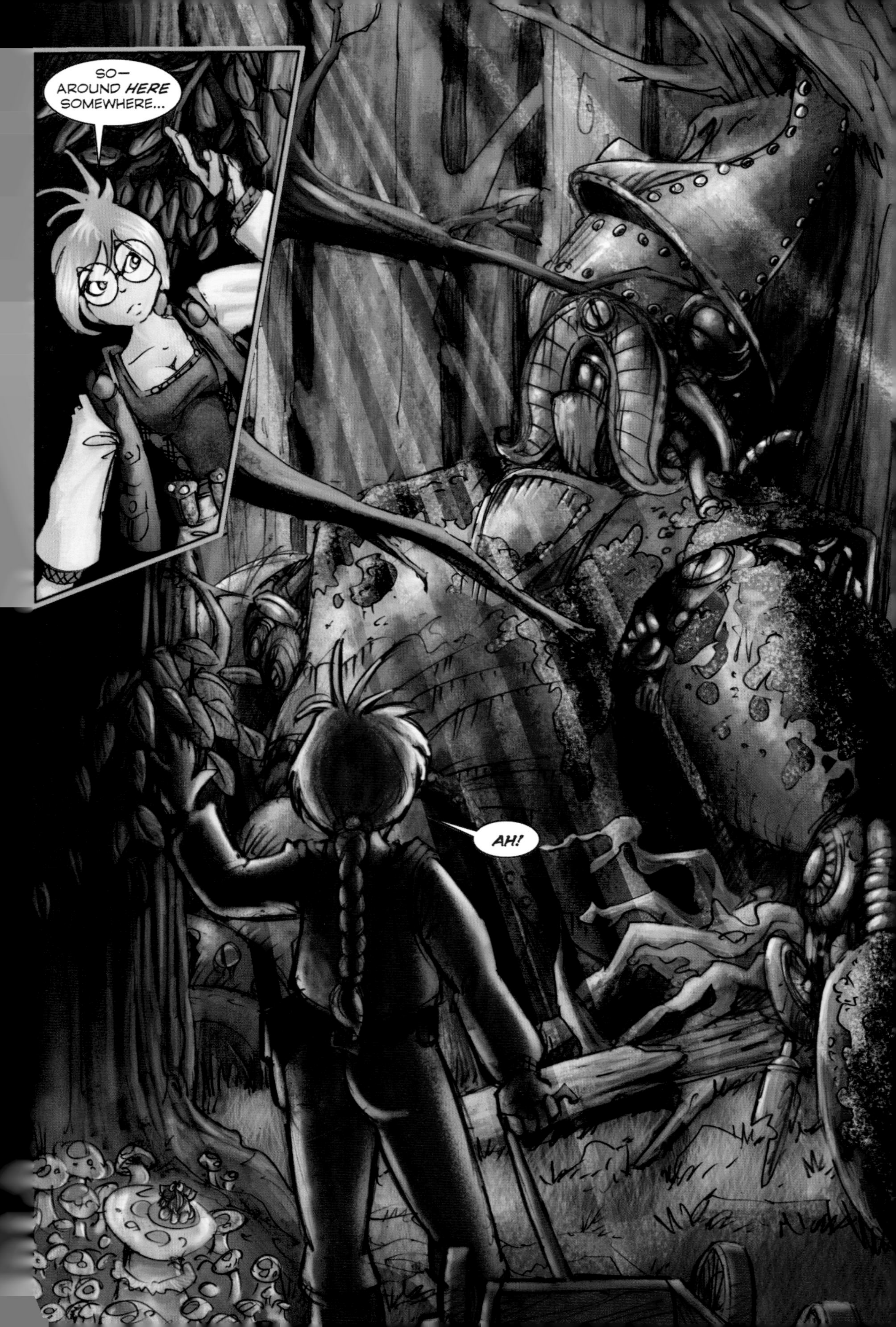
SO—
AROUND HERE
SOMEWHERE...
AH!

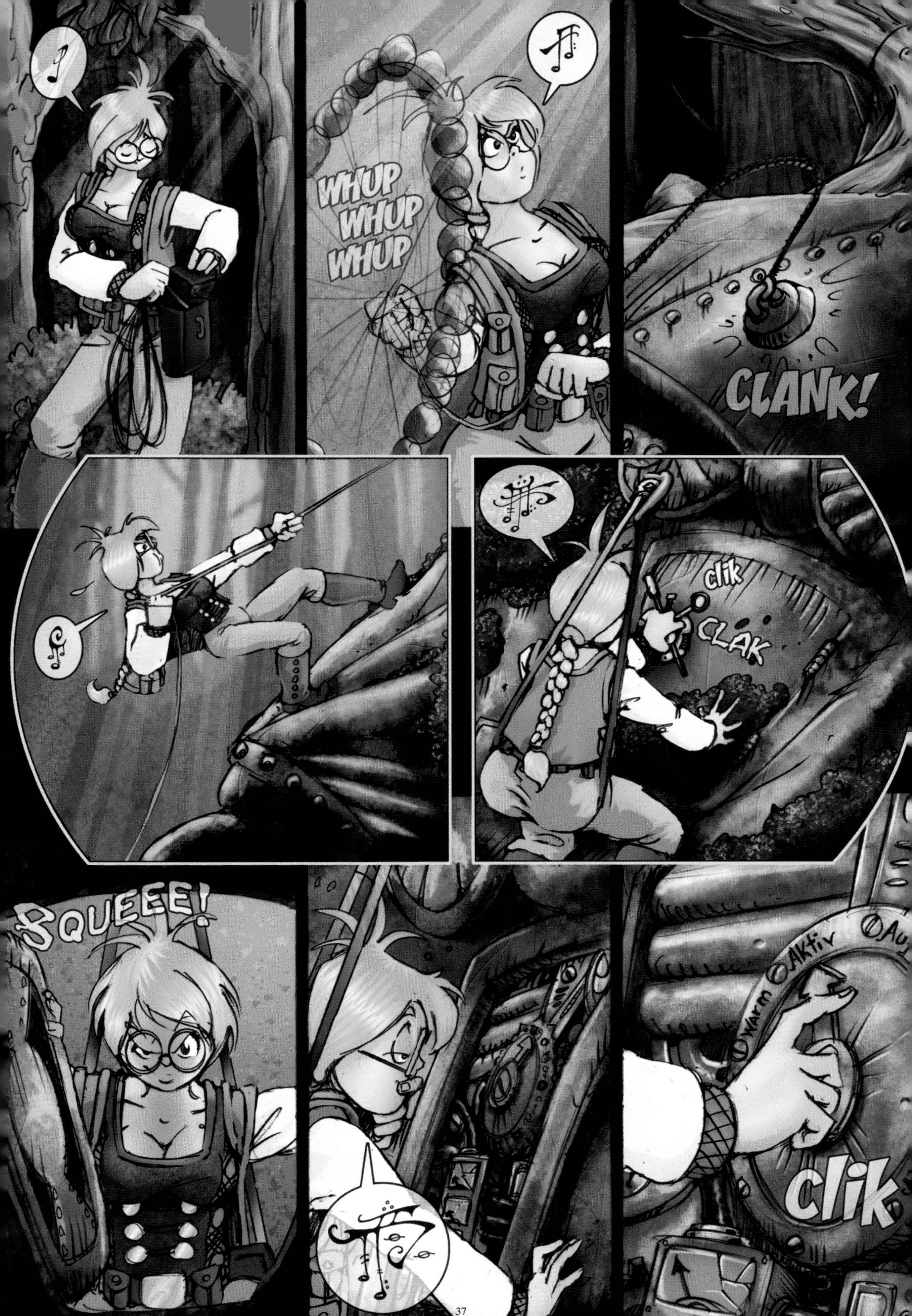
WHUP
WHUP
WHUP
CLANK!
clik
CLAK
SQUEEE!
warm
Aktiv
Au
clik

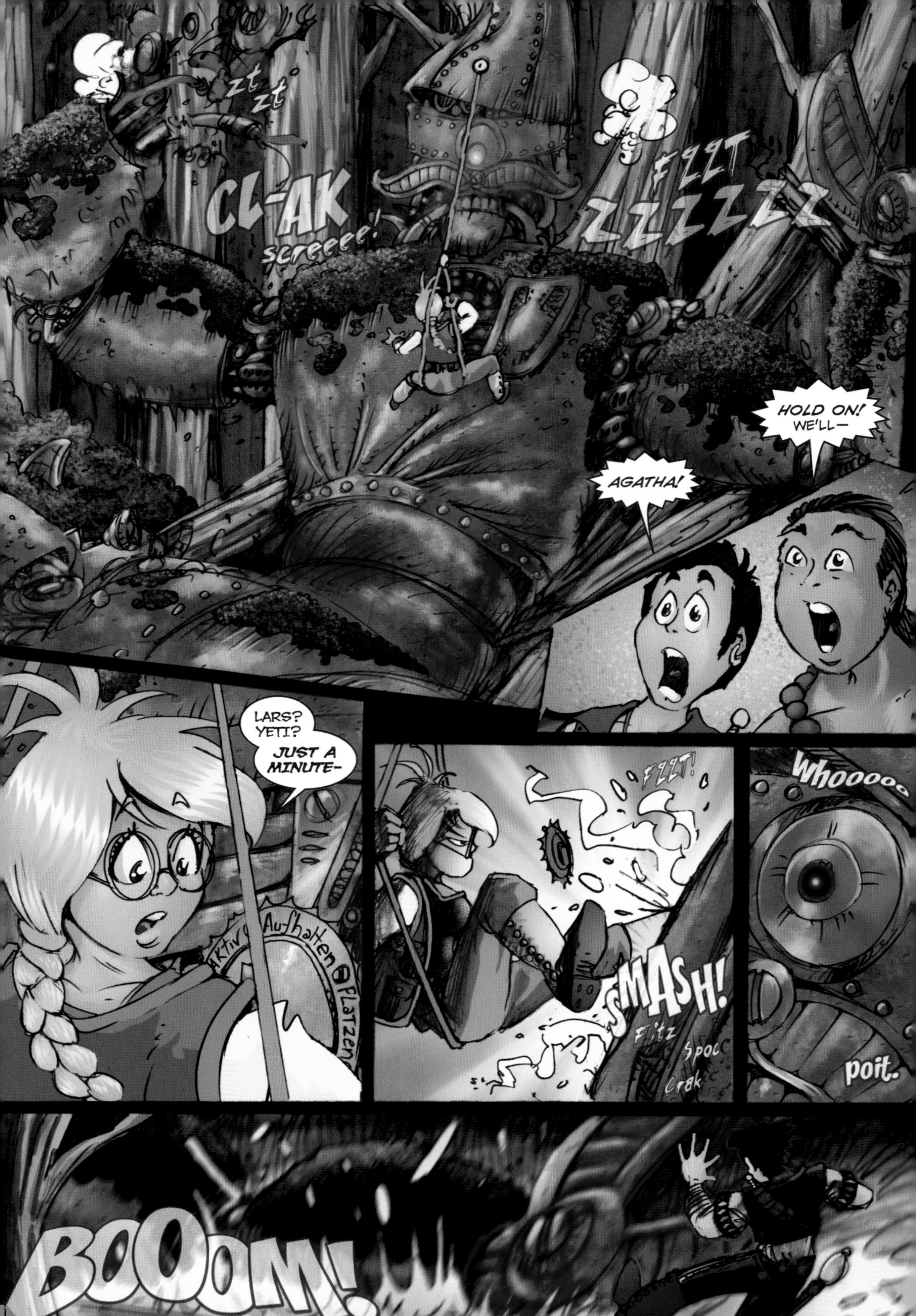
zt zt
CL-AK
screeeee!
FZZT
ZZZZZZ
HOLD ON! WE'LL—
AGATHA!
LARS? YETI?
JUST A MINUTE-
Aktiv
Aufhalten
Platzen
FZZT!
SMASH!
Fitz
Spoc
Crak
Whooooo
poit.
BOOOM!

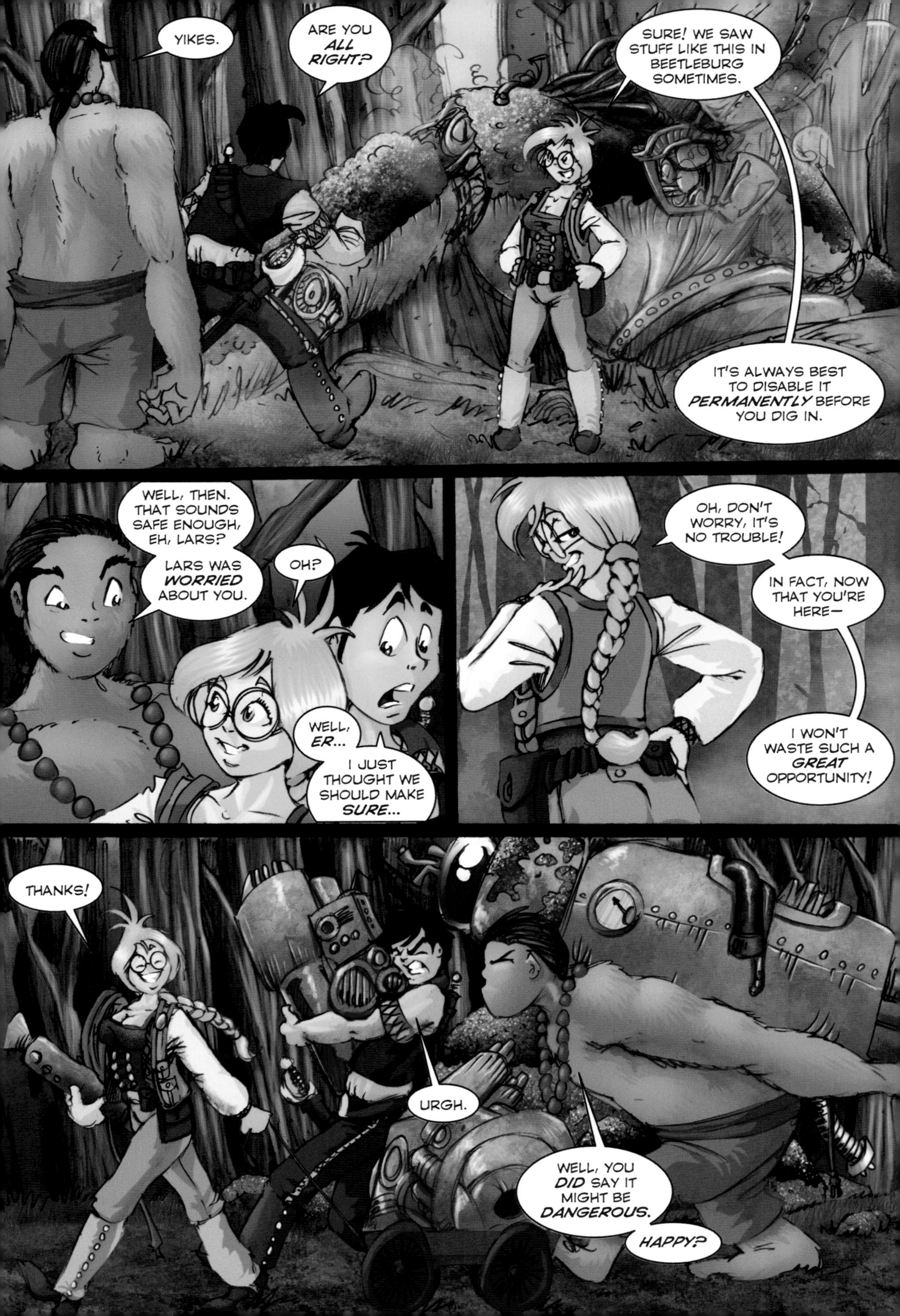
YIKES.
ARE YOU ALL RIGHT?
SURE! WE SAW STUFF LIKE THIS IN BEETLEBURG SOMETIMES.
IT'S ALWAYS BEST TO DISABLE IT PERMANENTLY BEFORE YOU DIG IN.
WELL, THEN. THAT SOUNDS SAFE ENOUGH, EH, LARS?
LARS WAS WORRIED ABOUT YOU.
OH?
WELL, ER...
I JUST THOUGHT WE SHOULD MAKE SURE...
OH, DON'T WORRY, IT'S NO TROUBLE!
IN FACT, NOW THAT YOU'RE HERE—
I WON'T WASTE SUCH A GREAT OPPORTUNITY!
THANKS!
URGH.
WELL, YOU DID SAY IT MIGHT BE DANGEROUS.
HAPPY?

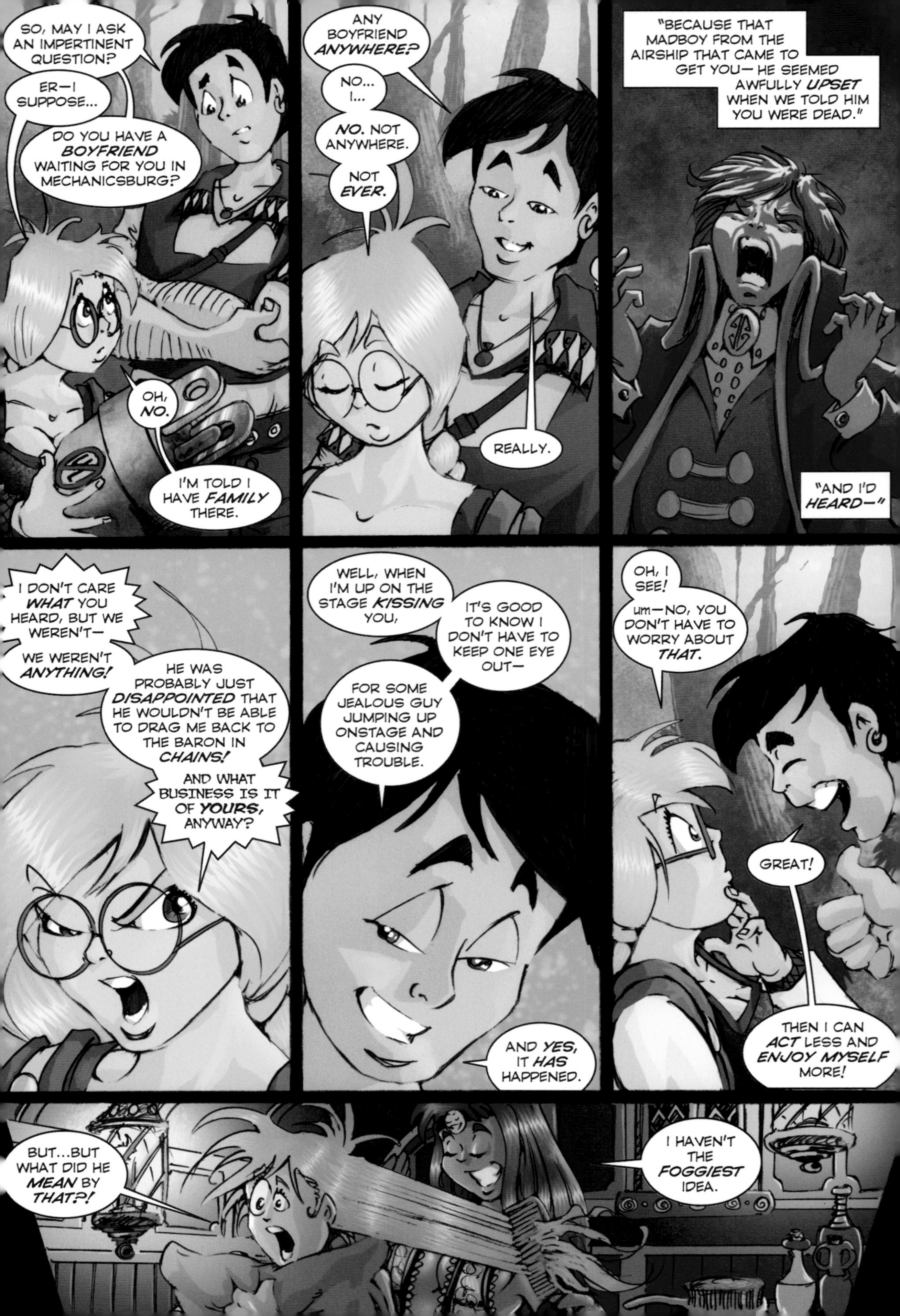
SO, MAY I ASK AN IMPERTINENT QUESTION?
ER—I SUPPOSE...
DO YOU HAVE A BOYFRIEND WAITING FOR YOU IN MECHANICSBURG?
OH, NO.
I'M TOLD I HAVE FAMILY THERE.
ANY BOYFRIEND ANYWHERE?
NO... I...
NO. NOT ANYWHERE.
NOT EVER.
REALLY.
"BECAUSE THAT MADBOY FROM THE AIRSHIP THAT CAME TO GET YOU— HE SEEMED AWFULLY UPSET WHEN WE TOLD HIM YOU WERE DEAD."
"AND I'D HEARD—"
I DON'T CARE WHAT YOU HEARD, BUT WE WEREN'T—
WE WEREN'T ANYTHING!
HE WAS PROBABLY JUST DISAPPOINTED THAT HE WOULDN'T BE ABLE TO DRAG ME BACK TO THE BARON IN CHAINS!
AND WHAT BUSINESS IS IT OF YOURS, ANYWAY?
WELL, WHEN I'M UP ON THE STAGE KISSING YOU,
IT'S GOOD TO KNOW I DON'T HAVE TO KEEP ONE EYE OUT—
FOR SOME JEALOUS GUY JUMPING UP ONSTAGE AND CAUSING TROUBLE.
AND YES, IT HAS HAPPENED.
OH, I SEE!
um—NO, YOU DON'T HAVE TO WORRY ABOUT THAT.
GREAT!
THEN I CAN ACT LESS AND ENJOY MYSELF MORE!
BUT...BUT WHAT DID HE MEAN BY THAT?!
I HAVEN'T THE FOGGIEST IDEA.

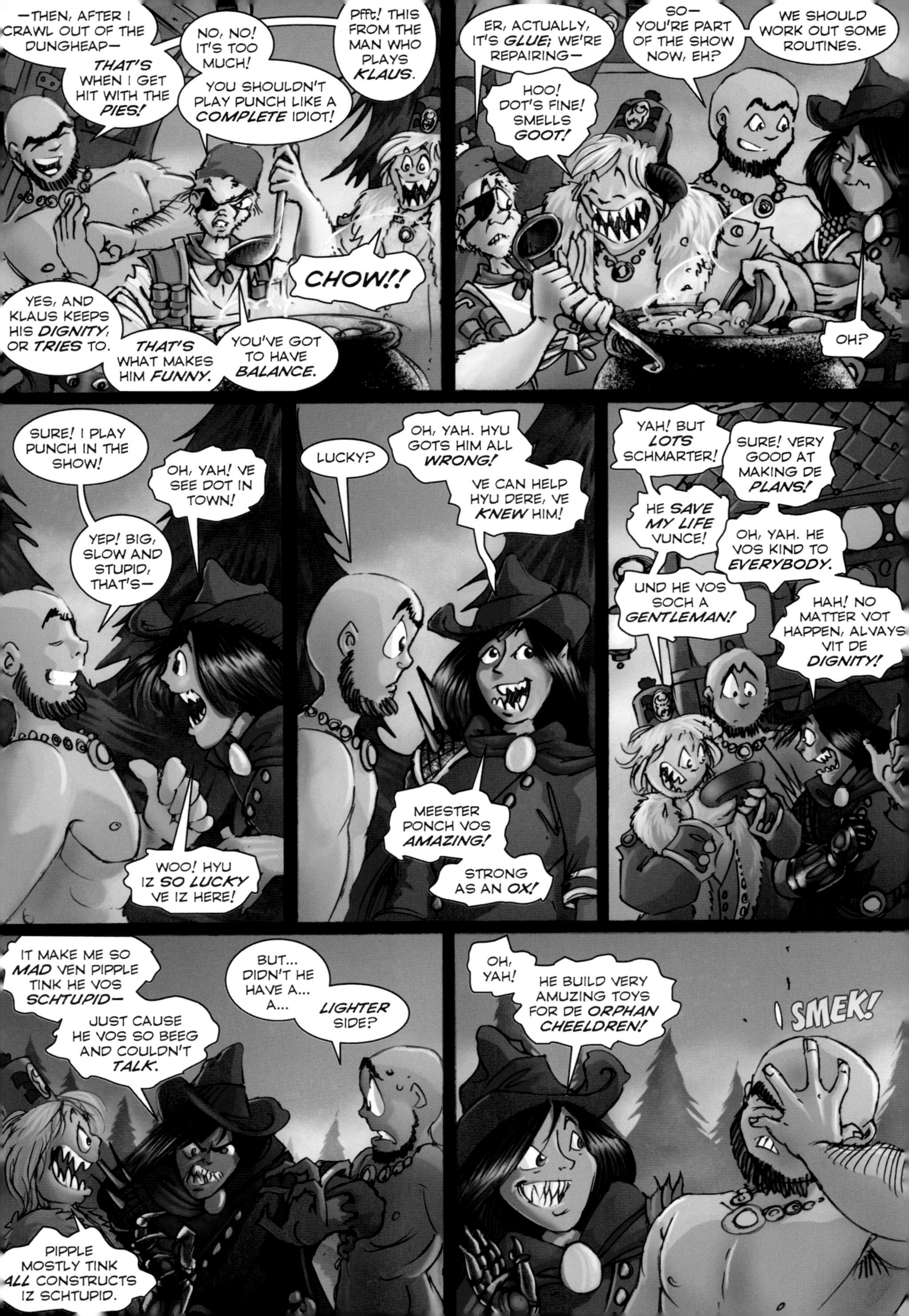
—THEN, AFTER I CRAWL OUT OF THE DUNGHEAP—
THAT'S WHEN I GET HIT WITH THE *PIES!*
NO, NO! IT'S TOO MUCH!
YOU SHOULDN'T PLAY PUNCH LIKE A *COMPLETE* IDIOT!
Pffft! THIS FROM THE MAN WHO PLAYS *KLAUS*.
CHOW!!
YES, AND KLAUS KEEPS HIS *DIGNITY*, OR *TRIES* TO.
THAT'S WHAT MAKES HIM *FUNNY*.
YOU'VE GOT TO HAVE *BALANCE*.
ER, ACTUALLY, IT'S *GLUE*; WE'RE REPAIRING—
HOO! DOT'S FINE! SMELLS *GOOT!*
SO— YOU'RE PART OF THE SHOW NOW, EH?
WE SHOULD WORK OUT SOME ROUTINES.
OH?
SURE! I PLAY PUNCH IN THE SHOW!
OH, YAH! VE SEE DOT IN TOWN!
YEP! BIG, SLOW AND STUPID, THAT'S—
WOO! HYU IZ *SO LUCKY* VE IZ HERE!
LUCKY?
OH, YAH. HYU GOTS HIM ALL *WRONG!*
VE CAN HELP HYU DERE, VE *KNEW* HIM!
MEESTER PONCH VOS *AMAZING!*
STRONG AS AN *OX!*
YAH! BUT *LOTS* SCHMARTER!
SURE! VERY GOOD AT MAKING DE *PLANS!*
HE *SAVE MY LIFE* VUNCE!
OH, YAH. HE VOS KIND TO *EVERYBODY*.
UND HE VOS SOCH A *GENTLEMAN!*
HAH! NO MATTER VOT HAPPEN, ALVAYS VIT DE *DIGNITY!*
IT MAKE ME SO *MAD* VEN PIPPLE TINK HE VOS *SCHTUPID*—
JUST CAUSE HE VOS SO BEEG AND COULDN'T *TALK*.
BUT... DIDN'T HE HAVE A... A... *LIGHTER* SIDE?
PIPPLE MOSTLY TINK *ALL* CONSTRUCTS IZ SCHTUPID.
OH, YAH!
HE BUILD VERY AMUZING TOYS FOR DE *ORPHAN CHEELDREN!*
SMEK!

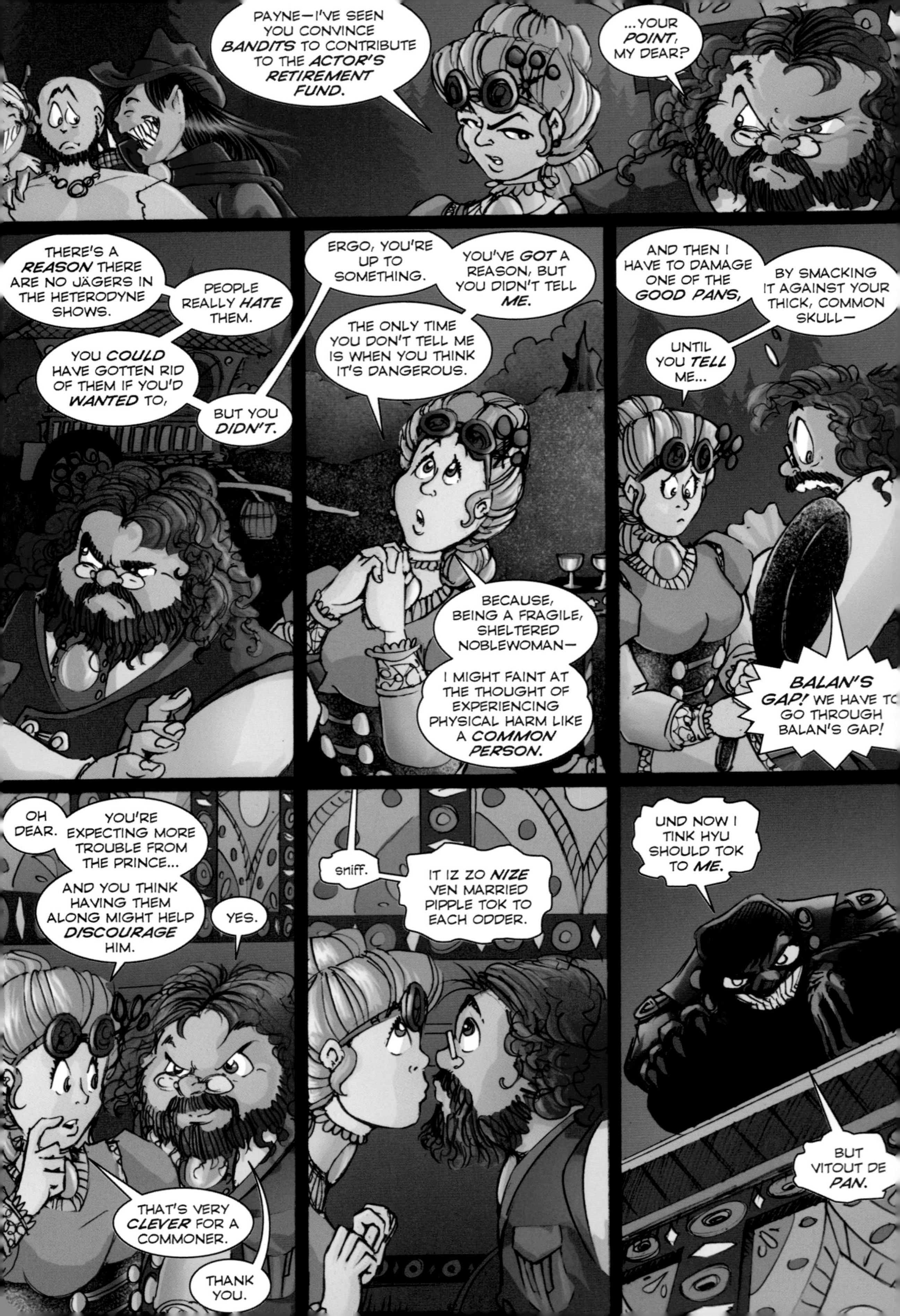
PAYNE—I'VE SEEN YOU CONVINCE BANDITS TO CONTRIBUTE TO THE ACTOR'S RETIREMENT FUND.
...YOUR POINT, MY DEAR?
THERE'S A REASON THERE ARE NO JÄGERS IN THE HETERODYNE SHOWS.
PEOPLE REALLY HATE THEM.
YOU COULD HAVE GOTTEN RID OF THEM IF YOU'D WANTED TO,
BUT YOU DIDN'T.
ERGO, YOU'RE UP TO SOMETHING.
YOU'VE GOT A REASON, BUT YOU DIDN'T TELL ME.
THE ONLY TIME YOU DON'T TELL ME IS WHEN YOU THINK IT'S DANGEROUS.
BECAUSE, BEING A FRAGILE, SHELTERED NOBLEWOMAN—
I MIGHT FAINT AT THE THOUGHT OF EXPERIENCING PHYSICAL HARM LIKE A COMMON PERSON.
AND THEN I HAVE TO DAMAGE ONE OF THE GOOD PANS,
BY SMACKING IT AGAINST YOUR THICK, COMMON SKULL—
UNTIL YOU TELL ME...
BALAN'S GAP! WE HAVE TO GO THROUGH BALAN'S GAP!
OH DEAR.
YOU'RE EXPECTING MORE TROUBLE FROM THE PRINCE...
AND YOU THINK HAVING THEM ALONG MIGHT HELP DISCOURAGE HIM.
YES.
THAT'S VERY CLEVER FOR A COMMONER.
THANK YOU.
sniff.
IT IZ ZO NIZE VEN MARRIED PIPPLE TOK TO EACH ODDER.
UND NOW I TINK HYU SHOULD TOK TO ME.
BUT VITOUT DE PAN.

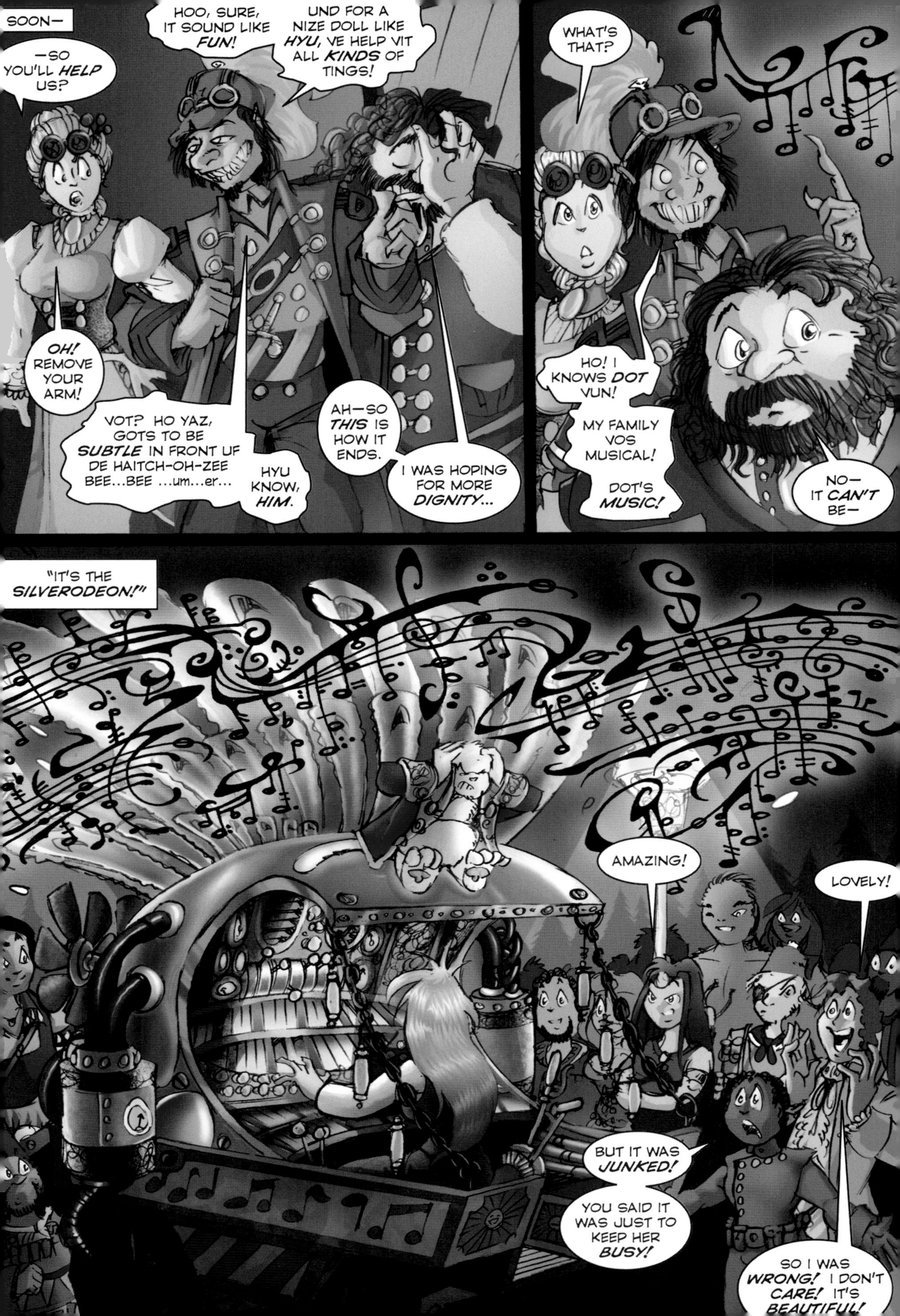

SOON—
—SO YOU'LL *HELP* US?
HOO, SURE, IT SOUND LIKE *FUN!*
UND FOR A NIZE DOLL LIKE *HYU,* VE HELP VIT ALL *KINDS* OF TINGS!
OH! REMOVE YOUR ARM!
VOT? HO YAZ, GOTS TO BE *SUBTLE* IN FRONT UF DE HAITCH-OH-ZEE BEE...BEE ...um...er...
HYU KNOW, *HIM*.
AH—SO *THIS* IS HOW IT ENDS.
I WAS HOPING FOR MORE *DIGNITY...*
WHAT'S THAT?
HO! I KNOWS *DOT* VUN!
MY FAMILY VOS MUSICAL!
DOT'S *MUSIC!*
NO— IT *CAN'T* BE—
"IT'S THE *SILVERODEON!*"
AMAZING!
LOVELY!
BUT IT WAS *JUNKED!*
YOU SAID IT WAS JUST TO KEEP HER *BUSY!*
SO I WAS *WRONG!* I DON'T *CARE!* IT'S *BEAUTIFUL!*

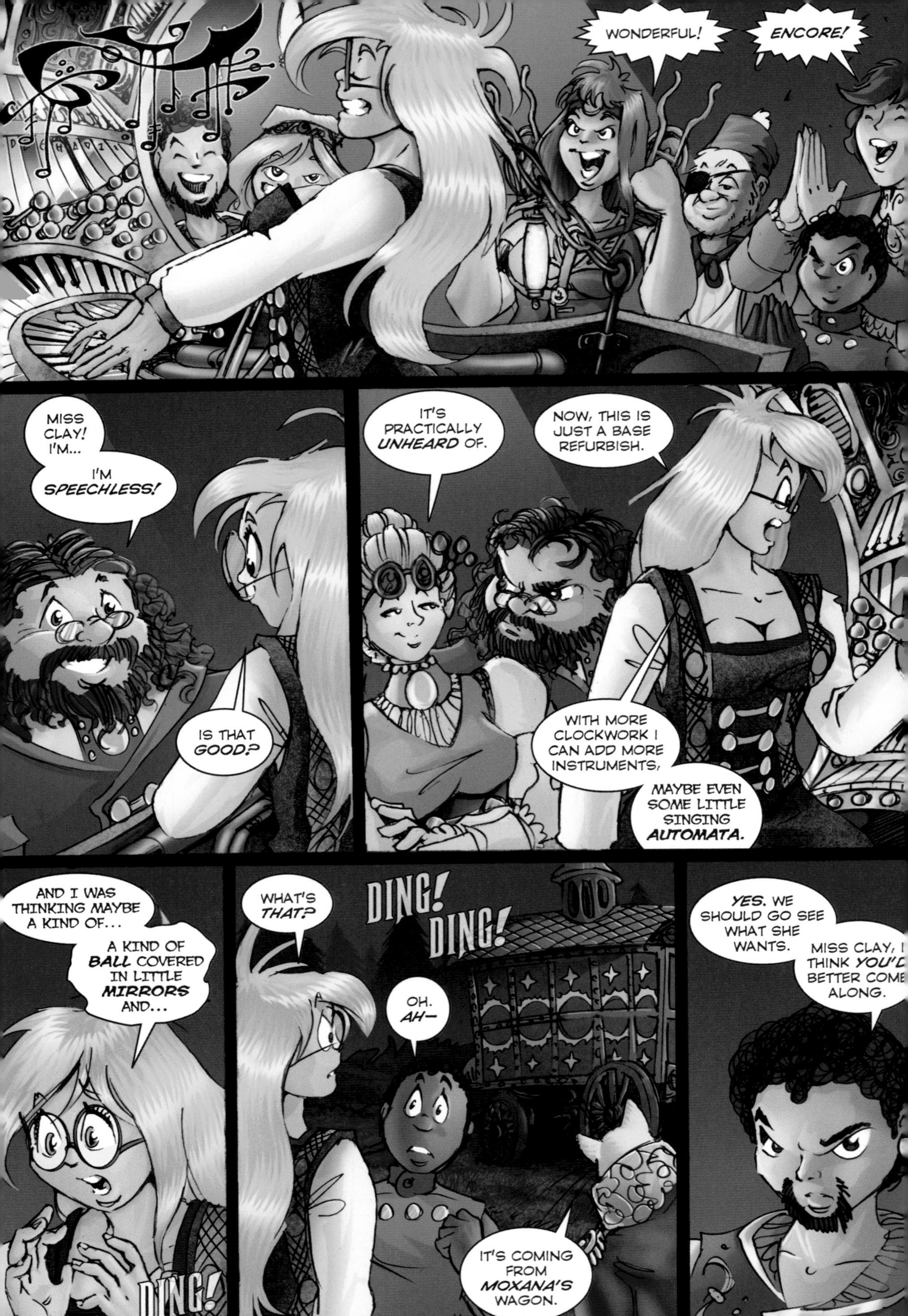
WONDERFUL!
ENCORE!
MISS CLAY! I'M...
I'M SPEECHLESS!
IS THAT GOOD?
IT'S PRACTICALLY UNHEARD OF.
NOW, THIS IS JUST A BASE REFURBISH.
WITH MORE CLOCKWORK I CAN ADD MORE INSTRUMENTS,
MAYBE EVEN SOME LITTLE SINGING AUTOMATA.
AND I WAS THINKING MAYBE A KIND OF...
A KIND OF BALL COVERED IN LITTLE MIRRORS AND...
DING!
WHAT'S THAT?
DING! DING!
OH. AH—
IT'S COMING FROM MOXANA'S WAGON.
YES. WE SHOULD GO SEE WHAT SHE WANTS.
MISS CLAY, I THINK YOU'D BETTER COME ALONG.

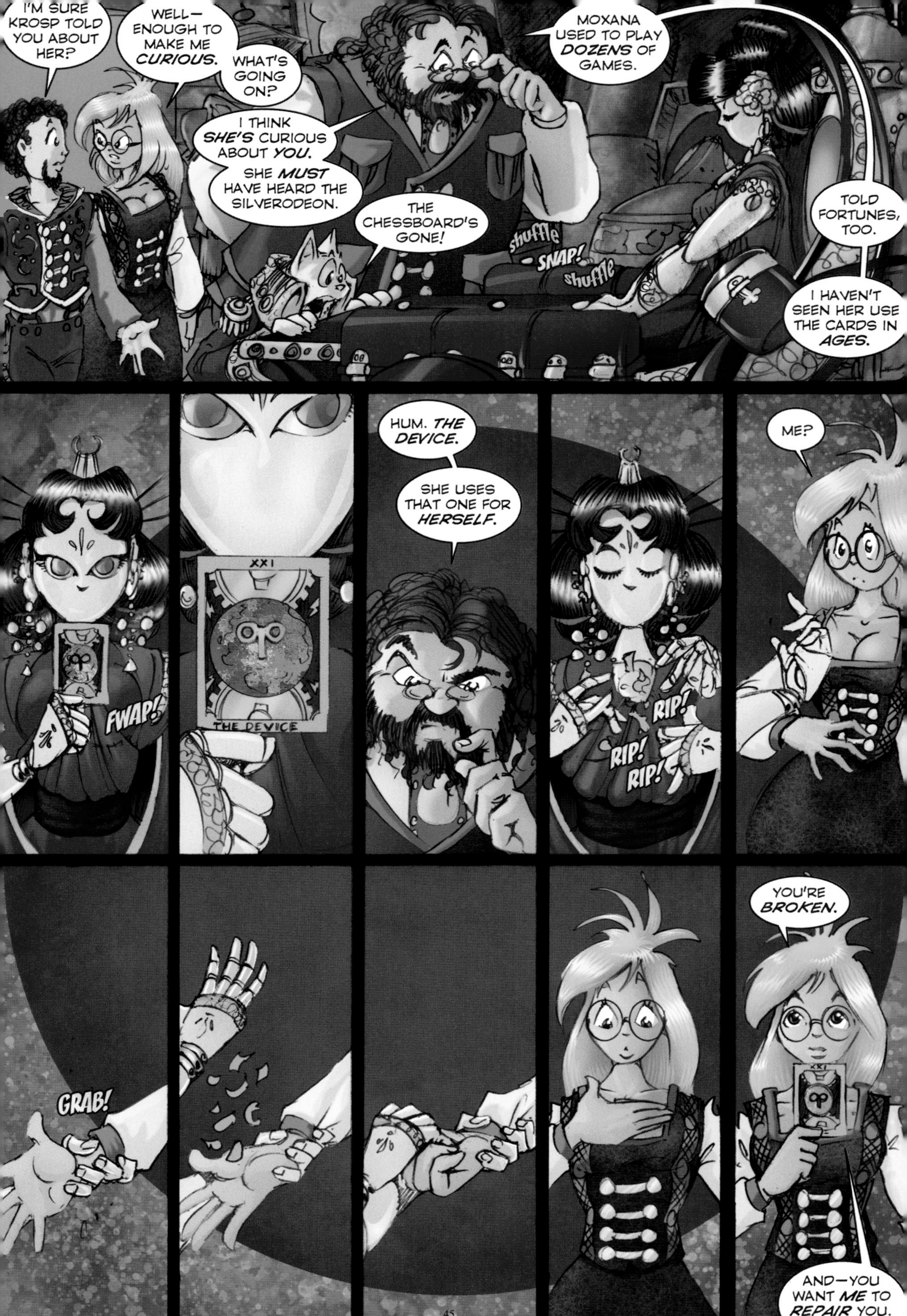

I'M SURE KROSP TOLD YOU ABOUT HER?
WELL— ENOUGH TO MAKE ME *CURIOUS.*
WHAT'S GOING ON?
I THINK *SHE'S* CURIOUS ABOUT *YOU.*
SHE *MUST* HAVE HEARD THE SILVERODEON.
THE CHESSBOARD'S GONE!
MOXANA USED TO PLAY *DOZENS* OF GAMES.
shuffle
SNAP!
shuffle
TOLD FORTUNES, TOO.
I HAVEN'T SEEN HER USE THE CARDS IN *AGES.*
FWAP!
XXI
THE DEVICE
HUM. *THE DEVICE.*
SHE USES THAT ONE FOR *HERSELF.*
RIP!
RIP!
RIP!
ME?
GRAB!
YOU'RE *BROKEN.*
AND—YOU WANT *ME* TO *REPAIR* YOU.

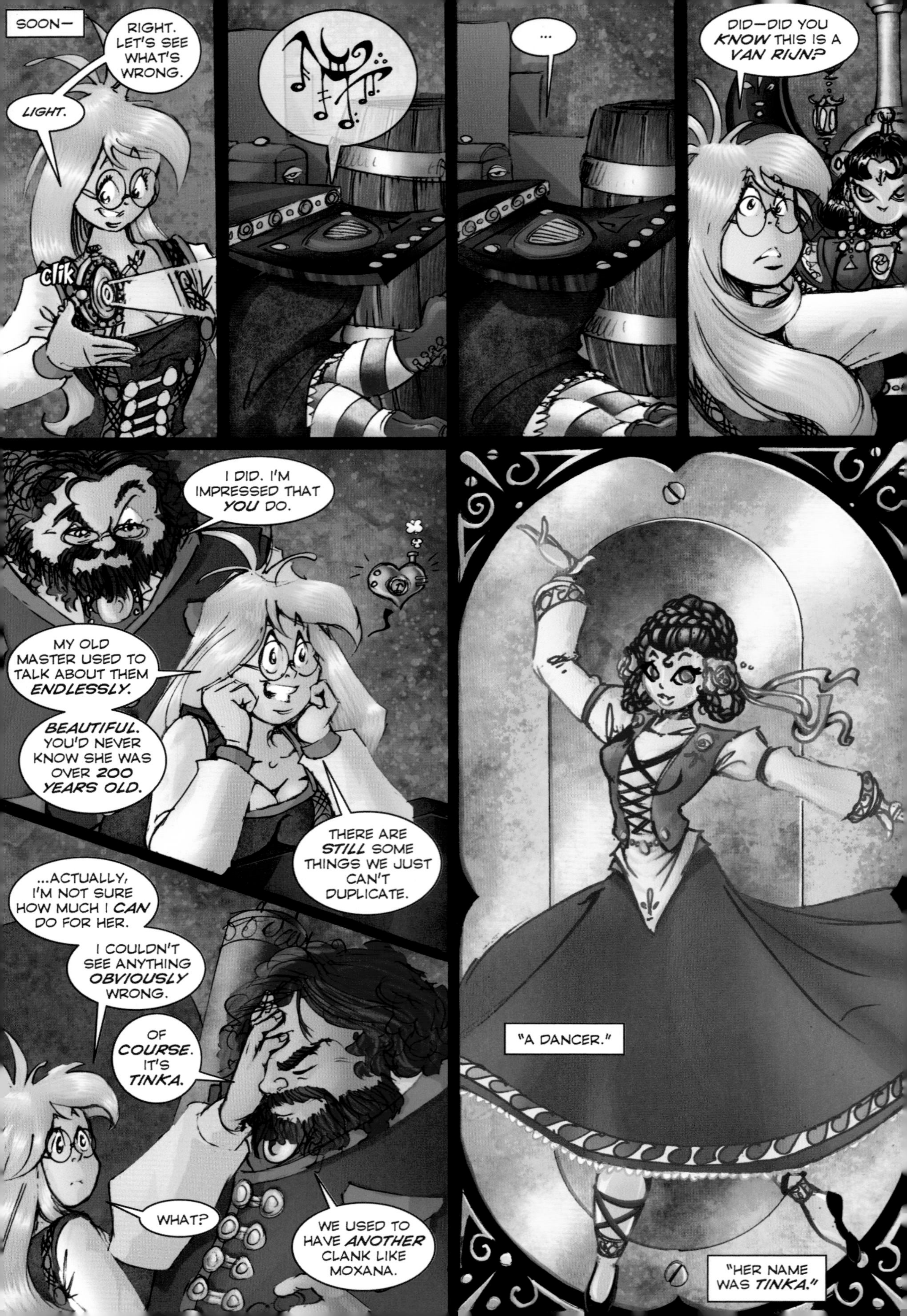
SOON—
RIGHT. LET'S SEE WHAT'S WRONG.
LIGHT.
clik
...
DID—DID YOU KNOW THIS IS A VAN RIJN?
I DID. I'M IMPRESSED THAT YOU DO.
MY OLD MASTER USED TO TALK ABOUT THEM ENDLESSLY.
BEAUTIFUL. YOU'D NEVER KNOW SHE WAS OVER 200 YEARS OLD.
THERE ARE STILL SOME THINGS WE JUST CAN'T DUPLICATE.
...ACTUALLY, I'M NOT SURE HOW MUCH I CAN DO FOR HER.
I COULDN'T SEE ANYTHING OBVIOUSLY WRONG.
OF COURSE. IT'S TINKA.
WHAT?
WE USED TO HAVE ANOTHER CLANK LIKE MOXANA.
"A DANCER."
"HER NAME WAS TINKA."

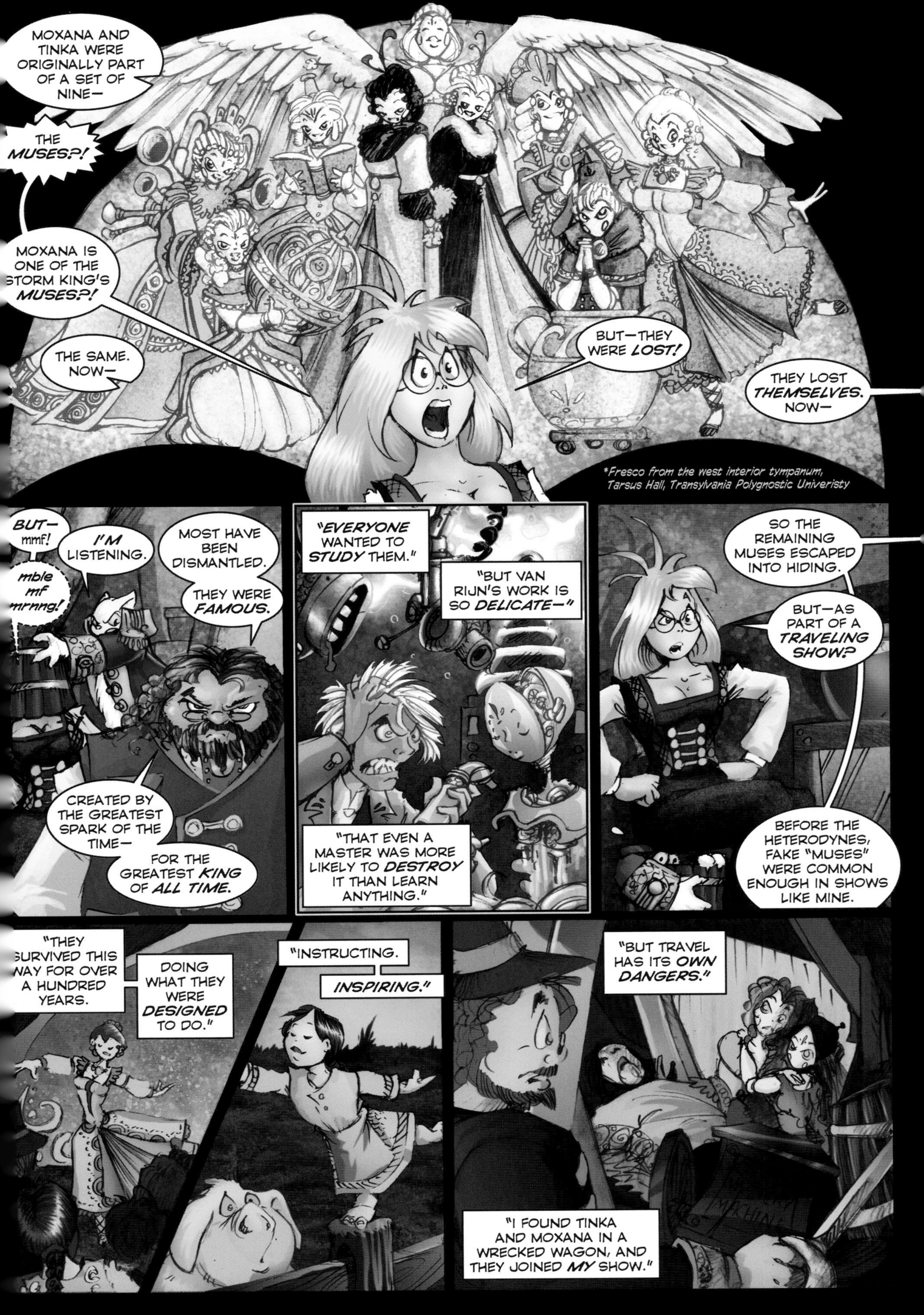
MOXANA AND TINKA WERE ORIGINALLY PART OF A SET OF NINE—
THE *MUSES?!*
MOXANA IS ONE OF THE STORM KING'S *MUSES?!*
THE SAME. NOW—
BUT—THEY WERE *LOST!*
THEY LOST *THEMSELVES.* NOW—
*Fresco from the west interior tympanum, Tarsus Hall, Transylvania Polygnostic Univeristy
BUT— mmf!
mble mf mrnng!
I'M LISTENING.
MOST HAVE BEEN DISMANTLED.
THEY WERE *FAMOUS.*
CREATED BY THE GREATEST SPARK OF THE TIME—
FOR THE GREATEST *KING* OF *ALL TIME.*
"*EVERYONE* WANTED TO *STUDY* THEM."
"BUT VAN RIJN'S WORK IS SO *DELICATE*—"
"THAT EVEN A MASTER WAS MORE LIKELY TO *DESTROY* IT THAN LEARN ANYTHING."
SO THE REMAINING MUSES ESCAPED INTO HIDING.
BUT—AS PART OF A *TRAVELING SHOW?*
BEFORE THE HETERODYNES, FAKE "MUSES" WERE COMMON ENOUGH IN SHOWS LIKE MINE.
"THEY SURVIVED THIS WAY FOR OVER A HUNDRED YEARS.
DOING WHAT THEY WERE *DESIGNED* TO DO."
"INSTRUCTING.
INSPIRING."
"BUT TRAVEL HAS ITS *OWN DANGERS.*"
"I FOUND TINKA AND MOXANA IN A WRECKED WAGON, AND THEY JOINED *MY* SHOW."

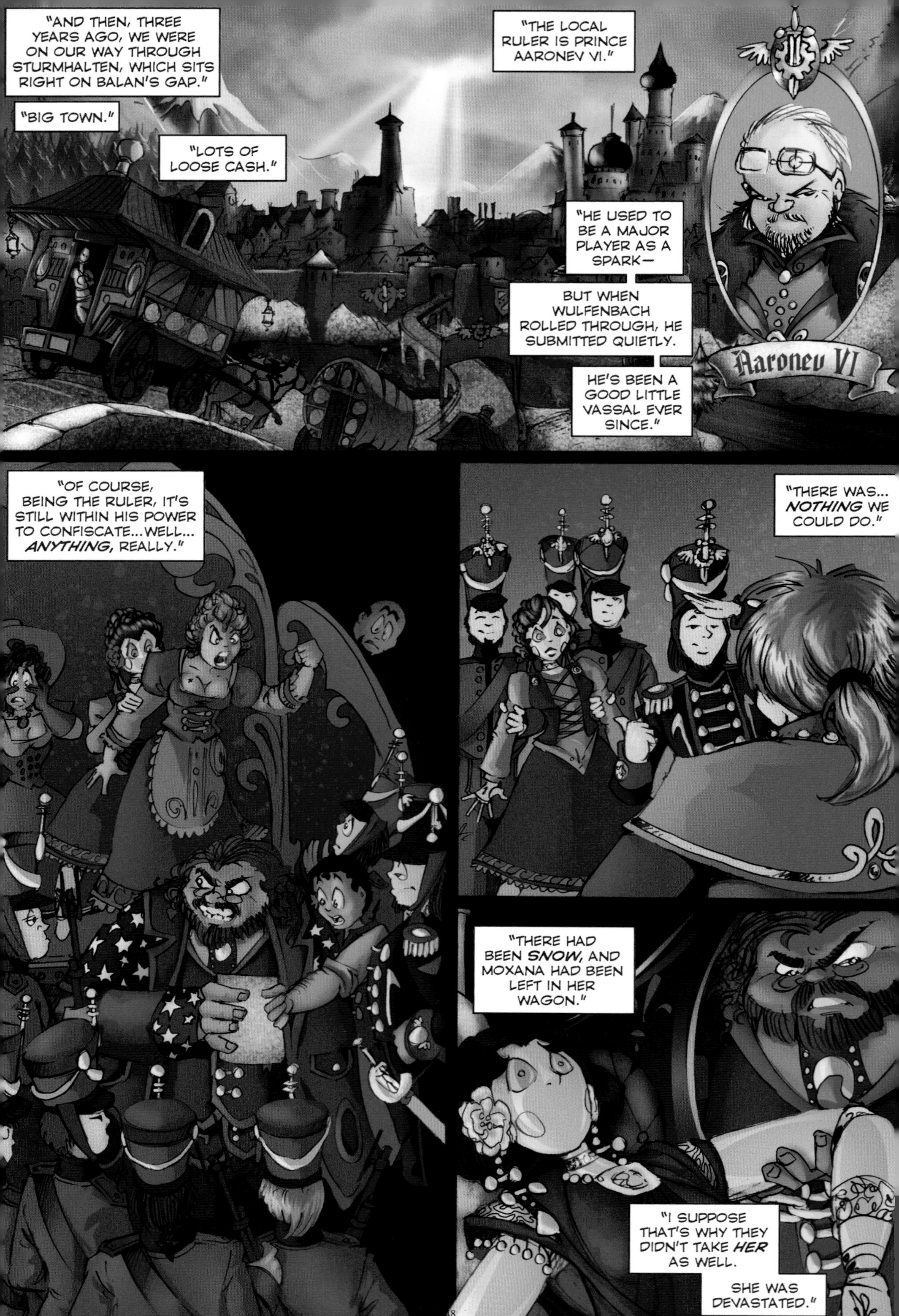
"AND THEN, THREE YEARS AGO, WE WERE ON OUR WAY THROUGH STURMHALTEN, WHICH SITS RIGHT ON BALAN'S GAP."
"BIG TOWN."
"LOTS OF LOOSE CASH."
"THE LOCAL RULER IS PRINCE AARONEV VI."
Aaronev VI
"HE USED TO BE A MAJOR PLAYER AS A SPARK—
BUT WHEN WULFENBACH ROLLED THROUGH, HE SUBMITTED QUIETLY.
HE'S BEEN A GOOD LITTLE VASSAL EVER SINCE."
"OF COURSE, BEING THE RULER, IT'S STILL WITHIN HIS POWER TO CONFISCATE...WELL... *ANYTHING*, REALLY."
"THERE WAS... *NOTHING* WE COULD DO."
"THERE HAD BEEN *SNOW*, AND MOXANA HAD BEEN LEFT IN HER WAGON."
"I SUPPOSE THAT'S WHY THEY DIDN'T TAKE *HER* AS WELL.
SHE WAS DEVASTATED."

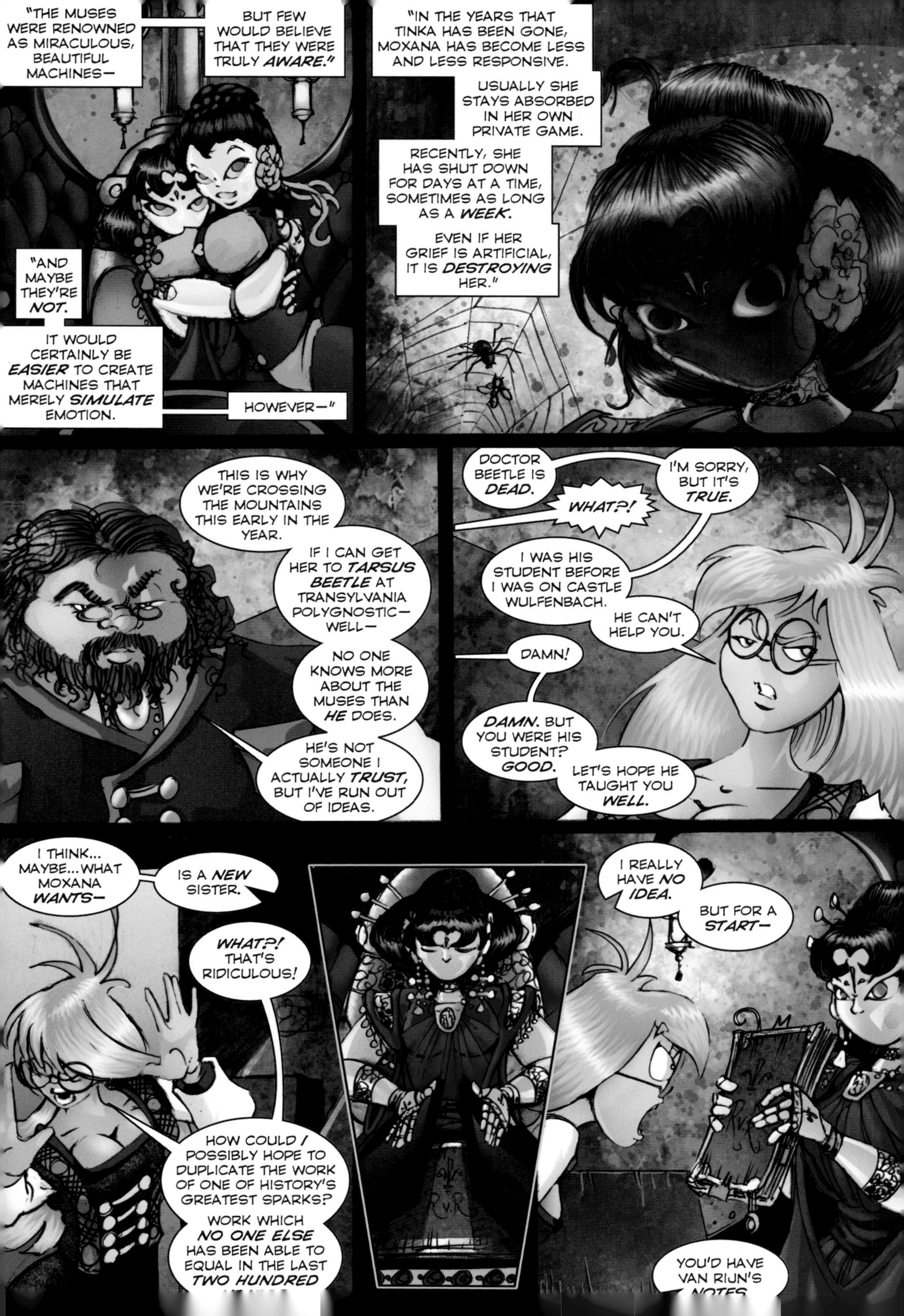
"THE MUSES WERE RENOWNED AS MIRACULOUS, BEAUTIFUL MACHINES—
BUT FEW WOULD BELIEVE THAT THEY WERE TRULY *AWARE.*"
"AND MAYBE THEY'RE *NOT*.
IT WOULD CERTAINLY BE *EASIER* TO CREATE MACHINES THAT MERELY *SIMULATE* EMOTION.
HOWEVER—"
"IN THE YEARS THAT TINKA HAS BEEN GONE, MOXANA HAS BECOME LESS AND LESS RESPONSIVE.
USUALLY SHE STAYS ABSORBED IN HER OWN PRIVATE GAME.
RECENTLY, SHE HAS SHUT DOWN FOR DAYS AT A TIME, SOMETIMES AS LONG AS A *WEEK*.
EVEN IF HER GRIEF IS ARTIFICIAL, IT IS *DESTROYING* HER."
THIS IS WHY WE'RE CROSSING THE MOUNTAINS THIS EARLY IN THE YEAR.
IF I CAN GET HER TO *TARSUS BEETLE* AT TRANSYLVANIA POLYGNOSTIC— WELL—
NO ONE KNOWS MORE ABOUT THE MUSES THAN *HE* DOES.
HE'S NOT SOMEONE I ACTUALLY *TRUST*, BUT I'VE RUN OUT OF IDEAS.
DOCTOR BEETLE IS *DEAD*.
WHAT?!
I'M SORRY, BUT IT'S *TRUE*.
I WAS HIS STUDENT BEFORE I WAS ON CASTLE WULFENBACH.
HE CAN'T HELP YOU.
DAMN!
DAMN. BUT YOU WERE HIS STUDENT? *GOOD*.
LET'S HOPE HE TAUGHT YOU *WELL*.
I THINK... MAYBE... WHAT MOXANA *WANTS*—
IS A *NEW* SISTER.
WHAT?! THAT'S RIDICULOUS!
HOW COULD *I* POSSIBLY HOPE TO DUPLICATE THE WORK OF ONE OF HISTORY'S GREATEST SPARKS?
WORK WHICH *NO ONE ELSE* HAS BEEN ABLE TO EQUAL IN THE LAST *TWO HUNDRED*
I REALLY HAVE *NO IDEA*.
BUT FOR A *START*—
YOU'D HAVE VAN RIJN'S

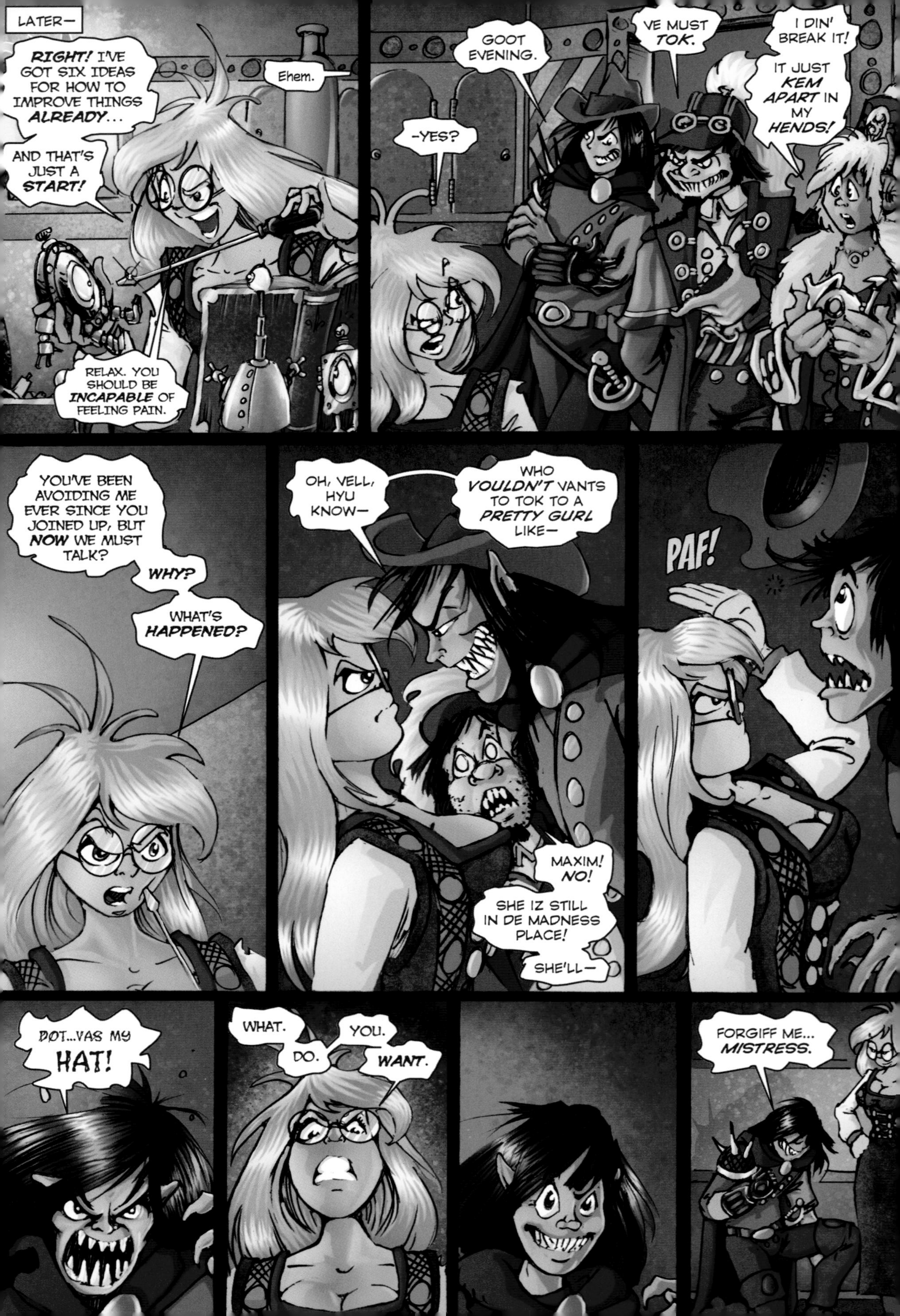

LATER—
RIGHT! I'VE GOT SIX IDEAS FOR HOW TO IMPROVE THINGS ALREADY...
AND THAT'S JUST A START!
Ehem.
RELAX. YOU SHOULD BE INCAPABLE OF FEELING PAIN.
GOOT EVENING.
-YES?
VE MUST TOK.
I DIN' BREAK IT!
IT JUST KEM APART IN MY HENDS!
YOU'VE BEEN AVOIDING ME EVER SINCE YOU JOINED UP, BUT NOW WE MUST TALK?
WHY?
WHAT'S HAPPENED?
OH, VELL, HYU KNOW—
WHO VOULDN'T VANTS TO TOK TO A PRETTY GURL LIKE—
MAXIM! NO!
SHE IZ STILL IN DE MADNESS PLACE!
SHE'LL—
PAF!
DOT...VAS MY HAT!
WHAT.
DO.
YOU.
WANT.
FORGIFF ME... MISTRESS.

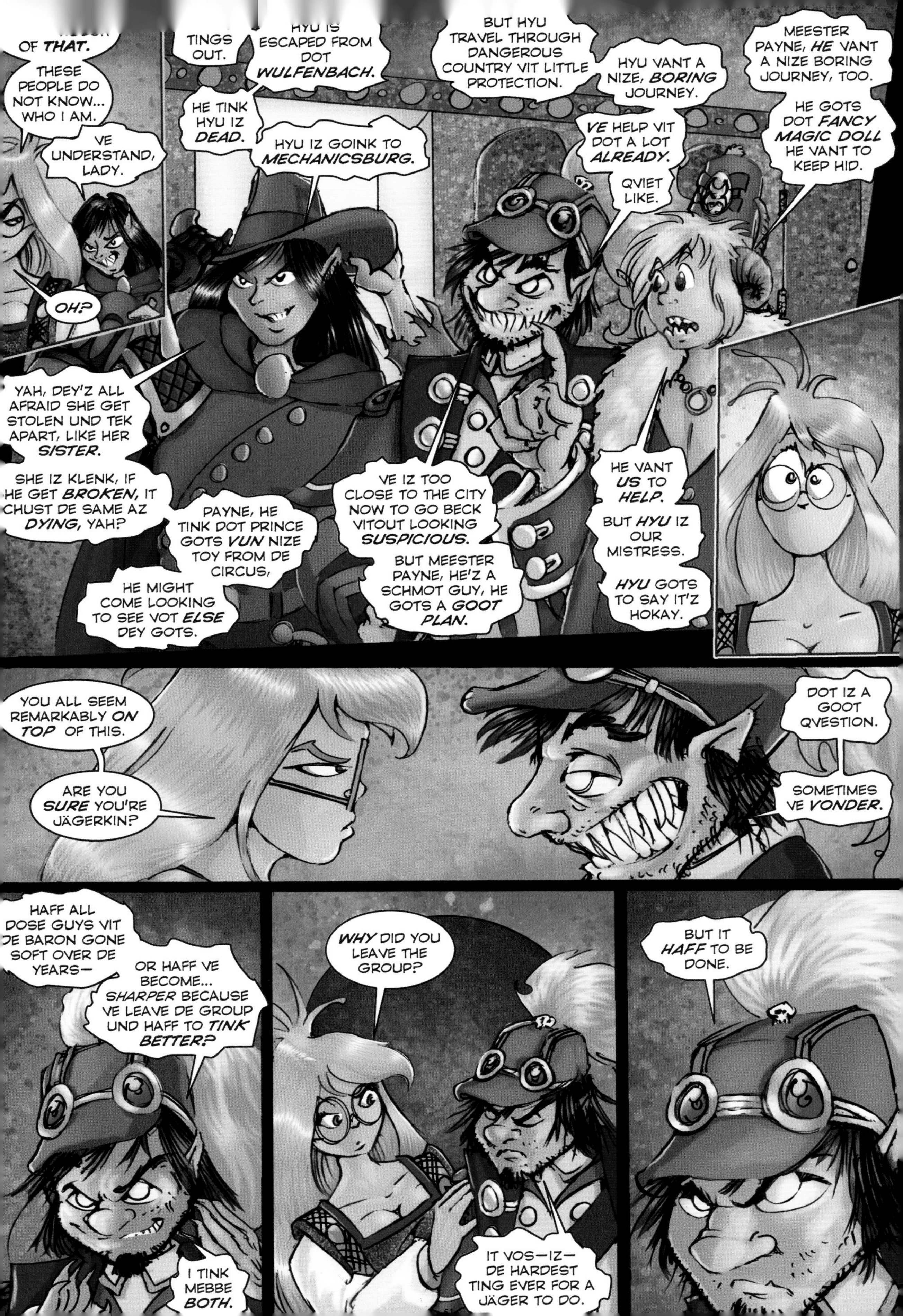
OF THAT.
THESE PEOPLE DO NOT KNOW... WHO I AM.
VE UNDERSTAND, LADY.
OH?
TINGS OUT.
HYU IS ESCAPED FROM DOT WULFENBACH.
HE TINK HYU IZ DEAD.
HYU IZ GOINK TO MECHANICSBURG.
BUT HYU TRAVEL THROUGH DANGEROUS COUNTRY VIT LITTLE PROTECTION.
HYU VANT A NIZE, BORING JOURNEY.
VE HELP VIT DOT A LOT ALREADY.
QVIET LIKE.
MEESTER PAYNE, HE VANT A NIZE BORING JOURNEY, TOO.
HE GOTS DOT FANCY MAGIC DOLL HE VANT TO KEEP HID.
YAH, DEY'Z ALL AFRAID SHE GET STOLEN UND TEK APART, LIKE HER SISTER.
SHE IZ KLENK, IF HE GET BROKEN, IT CHUST DE SAME AZ DYING, YAH?
PAYNE, HE TINK DOT PRINCE GOTS VUN NIZE TOY FROM DE CIRCUS,
HE MIGHT COME LOOKING TO SEE VOT ELSE DEY GOTS.
VE IZ TOO CLOSE TO THE CITY NOW TO GO BECK VITOUT LOOKING SUSPICIOUS.
BUT MEESTER PAYNE, HE'Z A SCHMOT GUY, HE GOTS A GOOT PLAN.
HE VANT US TO HELP.
BUT HYU IZ OUR MISTRESS.
HYU GOTS TO SAY IT'Z HOKAY.
YOU ALL SEEM REMARKABLY ON TOP OF THIS.
ARE YOU SURE YOU'RE JÄGERKIN?
DOT IZ A GOOT QVESTION.
SOMETIMES VE VONDER.
HAFF ALL DOSE GUYS VIT DE BARON GONE SOFT OVER DE YEARS—
OR HAFF VE BECOME... SHARPER BECAUSE VE LEAVE DE GROUP UND HAFF TO TINK BETTER?
I TINK MEBBE BOTH.
WHY DID YOU LEAVE THE GROUP?
IT VOS—IZ— DE HARDEST TING EVER FOR A JÄGER TO DO.
BUT IT HAFF TO BE DONE.

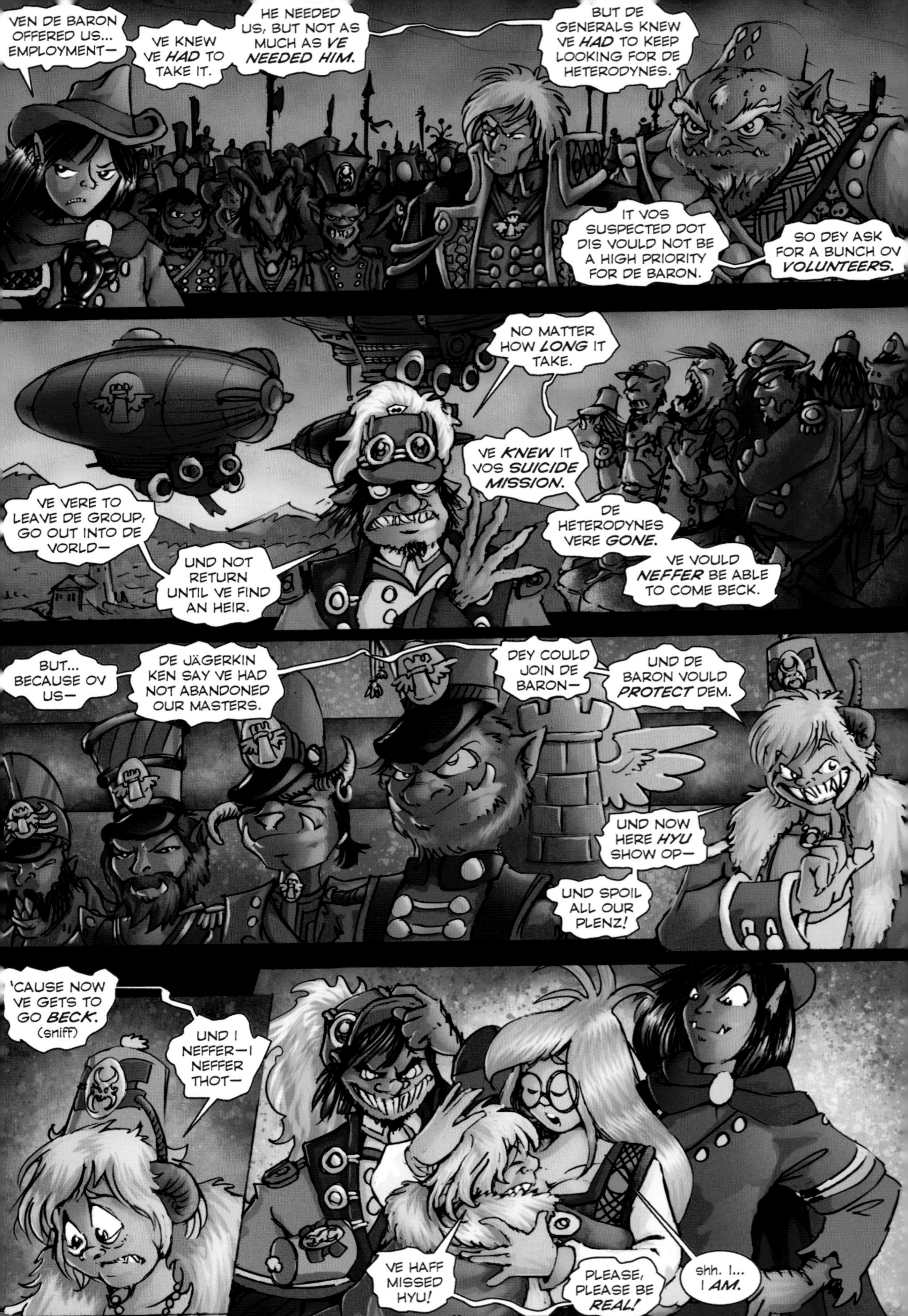
VEN DE BARON OFFERED US... EMPLOYMENT—
VE KNEW VE HAD TO TAKE IT.
HE NEEDED US, BUT NOT AS MUCH AS VE NEEDED HIM.
BUT DE GENERALS KNEW VE HAD TO KEEP LOOKING FOR DE HETERODYNES.
IT VOS SUSPECTED DOT DIS VOULD NOT BE A HIGH PRIORITY FOR DE BARON.
SO DEY ASK FOR A BUNCH OV VOLUNTEERS.
VE VERE TO LEAVE DE GROUP, GO OUT INTO DE VORLD—
UND NOT RETURN UNTIL VE FIND AN HEIR.
NO MATTER HOW LONG IT TAKE.
VE KNEW IT VOS SUICIDE MISSION.
DE HETERODYNES VERE GONE.
VE VOULD NEFFER BE ABLE TO COME BECK.
BUT... BECAUSE OV US—
DE JÄGERKIN KEN SAY VE HAD NOT ABANDONED OUR MASTERS.
DEY COULD JOIN DE BARON—
UND DE BARON VOULD PROTECT DEM.
UND NOW HERE HYU SHOW OP—
UND SPOIL ALL OUR PLENZ!
'CAUSE NOW VE GETS TO GO BECK. (sniff)
UND I NEFFER—I NEFFER THOT—
VE HAFF MISSED HYU!
PLEASE, PLEASE BE REAL!
shh. I... I AM.

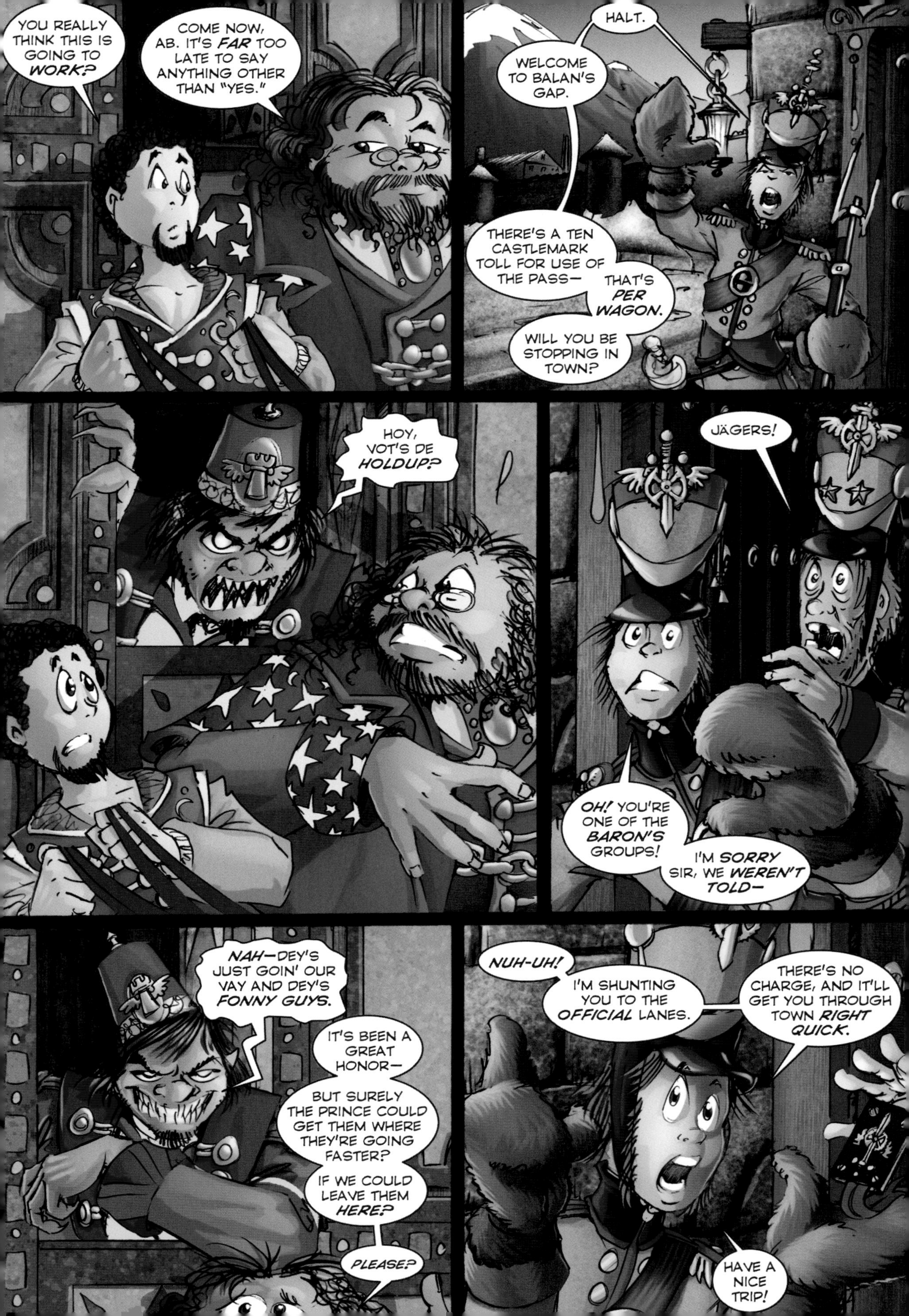
YOU REALLY THINK THIS IS GOING TO WORK?
COME NOW, AB. IT'S FAR TOO LATE TO SAY ANYTHING OTHER THAN "YES."
HALT.
WELCOME TO BALAN'S GAP.
THERE'S A TEN CASTLEMARK TOLL FOR USE OF THE PASS—
THAT'S PER WAGON.
WILL YOU BE STOPPING IN TOWN?
HOY, VOT'S DE HOLDUP?
!
JÄGERS!
OH! YOU'RE ONE OF THE BARON'S GROUPS!
I'M SORRY SIR, WE WEREN'T TOLD—
NAH—DEY'S JUST GOIN' OUR VAY AND DEY'S FONNY GUYS.
IT'S BEEN A GREAT HONOR—
BUT SURELY THE PRINCE COULD GET THEM WHERE THEY'RE GOING FASTER?
IF WE COULD LEAVE THEM HERE?
PLEASE?
NUH-UH!
I'M SHUNTING YOU TO THE OFFICIAL LANES.
THERE'S NO CHARGE, AND IT'LL GET YOU THROUGH TOWN RIGHT QUICK.
HAVE A NICE TRIP!

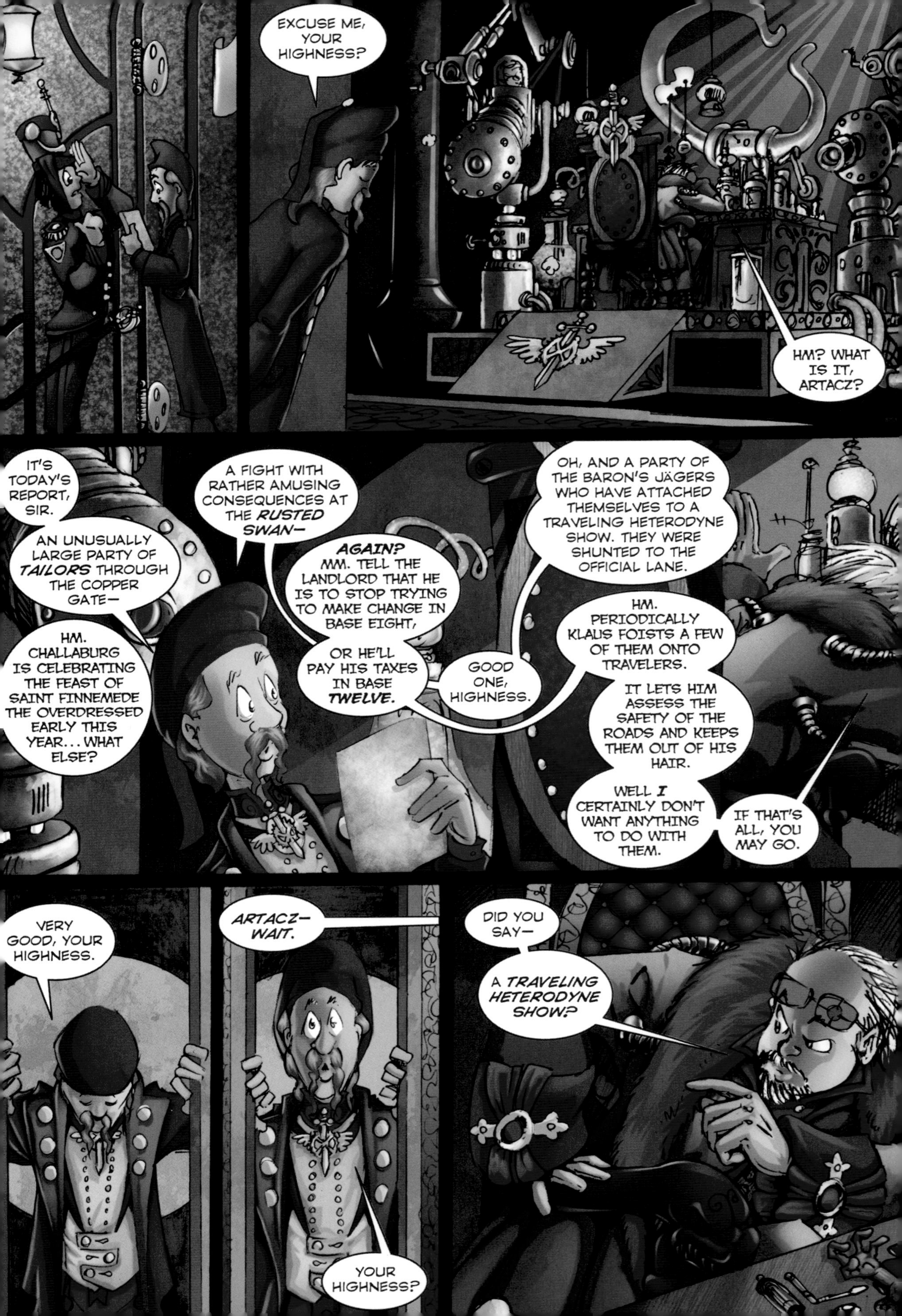
EXCUSE ME, YOUR HIGHNESS?
HM? WHAT IS IT, ARTACZ?
IT'S TODAY'S REPORT, SIR.
AN UNUSUALLY LARGE PARTY OF *TAILORS* THROUGH THE COPPER GATE—
HM. CHALLABURG IS CELEBRATING THE FEAST OF SAINT FINNEMEDE THE OVERDRESSED EARLY THIS YEAR... WHAT ELSE?
A FIGHT WITH RATHER AMUSING CONSEQUENCES AT THE *RUSTED SWAN*—
AGAIN? MM. TELL THE LANDLORD THAT HE IS TO STOP TRYING TO MAKE CHANGE IN BASE EIGHT,
OR HE'LL PAY HIS TAXES IN BASE *TWELVE*.
GOOD ONE, HIGHNESS.
OH, AND A PARTY OF THE BARON'S JÄGERS WHO HAVE ATTACHED THEMSELVES TO A TRAVELING HETERODYNE SHOW. THEY WERE SHUNTED TO THE OFFICIAL LANE.
HM. PERIODICALLY KLAUS FOISTS A FEW OF THEM ONTO TRAVELERS.
IT LETS HIM ASSESS THE SAFETY OF THE ROADS AND KEEPS THEM OUT OF HIS HAIR.
WELL *I* CERTAINLY DON'T WANT ANYTHING TO DO WITH THEM.
IF THAT'S ALL, YOU MAY GO.
VERY GOOD, YOUR HIGHNESS.
ARTACZ— WAIT.
YOUR HIGHNESS?
DID YOU SAY—
A *TRAVELING HETERODYNE SHOW?*

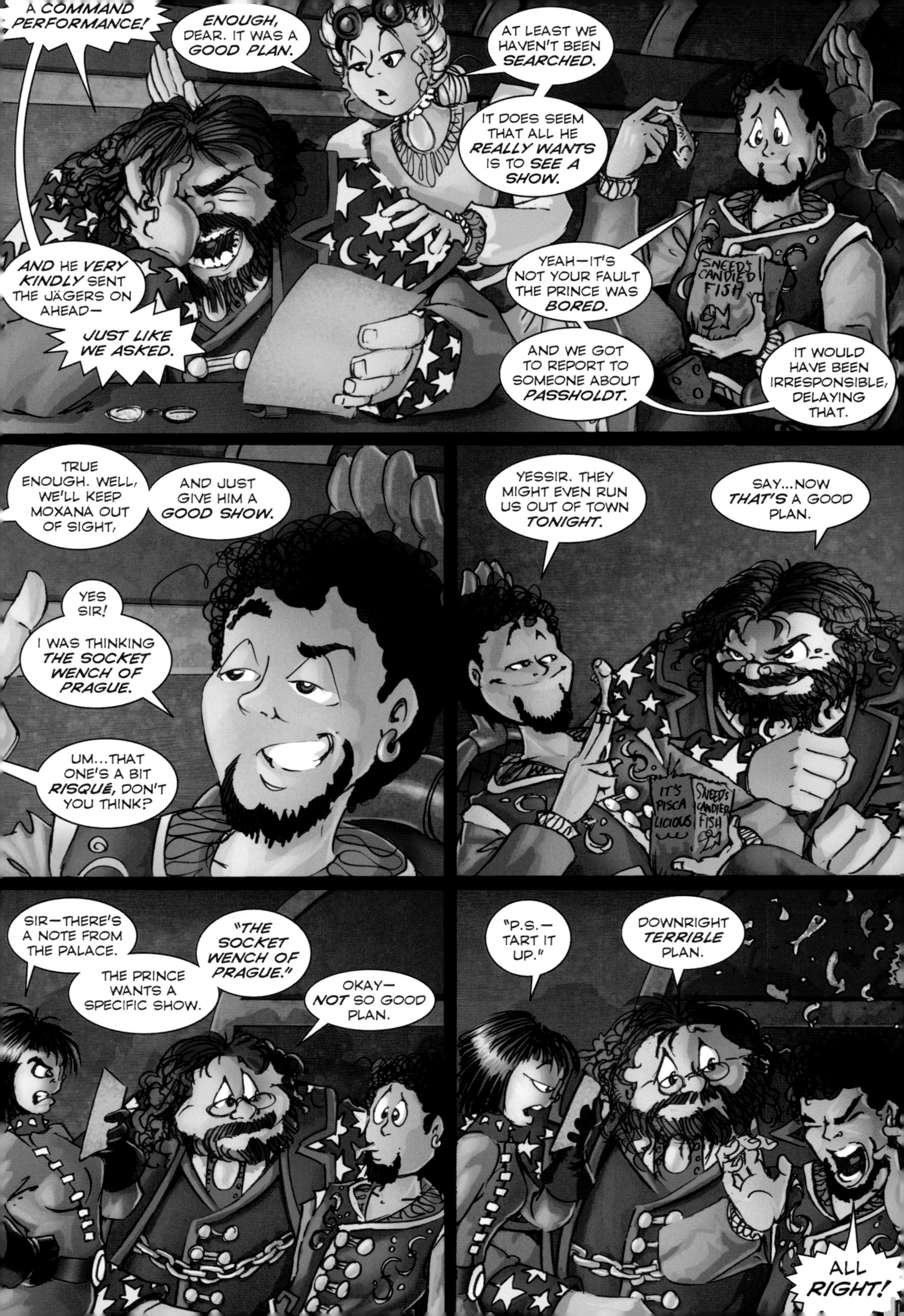
A COMMAND PERFORMANCE!
ENOUGH, DEAR. IT WAS A GOOD PLAN.
AT LEAST WE HAVEN'T BEEN SEARCHED.
IT DOES SEEM THAT ALL HE REALLY WANTS IS TO SEE A SHOW.
AND HE VERY KINDLY SENT THE JÄGERS ON AHEAD—
JUST LIKE WE ASKED.
SNEED'S CANDIED FISH
YEAH—IT'S NOT YOUR FAULT THE PRINCE WAS BORED.
AND WE GOT TO REPORT TO SOMEONE ABOUT PASSHOLDT.
IT WOULD HAVE BEEN IRRESPONSIBLE, DELAYING THAT.
TRUE ENOUGH. WELL, WE'LL KEEP MOXANA OUT OF SIGHT,
AND JUST GIVE HIM A GOOD SHOW.
YES SIR!
I WAS THINKING THE SOCKET WENCH OF PRAGUE.
UM...THAT ONE'S A BIT RISQUÉ, DON'T YOU THINK?
YESSIR. THEY MIGHT EVEN RUN US OUT OF TOWN TONIGHT.
SAY...NOW THAT'S A GOOD PLAN.
IT'S PISCA LICIOUS
SNEED'S CANDIED FISH
SIR—THERE'S A NOTE FROM THE PALACE.
THE PRINCE WANTS A SPECIFIC SHOW.
"THE SOCKET WENCH OF PRAGUE."
OKAY—NOT SO GOOD PLAN.
"P.S.—TART IT UP."
DOWNRIGHT TERRIBLE PLAN.
ALL RIGHT!

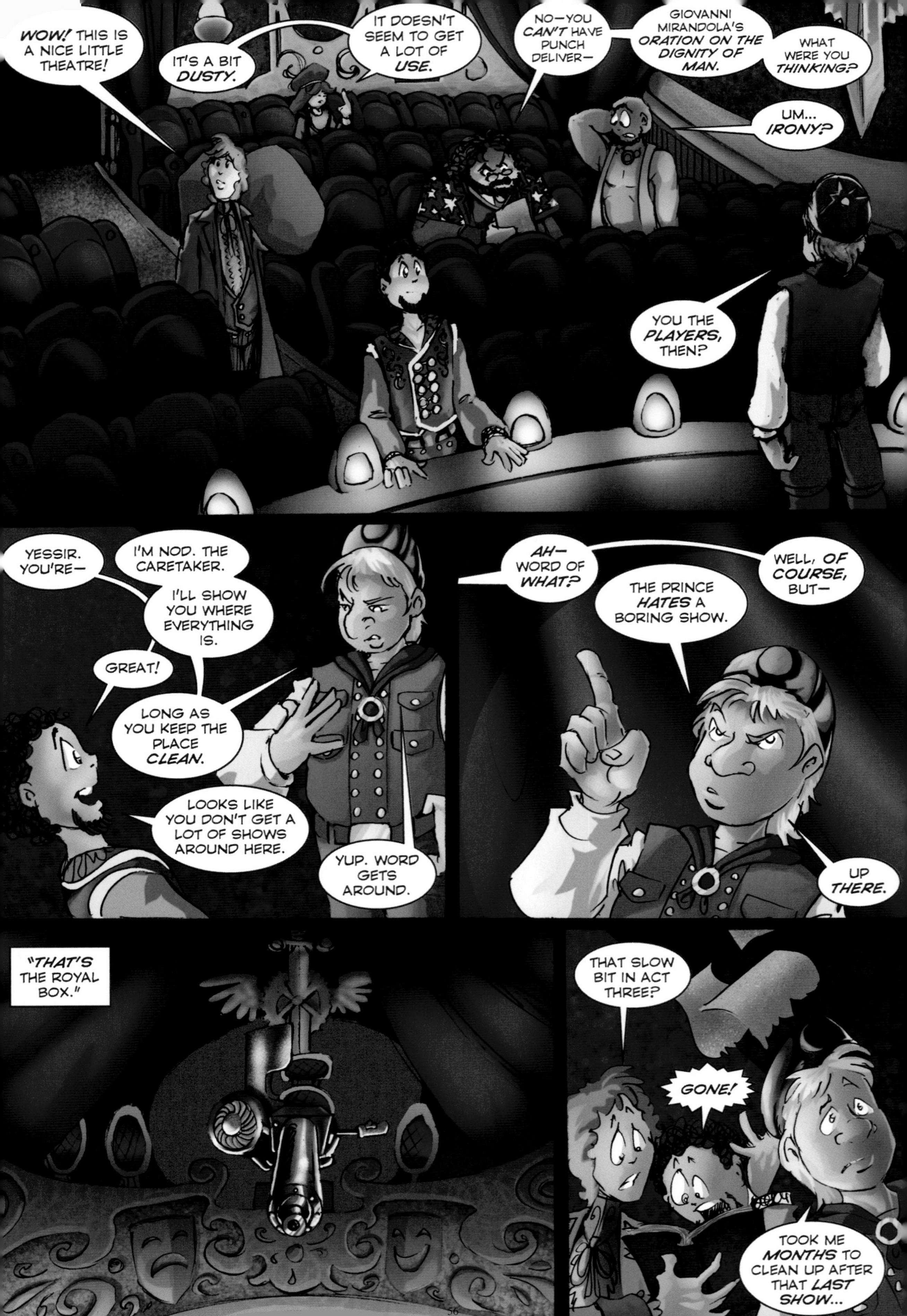
WOW! THIS IS A NICE LITTLE THEATRE!
IT'S A BIT DUSTY.
IT DOESN'T SEEM TO GET A LOT OF USE.
NO—YOU CAN'T HAVE PUNCH DELIVER—
GIOVANNI MIRANDOLA'S ORATION ON THE DIGNITY OF MAN.
WHAT WERE YOU THINKING?
UM... IRONY?
YOU THE PLAYERS, THEN?
YESSIR. YOU'RE—
I'M NOD. THE CARETAKER.
I'LL SHOW YOU WHERE EVERYTHING IS.
GREAT!
LONG AS YOU KEEP THE PLACE CLEAN.
LOOKS LIKE YOU DON'T GET A LOT OF SHOWS AROUND HERE.
YUP. WORD GETS AROUND.
AH— WORD OF WHAT?
THE PRINCE HATES A BORING SHOW.
WELL, OF COURSE, BUT—
UP THERE.
"THAT'S THE ROYAL BOX."
THAT SLOW BIT IN ACT THREE?
GONE!
TOOK ME MONTHS TO CLEAN UP AFTER THAT LAST SHOW...

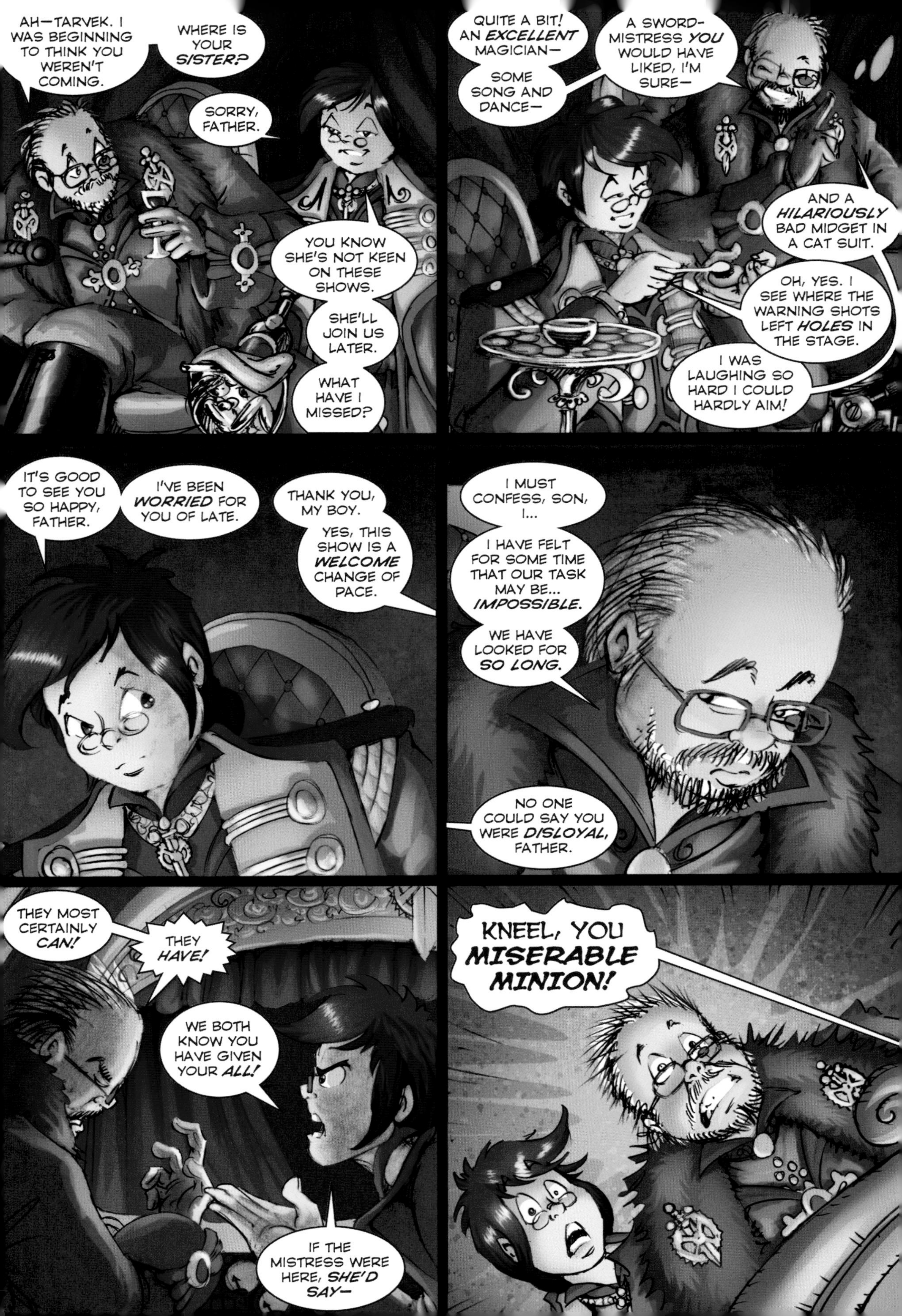

AH—TARVEK. I WAS BEGINNING TO THINK YOU WEREN'T COMING.
WHERE IS YOUR *SISTER?*
SORRY, FATHER.
YOU KNOW SHE'S NOT KEEN ON THESE SHOWS.
SHE'LL JOIN US LATER.
WHAT HAVE I MISSED?
QUITE A BIT! AN *EXCELLENT* MAGICIAN—
SOME SONG AND DANCE—
A SWORD-MISTRESS *YOU* WOULD HAVE LIKED, I'M SURE—
AND A *HILARIOUSLY* BAD MIDGET IN A CAT SUIT.
OH, YES. I SEE WHERE THE WARNING SHOTS LEFT *HOLES* IN THE STAGE.
I WAS LAUGHING SO HARD I COULD HARDLY AIM!
IT'S GOOD TO SEE YOU SO HAPPY, FATHER.
I'VE BEEN *WORRIED* FOR YOU OF LATE.
THANK YOU, MY BOY.
YES, THIS SHOW IS A *WELCOME* CHANGE OF PACE.
I MUST CONFESS, SON, I...
I HAVE FELT FOR SOME TIME THAT OUR TASK MAY BE... *IMPOSSIBLE.*
WE HAVE LOOKED FOR *SO LONG.*
NO ONE COULD SAY YOU WERE *DISLOYAL,* FATHER.
THEY MOST CERTAINLY *CAN!*
THEY *HAVE!*
WE BOTH KNOW YOU HAVE GIVEN YOUR *ALL!*
IF THE MISTRESS WERE HERE, *SHE'D* SAY—
KNEEL, YOU *MISERABLE MINION!*

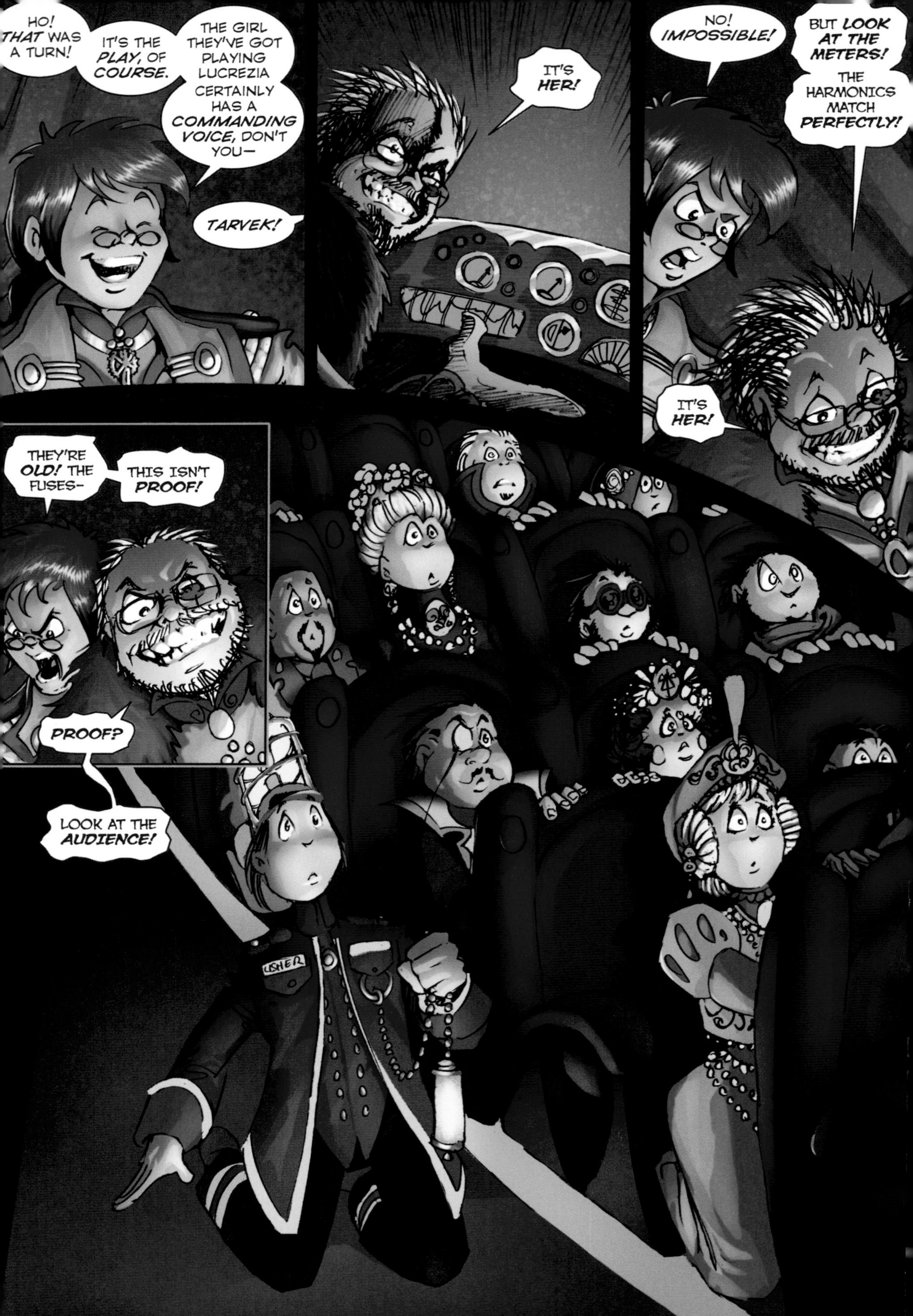
HO! THAT WAS A TURN!
IT'S THE PLAY, OF COURSE.
THE GIRL THEY'VE GOT PLAYING LUCREZIA CERTAINLY HAS A COMMANDING VOICE, DON'T YOU—
TARVEK!
IT'S HER!
NO! IMPOSSIBLE!
BUT LOOK AT THE METERS!
THE HARMONICS MATCH PERFECTLY!
IT'S HER!
THEY'RE OLD! THE FUSES-
THIS ISN'T PROOF!
PROOF?
LOOK AT THE AUDIENCE!
USHER

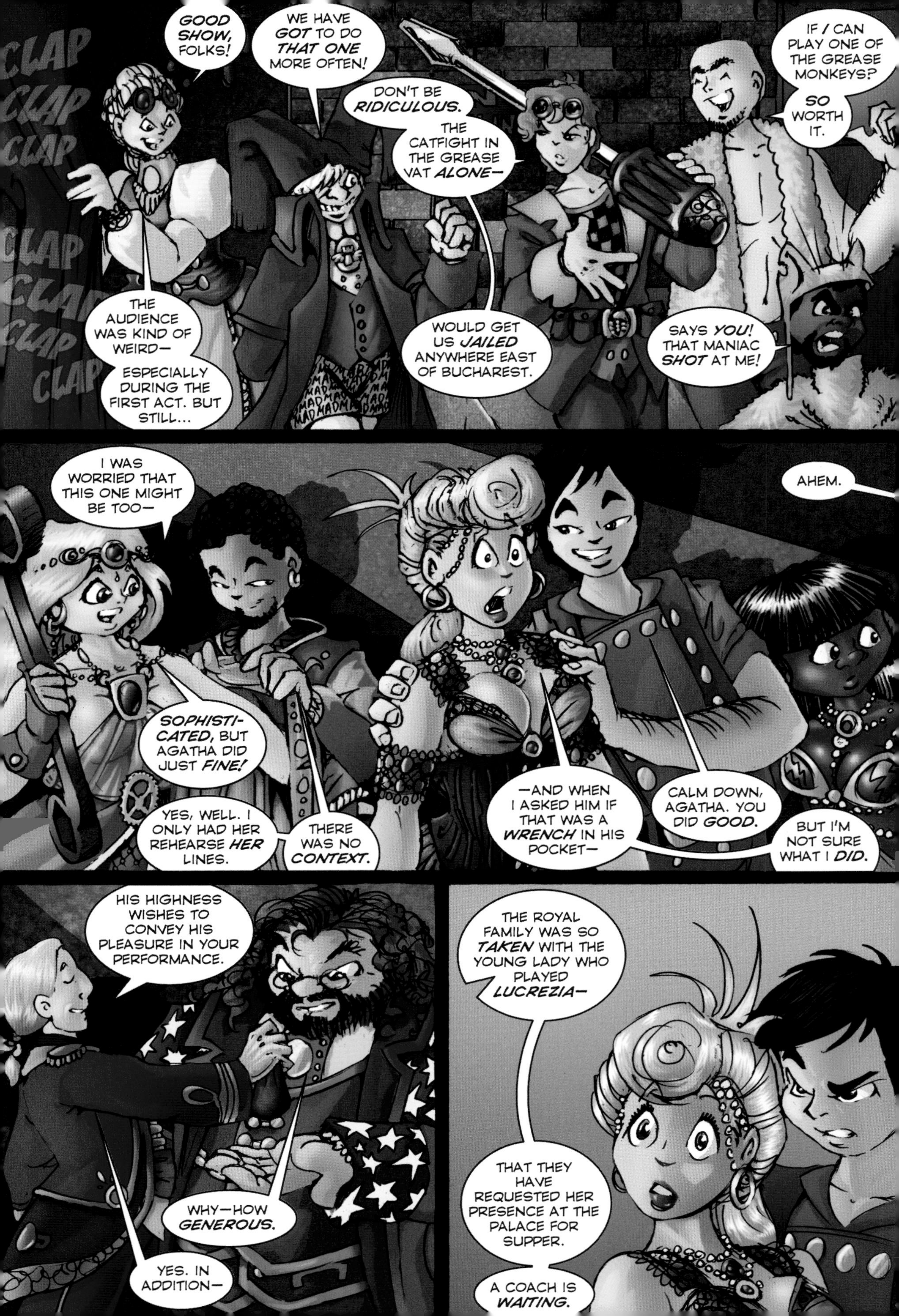
CLAP CLAP CLAP
GOOD SHOW, FOLKS!
WE HAVE GOT TO DO THAT ONE MORE OFTEN!
DON'T BE RIDICULOUS.
THE CATFIGHT IN THE GREASE VAT ALONE—
WOULD GET US JAILED ANYWHERE EAST OF BUCHAREST.
IF I CAN PLAY ONE OF THE GREASE MONKEYS?
SO WORTH IT.
SAYS YOU! THAT MANIAC SHOT AT ME!
CLAP CLAP CLAP CLAP
THE AUDIENCE WAS KIND OF WEIRD—
ESPECIALLY DURING THE FIRST ACT. BUT STILL...
I WAS WORRIED THAT THIS ONE MIGHT BE TOO—
SOPHISTI-CATED, BUT AGATHA DID JUST FINE!
YES, WELL. I ONLY HAD HER REHEARSE HER LINES.
THERE WAS NO CONTEXT.
—AND WHEN I ASKED HIM IF THAT WAS A WRENCH IN HIS POCKET—
CALM DOWN, AGATHA. YOU DID GOOD.
BUT I'M NOT SURE WHAT I DID.
AHEM.
HIS HIGHNESS WISHES TO CONVEY HIS PLEASURE IN YOUR PERFORMANCE.
WHY—HOW GENEROUS.
YES. IN ADDITION—
THE ROYAL FAMILY WAS SO TAKEN WITH THE YOUNG LADY WHO PLAYED LUCREZIA—
THAT THEY HAVE REQUESTED HER PRESENCE AT THE PALACE FOR SUPPER.
A COACH IS WAITING.

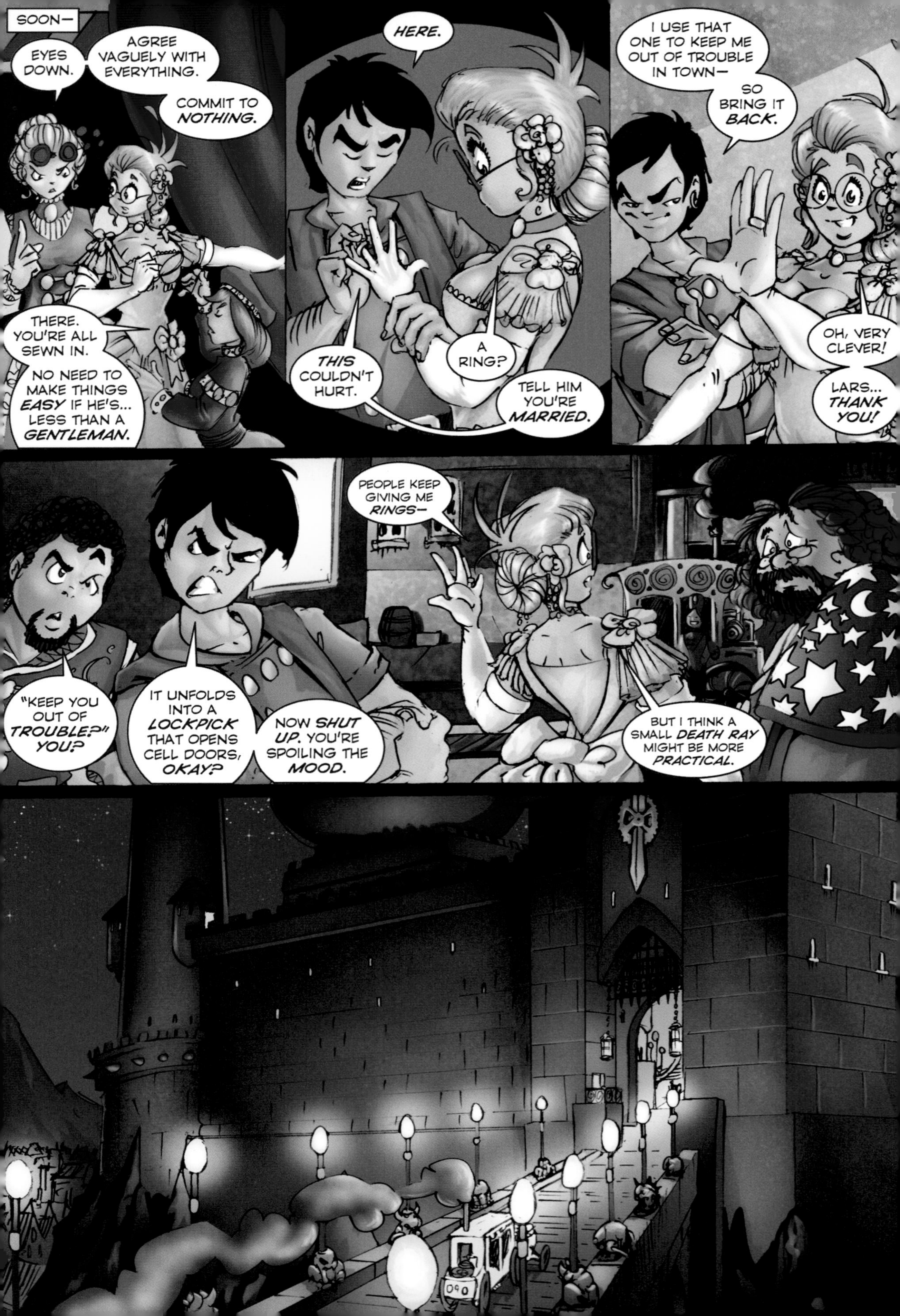
SOON—
EYES DOWN.
AGREE VAGUELY WITH EVERYTHING.
COMMIT TO NOTHING.
THERE. YOU'RE ALL SEWN IN.
NO NEED TO MAKE THINGS EASY IF HE'S... LESS THAN A GENTLEMAN.
HERE.
THIS COULDN'T HURT.
A RING?
TELL HIM YOU'RE MARRIED.
I USE THAT ONE TO KEEP ME OUT OF TROUBLE IN TOWN—
SO BRING IT BACK.
OH, VERY CLEVER!
LARS... THANK YOU!
"KEEP YOU OUT OF TROUBLE?" YOU?
IT UNFOLDS INTO A LOCKPICK THAT OPENS CELL DOORS, OKAY?
NOW SHUT UP. YOU'RE SPOILING THE MOOD.
PEOPLE KEEP GIVING ME RINGS—
BUT I THINK A SMALL DEATH RAY MIGHT BE MORE PRACTICAL.

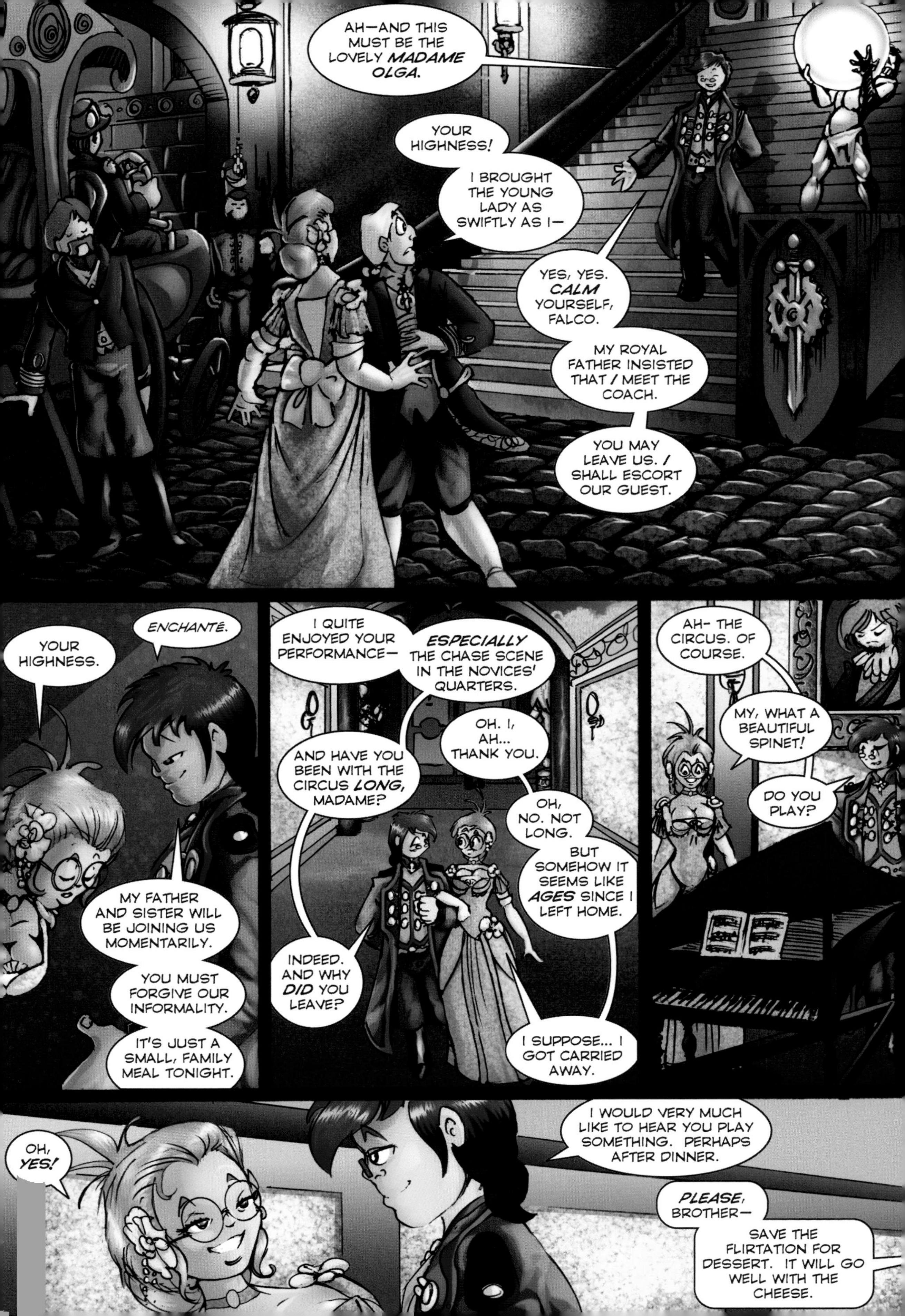
AH—AND THIS MUST BE THE LOVELY *MADAME OLGA.*
YOUR HIGHNESS!
I BROUGHT THE YOUNG LADY AS SWIFTLY AS I—
YES, YES. *CALM* YOURSELF, FALCO.
MY ROYAL FATHER INSISTED THAT *I* MEET THE COACH.
YOU MAY LEAVE US. *I* SHALL ESCORT OUR GUEST.
YOUR HIGHNESS.
ENCHANTÉ.
MY FATHER AND SISTER WILL BE JOINING US MOMENTARILY.
YOU MUST FORGIVE OUR INFORMALITY.
IT'S JUST A SMALL, FAMILY MEAL TONIGHT.
I QUITE ENJOYED YOUR PERFORMANCE—
ESPECIALLY THE CHASE SCENE IN THE NOVICES' QUARTERS.
OH. I, AH... THANK YOU.
AND HAVE YOU BEEN WITH THE CIRCUS *LONG,* MADAME?
OH, NO. NOT LONG.
BUT SOMEHOW IT SEEMS LIKE *AGES* SINCE I LEFT HOME.
INDEED. AND WHY *DID* YOU LEAVE?
I SUPPOSE... I GOT CARRIED AWAY.
AH- THE CIRCUS. OF COURSE.
MY, WHAT A BEAUTIFUL SPINET!
DO YOU PLAY?
OH, *YES!*
I WOULD VERY MUCH LIKE TO HEAR YOU PLAY SOMETHING. PERHAPS AFTER DINNER.
PLEASE, BROTHER—
SAVE THE FLIRTATION FOR DESSERT. IT WILL GO WELL WITH THE CHEESE.

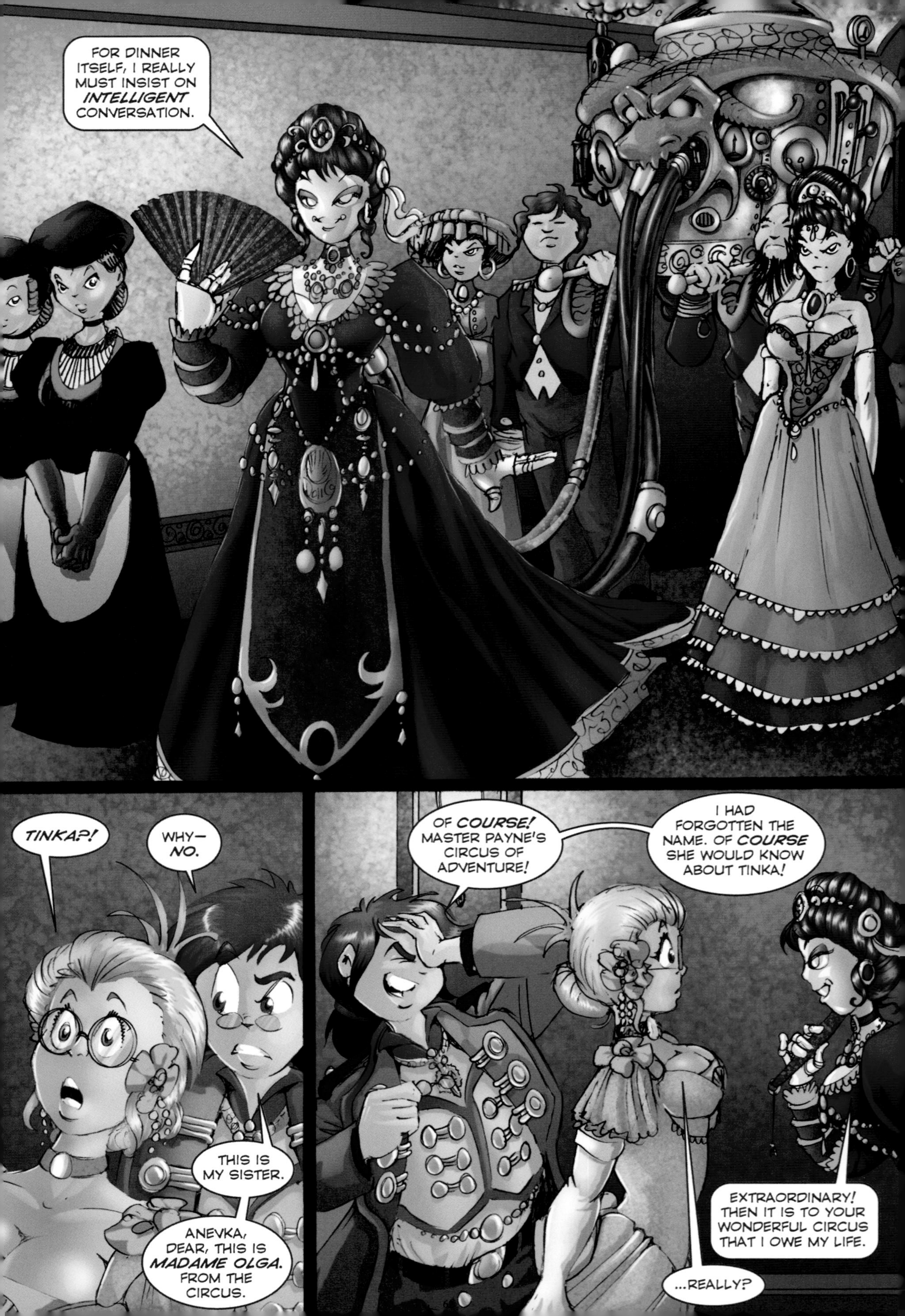
FOR DINNER ITSELF, I REALLY MUST INSIST ON *INTELLIGENT* CONVERSATION.
TINKA?!
WHY— *NO.*
THIS IS MY SISTER.
ANEVKA, DEAR, THIS IS ***MADAME OLGA.*** FROM THE CIRCUS.
OF ***COURSE!*** MASTER PAYNE'S CIRCUS OF ADVENTURE!
I HAD FORGOTTEN THE NAME. OF ***COURSE*** SHE WOULD KNOW ABOUT TINKA!
EXTRAORDINARY! THEN IT IS TO YOUR WONDERFUL CIRCUS THAT I OWE MY LIFE.
...REALLY?

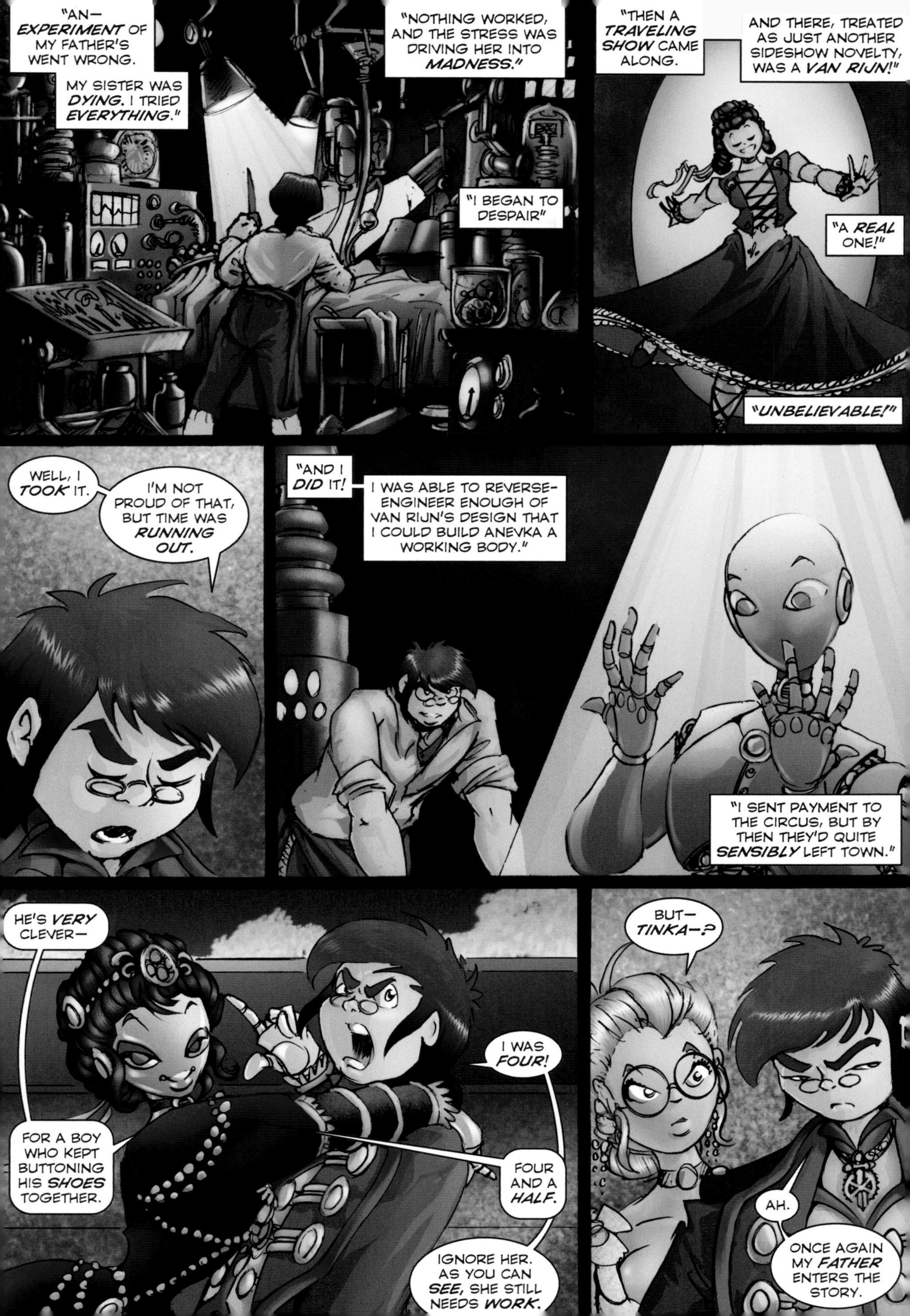
"AN—EXPERIMENT OF MY FATHER'S WENT WRONG.
MY SISTER WAS DYING. I TRIED EVERYTHING."
"NOTHING WORKED, AND THE STRESS WAS DRIVING HER INTO MADNESS."
"I BEGAN TO DESPAIR"
"THEN A TRAVELING SHOW CAME ALONG.
AND THERE, TREATED AS JUST ANOTHER SIDESHOW NOVELTY, WAS A VAN RIJN!"
"A REAL ONE!"
"UNBELIEVABLE!"
WELL, I TOOK IT.
I'M NOT PROUD OF THAT, BUT TIME WAS RUNNING OUT.
"AND I DID IT!
I WAS ABLE TO REVERSE-ENGINEER ENOUGH OF VAN RIJN'S DESIGN THAT I COULD BUILD ANEVKA A WORKING BODY."
"I SENT PAYMENT TO THE CIRCUS, BUT BY THEN THEY'D QUITE SENSIBLY LEFT TOWN."
HE'S VERY CLEVER—
FOR A BOY WHO KEPT BUTTONING HIS SHOES TOGETHER.
I WAS FOUR!
FOUR AND A HALF.
IGNORE HER. AS YOU CAN SEE, SHE STILL NEEDS WORK.
BUT—TINKA—?
AH.
ONCE AGAIN MY FATHER ENTERS THE STORY.

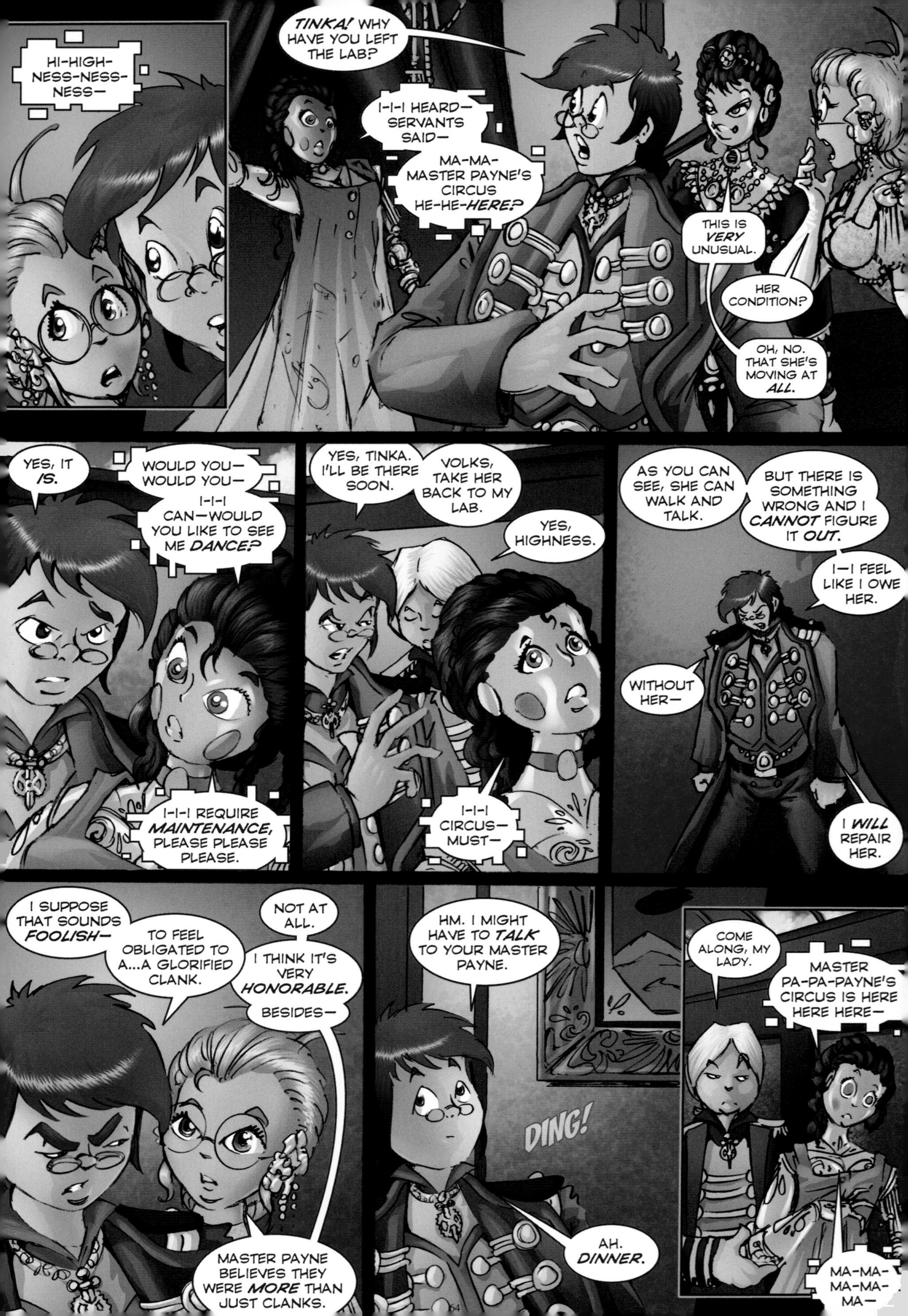
HI-HIGH-NESS-NESS-NESS—
TINKA! WHY HAVE YOU LEFT THE LAB?
I-I-I HEARD—SERVANTS SAID—
MA-MA-MASTER PAYNE'S CIRCUS HE-HE-HERE?
THIS IS VERY UNUSUAL.
HER CONDITION?
OH, NO. THAT SHE'S MOVING AT ALL.
YES, IT IS.
WOULD YOU—WOULD YOU—
I-I-I CAN—WOULD YOU LIKE TO SEE ME DANCE?
I-I-I REQUIRE MAINTENANCE, PLEASE PLEASE PLEASE.
YES, TINKA. I'LL BE THERE SOON.
VOLKS, TAKE HER BACK TO MY LAB.
YES, HIGHNESS.
I-I-I CIRCUS—MUST—
AS YOU CAN SEE, SHE CAN WALK AND TALK.
BUT THERE IS SOMETHING WRONG AND I CANNOT FIGURE IT OUT.
I—I FEEL LIKE I OWE HER.
WITHOUT HER—
I WILL REPAIR HER.
I SUPPOSE THAT SOUNDS FOOLISH—
TO FEEL OBLIGATED TO A...A GLORIFIED CLANK.
NOT AT ALL.
I THINK IT'S VERY HONORABLE.
BESIDES—
MASTER PAYNE BELIEVES THEY WERE MORE THAN JUST CLANKS.
HM. I MIGHT HAVE TO TALK TO YOUR MASTER PAYNE.
DING!
AH. DINNER.
COME ALONG, MY LADY.
MASTER PA-PA-PAYNE'S CIRCUS IS HERE HERE HERE—
MA-MA-MA-MA-MA—

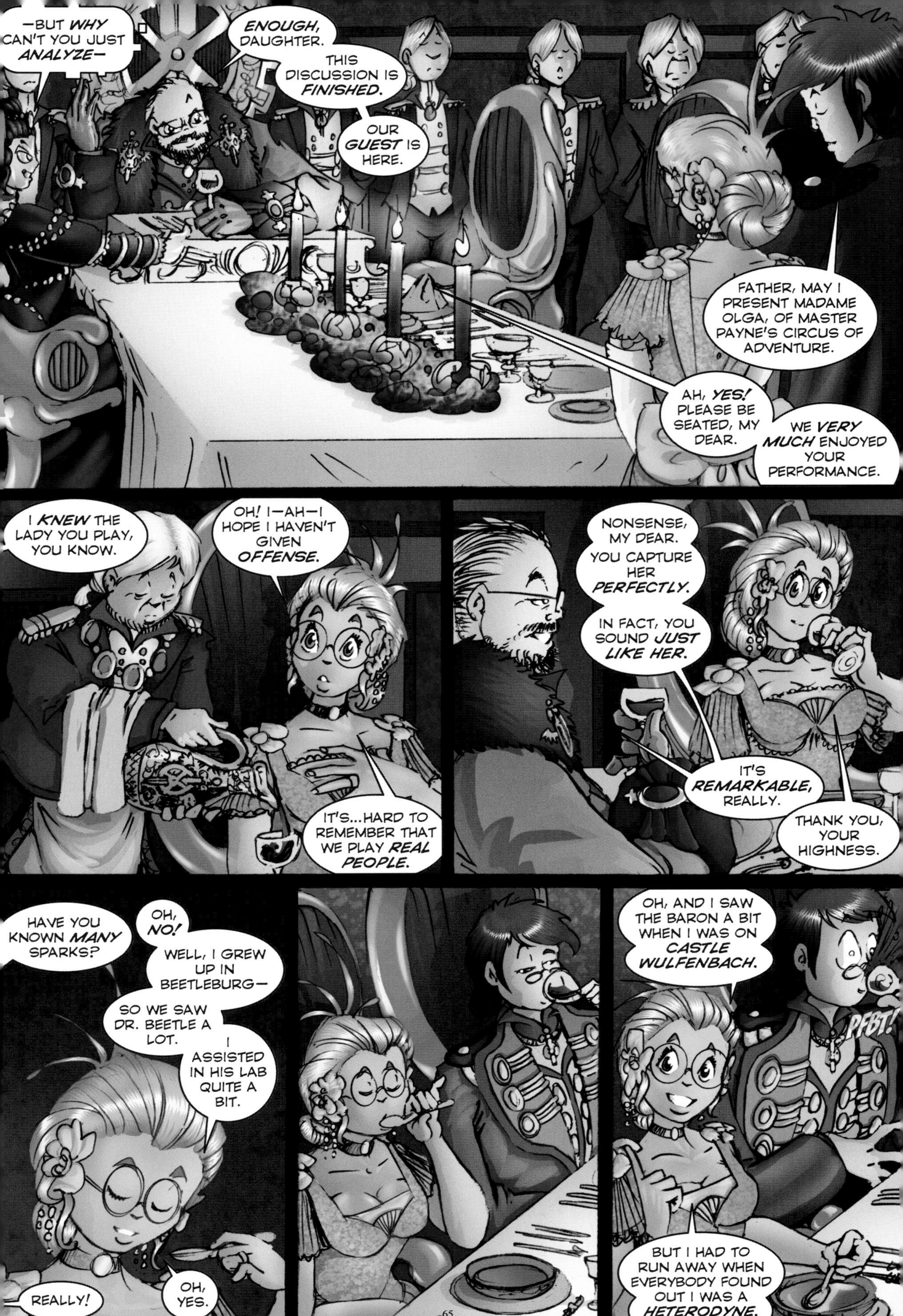

—BUT WHY CAN'T YOU JUST ANALYZE—
ENOUGH, DAUGHTER.
THIS DISCUSSION IS FINISHED.
OUR GUEST IS HERE.
FATHER, MAY I PRESENT MADAME OLGA, OF MASTER PAYNE'S CIRCUS OF ADVENTURE.
AH, YES! PLEASE BE SEATED, MY DEAR.
WE VERY MUCH ENJOYED YOUR PERFORMANCE.
I KNEW THE LADY YOU PLAY, YOU KNOW.
OH! I—AH—I HOPE I HAVEN'T GIVEN OFFENSE.
IT'S...HARD TO REMEMBER THAT WE PLAY REAL PEOPLE.
NONSENSE, MY DEAR.
YOU CAPTURE HER PERFECTLY.
IN FACT, YOU SOUND JUST LIKE HER.
IT'S REMARKABLE, REALLY.
THANK YOU, YOUR HIGHNESS.
HAVE YOU KNOWN MANY SPARKS?
OH, NO!
WELL, I GREW UP IN BEETLEBURG—
SO WE SAW DR. BEETLE A LOT.
I ASSISTED IN HIS LAB QUITE A BIT.
REALLY!
OH, YES.
OH, AND I SAW THE BARON A BIT WHEN I WAS ON CASTLE WULFENBACH.
PFBT!
BUT I HAD TO RUN AWAY WHEN EVERYBODY FOUND OUT I WAS A HETERODYNE.

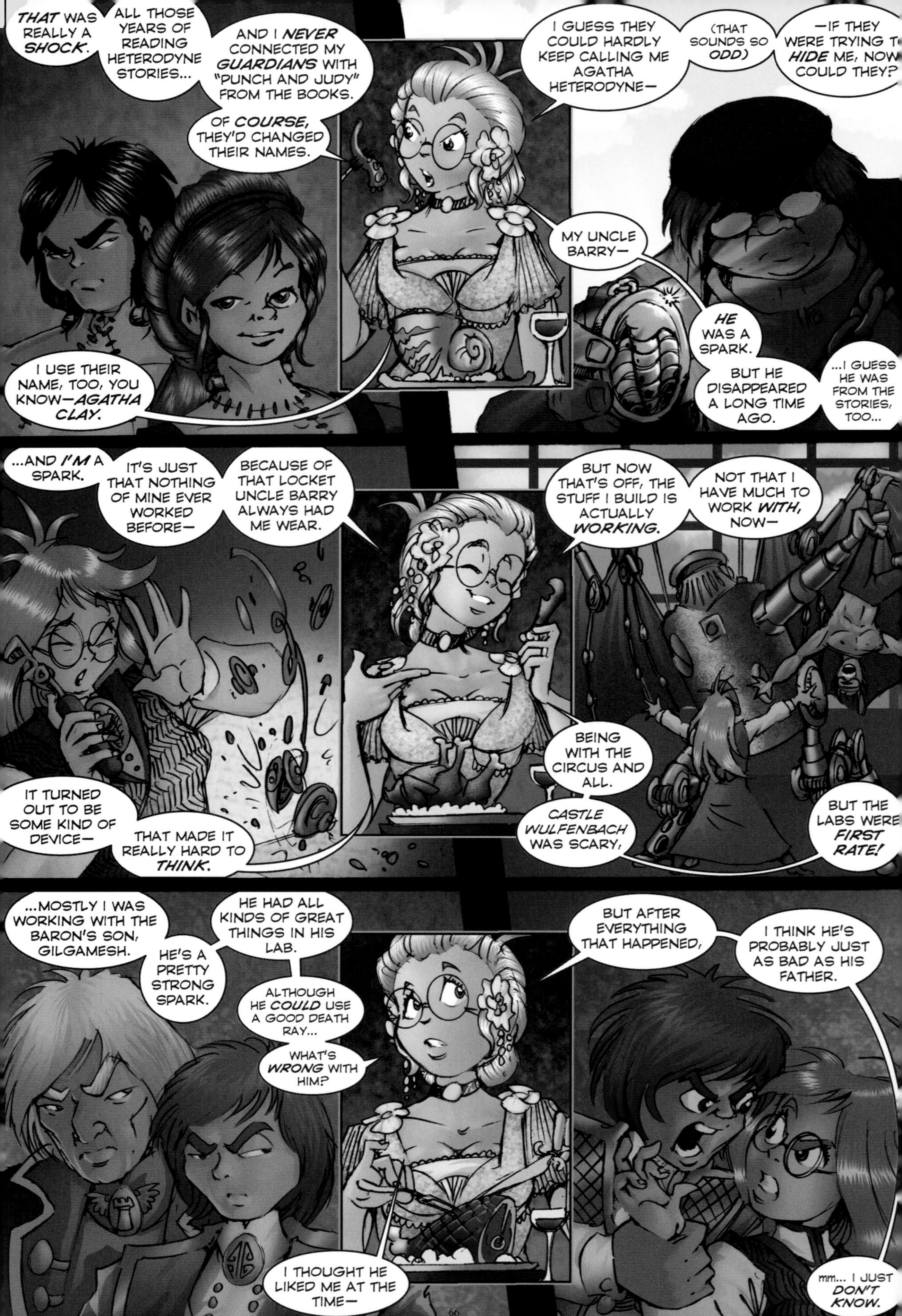

THAT WAS REALLY A SHOCK.
ALL THOSE YEARS OF READING HETERODYNE STORIES...
AND I NEVER CONNECTED MY GUARDIANS WITH "PUNCH AND JUDY" FROM THE BOOKS.
OF COURSE, THEY'D CHANGED THEIR NAMES.
I USE THEIR NAME, TOO, YOU KNOW—AGATHA CLAY.
I GUESS THEY COULD HARDLY KEEP CALLING ME AGATHA HETERODYNE—
(THAT SOUNDS SO ODD)
—IF THEY WERE TRYING TO HIDE ME, NOW COULD THEY?
MY UNCLE BARRY—
HE WAS A SPARK.
BUT HE DISAPPEARED A LONG TIME AGO.
...I GUESS HE WAS FROM THE STORIES, TOO...
...AND I'M A SPARK.
IT'S JUST THAT NOTHING OF MINE EVER WORKED BEFORE—
BECAUSE OF THAT LOCKET UNCLE BARRY ALWAYS HAD ME WEAR.
IT TURNED OUT TO BE SOME KIND OF DEVICE—
THAT MADE IT REALLY HARD TO THINK.
BUT NOW THAT'S OFF, THE STUFF I BUILD IS ACTUALLY WORKING.
NOT THAT I HAVE MUCH TO WORK WITH, NOW—
BEING WITH THE CIRCUS AND ALL.
CASTLE WULFENBACH WAS SCARY,
BUT THE LABS WERE FIRST RATE!
...MOSTLY I WAS WORKING WITH THE BARON'S SON, GILGAMESH.
HE'S A PRETTY STRONG SPARK.
HE HAD ALL KINDS OF GREAT THINGS IN HIS LAB.
ALTHOUGH HE COULD USE A GOOD DEATH RAY...
WHAT'S WRONG WITH HIM?
I THOUGHT HE LIKED ME AT THE TIME—
BUT AFTER EVERYTHING THAT HAPPENED,
I THINK HE'S PROBABLY JUST AS BAD AS HIS FATHER.
mm... I JUST DON'T KNOW.

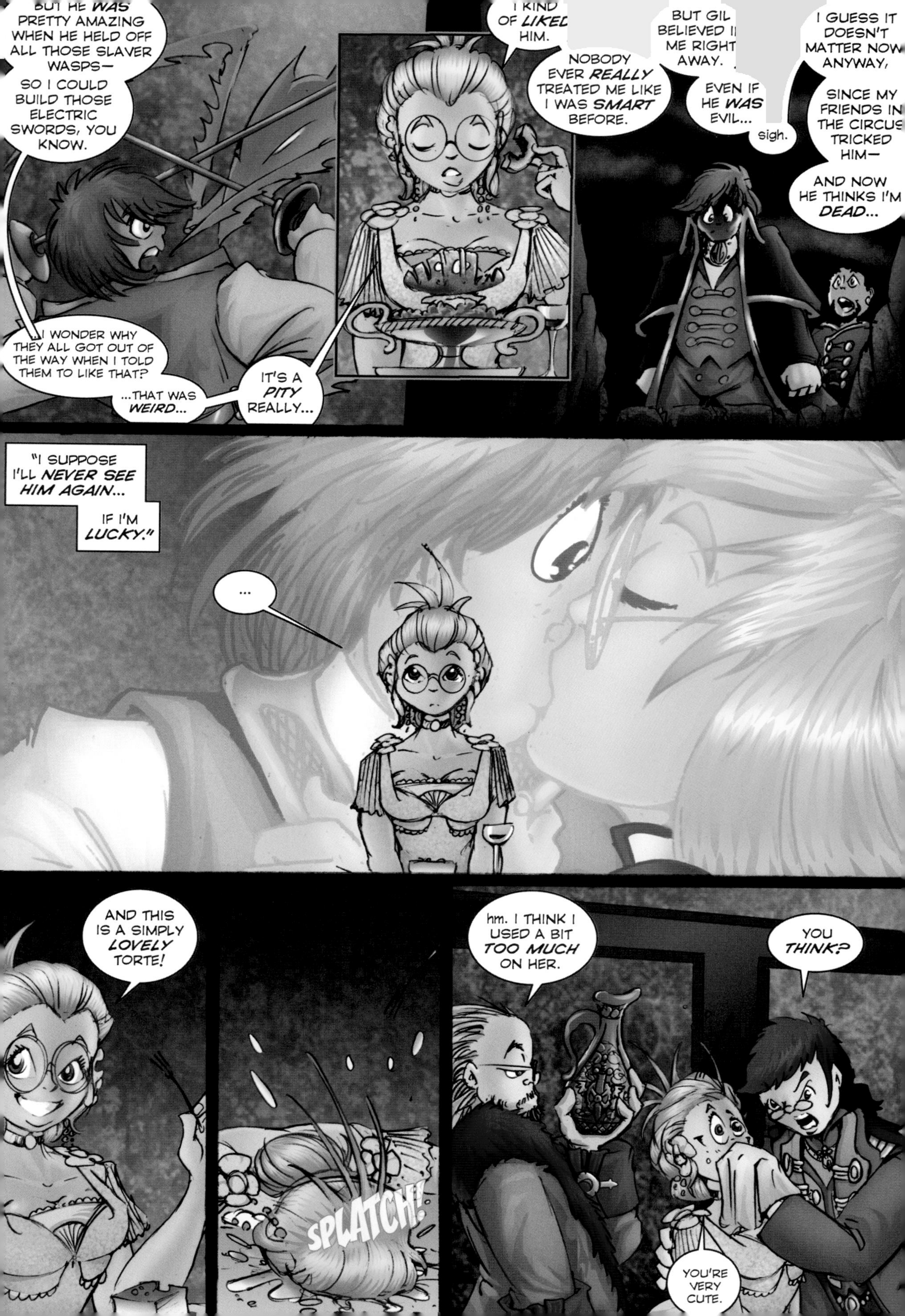

BUT HE WAS PRETTY AMAZING WHEN HE HELD OFF ALL THOSE SLAVER WASPS—
SO I COULD BUILD THOSE ELECTRIC SWORDS, YOU KNOW.
...I WONDER WHY THEY ALL GOT OUT OF THE WAY WHEN I TOLD THEM TO LIKE THAT?
...THAT WAS WEIRD...
IT'S A PITY REALLY...
I KIND OF LIKED HIM.
NOBODY EVER REALLY TREATED ME LIKE I WAS SMART BEFORE.
BUT GIL BELIEVED IN ME RIGHT AWAY.
EVEN IF HE WAS EVIL...
sigh.
I GUESS IT DOESN'T MATTER NOW ANYWAY,
SINCE MY FRIENDS IN THE CIRCUS TRICKED HIM—
AND NOW HE THINKS I'M DEAD...
"I SUPPOSE I'LL NEVER SEE HIM AGAIN...
IF I'M LUCKY."
...
AND THIS IS A SIMPLY LOVELY TORTE!
SPLATCH!
hm. I THINK I USED A BIT TOO MUCH ON HER.
YOU THINK?
YOU'RE VERY CUTE.

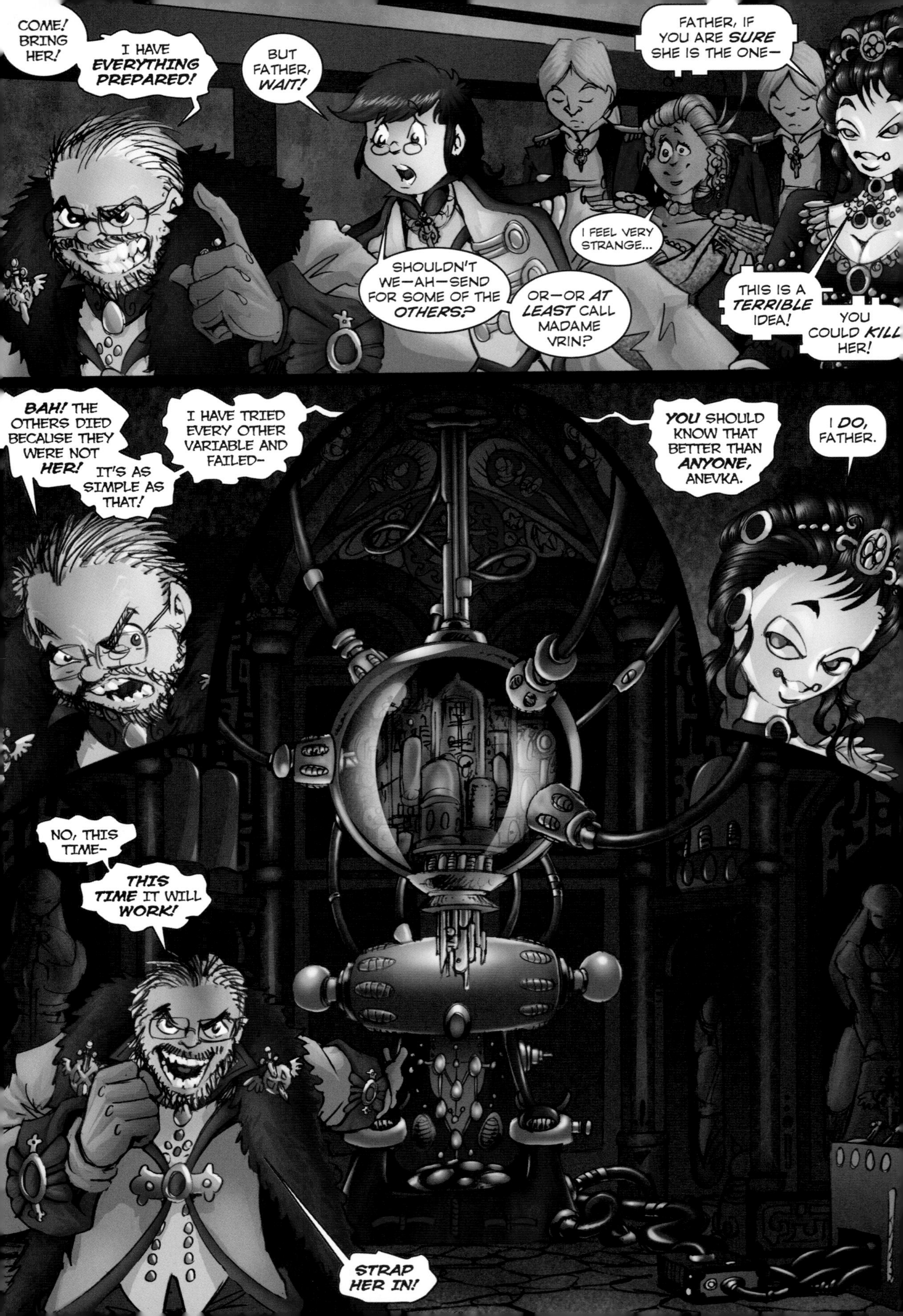
COME! BRING HER!
I HAVE EVERYTHING PREPARED!
BUT FATHER, WAIT!
SHOULDN'T WE—AH—SEND FOR SOME OF THE OTHERS?
I FEEL VERY STRANGE...
OR—OR AT LEAST CALL MADAME VRIN?
FATHER, IF YOU ARE SURE SHE IS THE ONE—
THIS IS A TERRIBLE IDEA!
YOU COULD KILL HER!
BAH! THE OTHERS DIED BECAUSE THEY WERE NOT HER!
IT'S AS SIMPLE AS THAT!
I HAVE TRIED EVERY OTHER VARIABLE AND FAILED-
YOU SHOULD KNOW THAT BETTER THAN ANYONE, ANEVKA.
I DO, FATHER.
NO, THIS TIME-
THIS TIME IT WILL WORK!
STRAP HER IN!

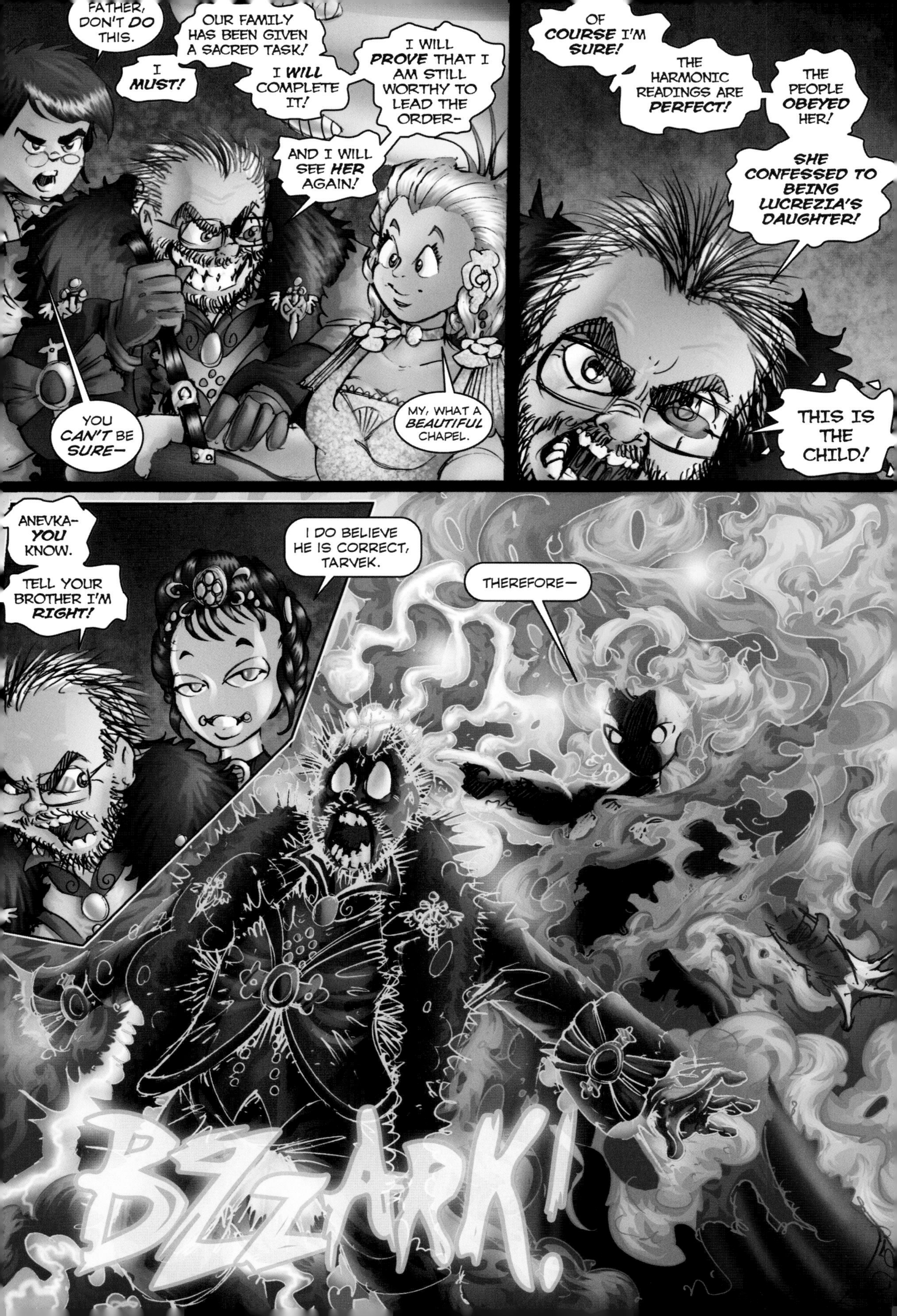
FATHER, DON'T DO THIS.
OUR FAMILY HAS BEEN GIVEN A SACRED TASK!
I MUST!
I WILL COMPLETE IT!
I WILL PROVE THAT I AM STILL WORTHY TO LEAD THE ORDER-
AND I WILL SEE HER AGAIN!
YOU CAN'T BE SURE-
MY, WHAT A BEAUTIFUL CHAPEL.
OF COURSE I'M SURE!
THE HARMONIC READINGS ARE PERFECT!
THE PEOPLE OBEYED HER!
SHE CONFESSED TO BEING LUCREZIA'S DAUGHTER!
THIS IS THE CHILD!
ANEVKA- YOU KNOW.
TELL YOUR BROTHER I'M RIGHT!
I DO BELIEVE HE IS CORRECT, TARVEK.
THEREFORE-
BZZARK!

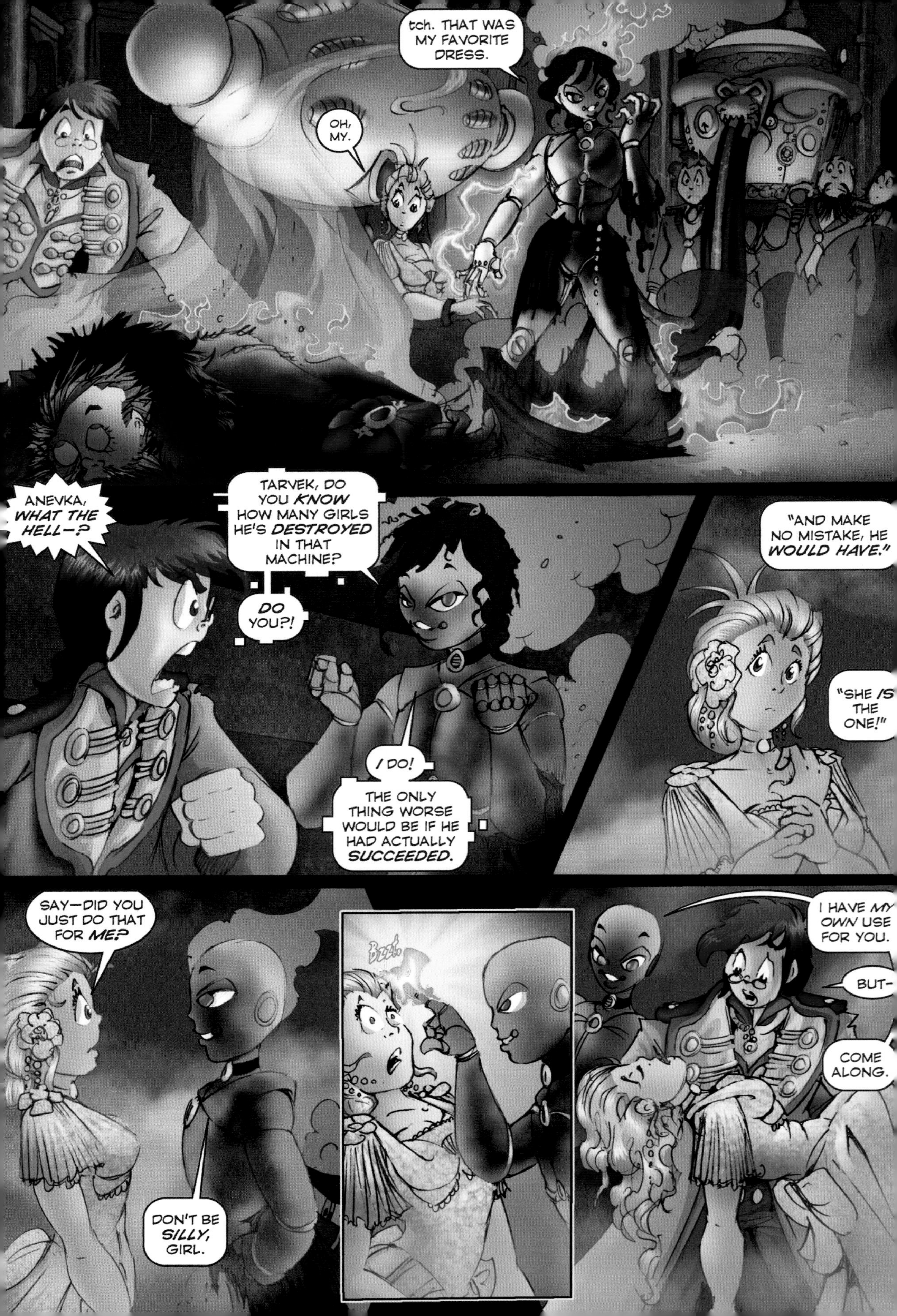
tch. THAT WAS MY FAVORITE DRESS.
OH, MY.
ANEVKA, WHAT THE HELL—?
TARVEK, DO YOU KNOW HOW MANY GIRLS HE'S DESTROYED IN THAT MACHINE?
DO YOU?!
I DO!
THE ONLY THING WORSE WOULD BE IF HE HAD ACTUALLY SUCCEEDED.
"AND MAKE NO MISTAKE, HE WOULD HAVE."
"SHE IS THE ONE!"
SAY—DID YOU JUST DO THAT FOR ME?
DON'T BE SILLY, GIRL.
I HAVE MY OWN USE FOR YOU.
BUT-
COME ALONG.

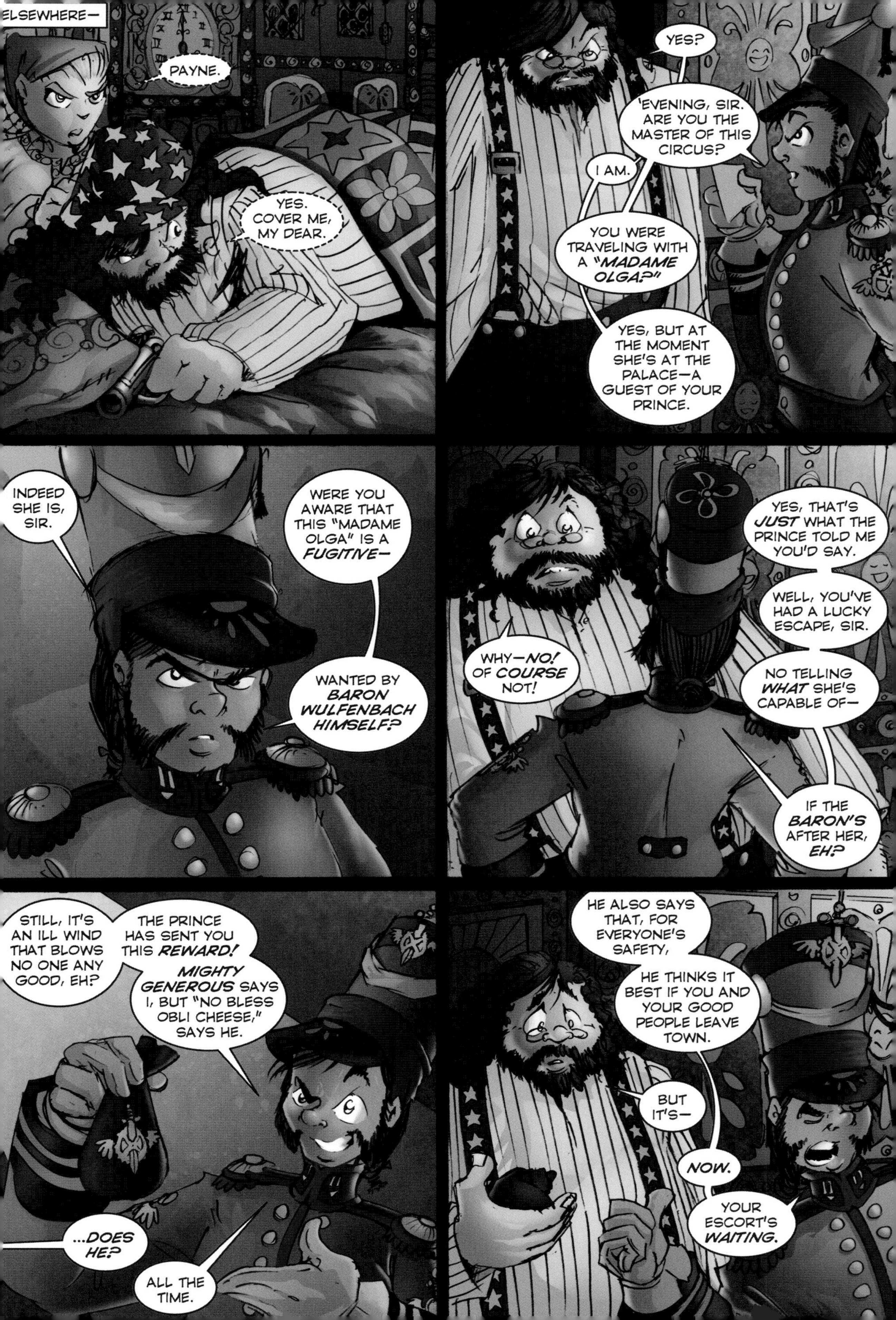
ELSEWHERE—
PAYNE.
YES. COVER ME, MY DEAR.
YES?
'EVENING, SIR. ARE YOU THE MASTER OF THIS CIRCUS?
I AM.
YOU WERE TRAVELING WITH A "MADAME OLGA?"
YES, BUT AT THE MOMENT SHE'S AT THE PALACE—A GUEST OF YOUR PRINCE.
INDEED SHE IS, SIR.
WERE YOU AWARE THAT THIS "MADAME OLGA" IS A FUGITIVE—
WANTED BY BARON WULFENBACH HIMSELF?
WHY—NO! OF COURSE NOT!
YES, THAT'S JUST WHAT THE PRINCE TOLD ME YOU'D SAY.
WELL, YOU'VE HAD A LUCKY ESCAPE, SIR.
NO TELLING WHAT SHE'S CAPABLE OF—
IF THE BARON'S AFTER HER, EH?
STILL, IT'S AN ILL WIND THAT BLOWS NO ONE ANY GOOD, EH?
THE PRINCE HAS SENT YOU THIS REWARD!
MIGHTY GENEROUS SAYS I, BUT "NO BLESS OBLI CHEESE," SAYS HE.
...DOES HE?
ALL THE TIME.
HE ALSO SAYS THAT, FOR EVERYONE'S SAFETY,
HE THINKS IT BEST IF YOU AND YOUR GOOD PEOPLE LEAVE TOWN.
BUT IT'S—
NOW.
YOUR ESCORT'S WAITING.

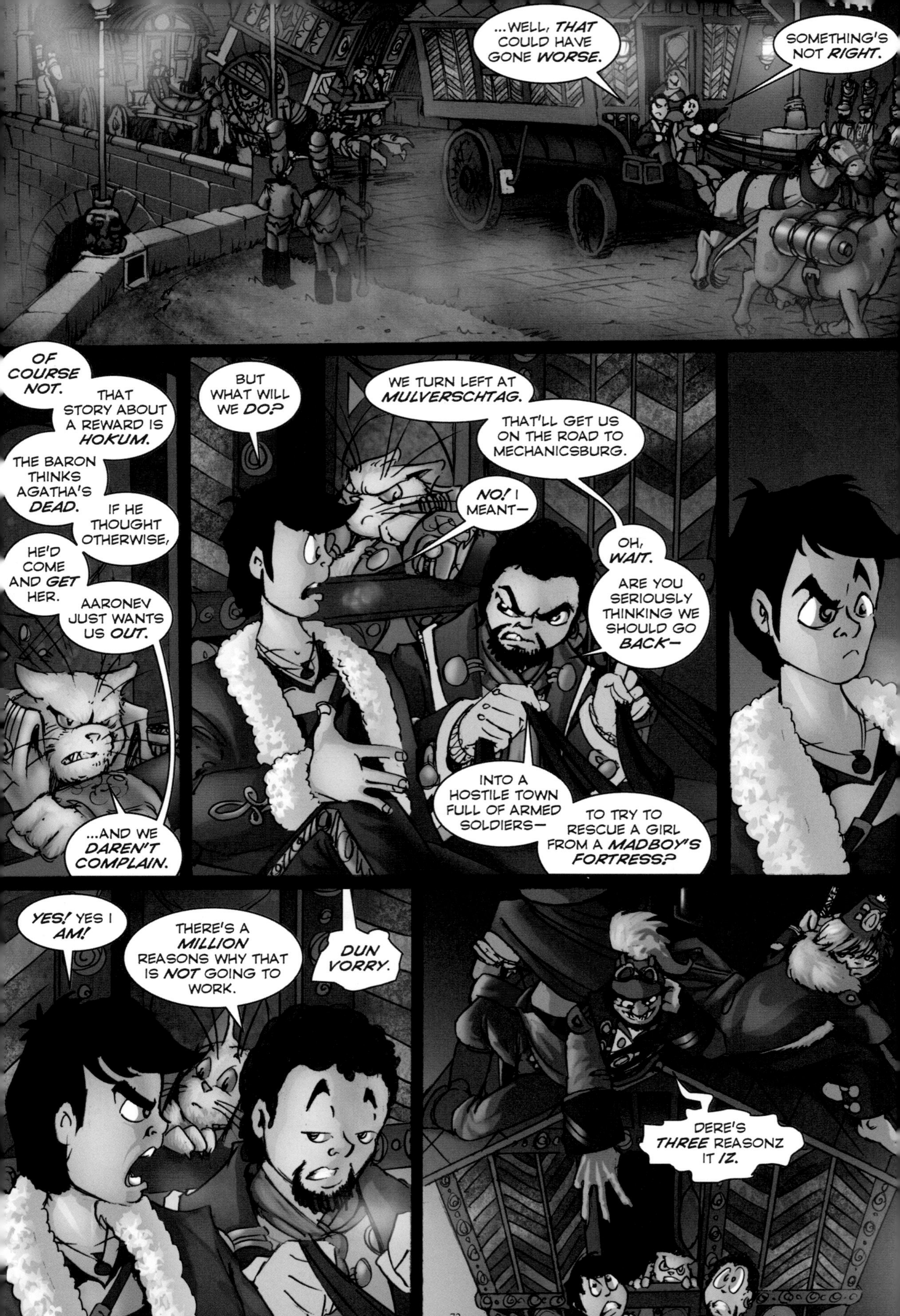

...WELL, *THAT* COULD HAVE GONE *WORSE*.
SOMETHING'S NOT *RIGHT*.
OF COURSE NOT.
THAT STORY ABOUT A REWARD IS *HOKUM*.
THE BARON THINKS AGATHA'S *DEAD*.
IF HE THOUGHT OTHERWISE,
HE'D COME AND *GET* HER.
AARONEV JUST WANTS US *OUT*.
...AND WE *DAREN'T COMPLAIN*.
BUT WHAT WILL WE *DO?*
WE TURN LEFT AT *MULVERSCHTAG*.
THAT'LL GET US ON THE ROAD TO MECHANICSBURG.
NO! I MEANT—
OH, *WAIT*.
ARE YOU SERIOUSLY THINKING WE SHOULD GO *BACK*—
INTO A HOSTILE TOWN FULL OF ARMED SOLDIERS—
TO TRY TO RESCUE A GIRL FROM A *MADBOY'S FORTRESS?*
YES! YES I *AM!*
THERE'S A *MILLION* REASONS WHY THAT IS *NOT* GOING TO WORK.
DUN VORRY.
DERE'S *THREE* REASONZ IT *IZ*.

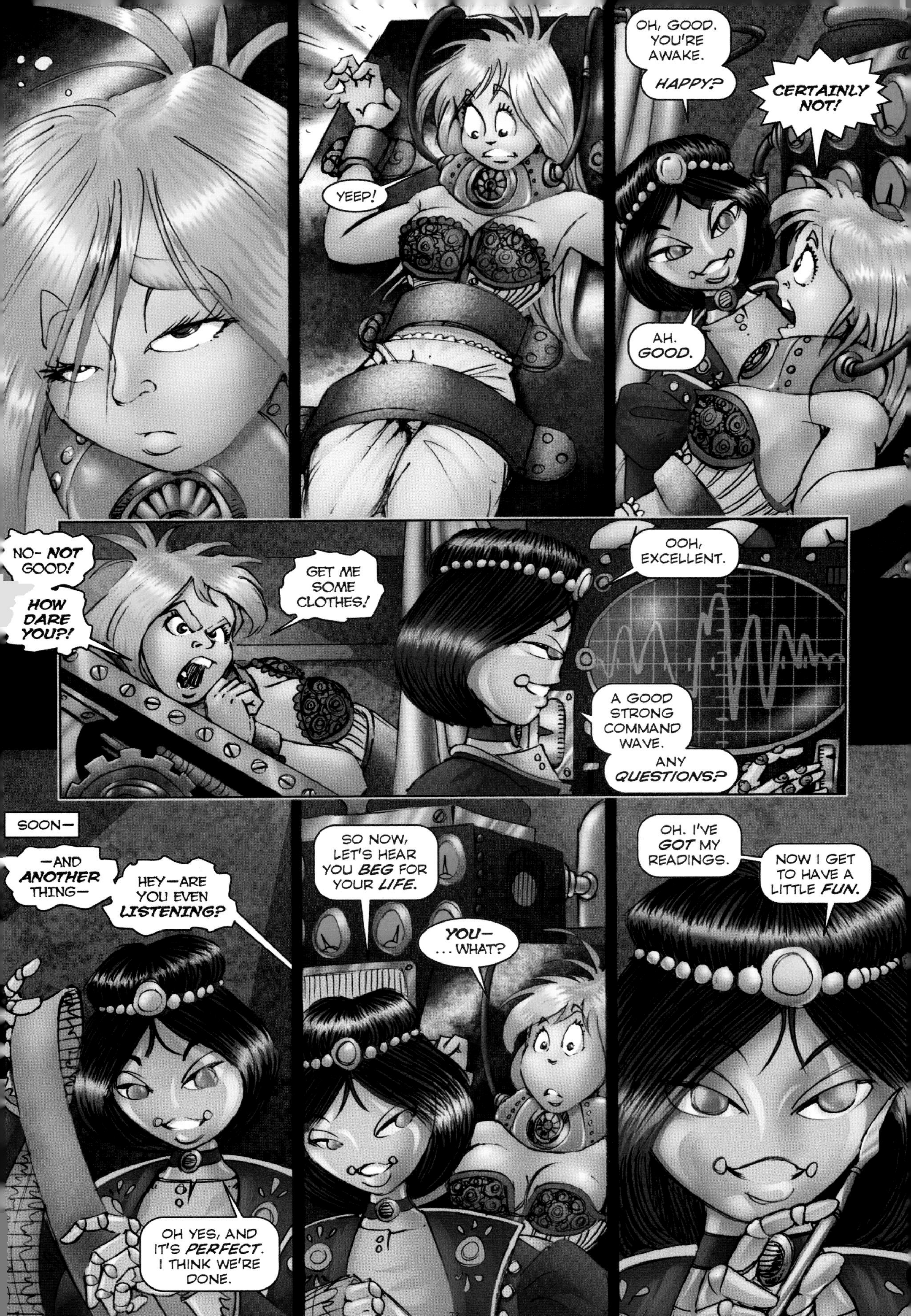
YEEP!
OH, GOOD. YOU'RE AWAKE.
HAPPY?
CERTAINLY NOT!
AH. GOOD.
NO- NOT GOOD!
HOW DARE YOU?!
GET ME SOME CLOTHES!
OOH, EXCELLENT.
A GOOD STRONG COMMAND WAVE.
ANY QUESTIONS?
SOON—
—AND ANOTHER THING—
HEY—ARE YOU EVEN LISTENING?
OH YES, AND IT'S PERFECT. I THINK WE'RE DONE.
SO NOW, LET'S HEAR YOU BEG FOR YOUR LIFE.
YOU— ...WHAT?
OH. I'VE GOT MY READINGS.
NOW I GET TO HAVE A LITTLE FUN.

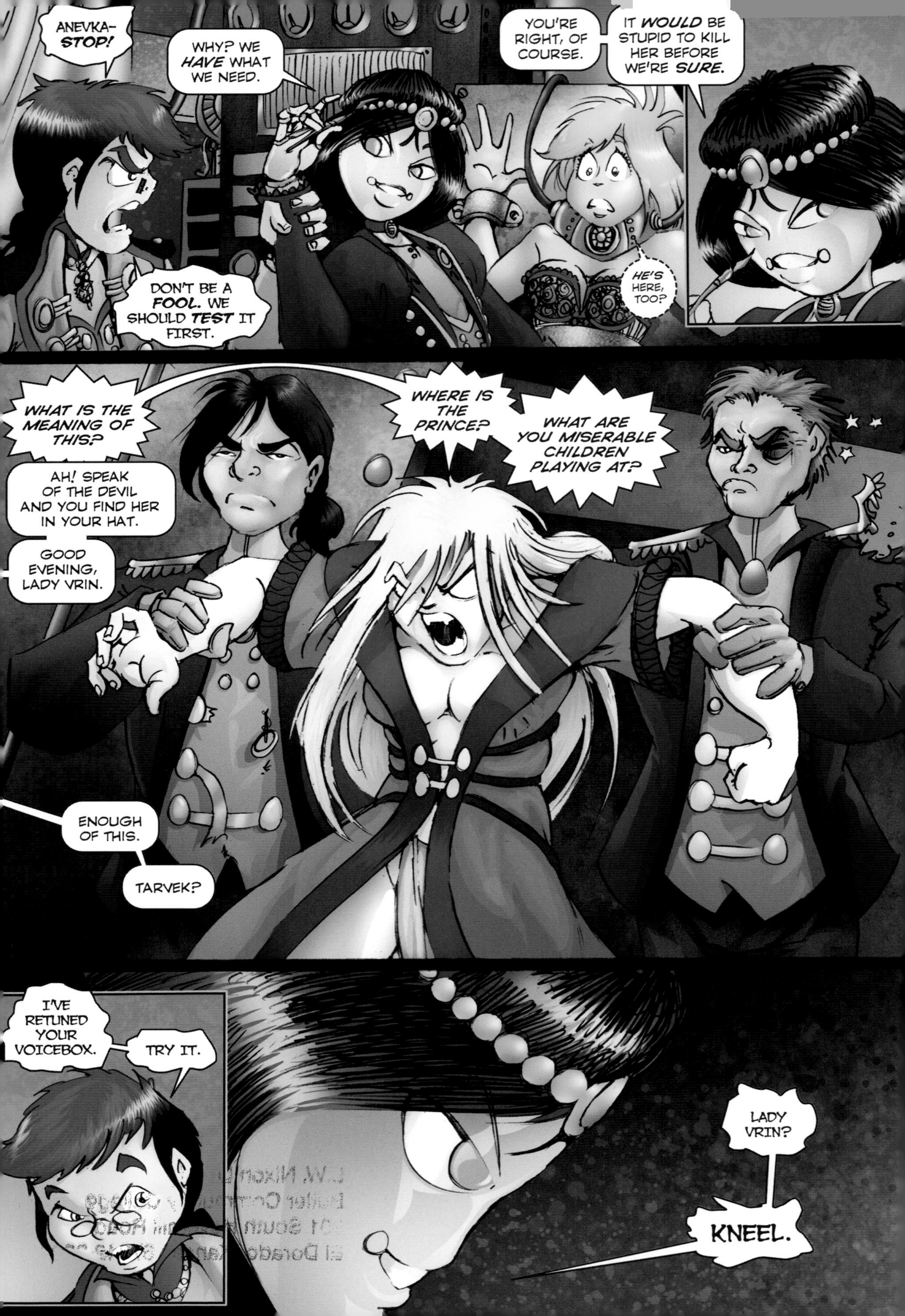

ANEVKA- STOP!
WHY? WE HAVE WHAT WE NEED.
DON'T BE A FOOL. WE SHOULD TEST IT FIRST.
HE'S HERE, TOO?
YOU'RE RIGHT, OF COURSE.
IT WOULD BE STUPID TO KILL HER BEFORE WE'RE SURE.
WHAT IS THE MEANING OF THIS?
WHERE IS THE PRINCE?
WHAT ARE YOU MISERABLE CHILDREN PLAYING AT?
AH! SPEAK OF THE DEVIL AND YOU FIND HER IN YOUR HAT.
GOOD EVENING, LADY VRIN.
ENOUGH OF THIS.
TARVEK?
I'VE RETUNED YOUR VOICEBOX.
TRY IT.
LADY VRIN?
KNEEL.

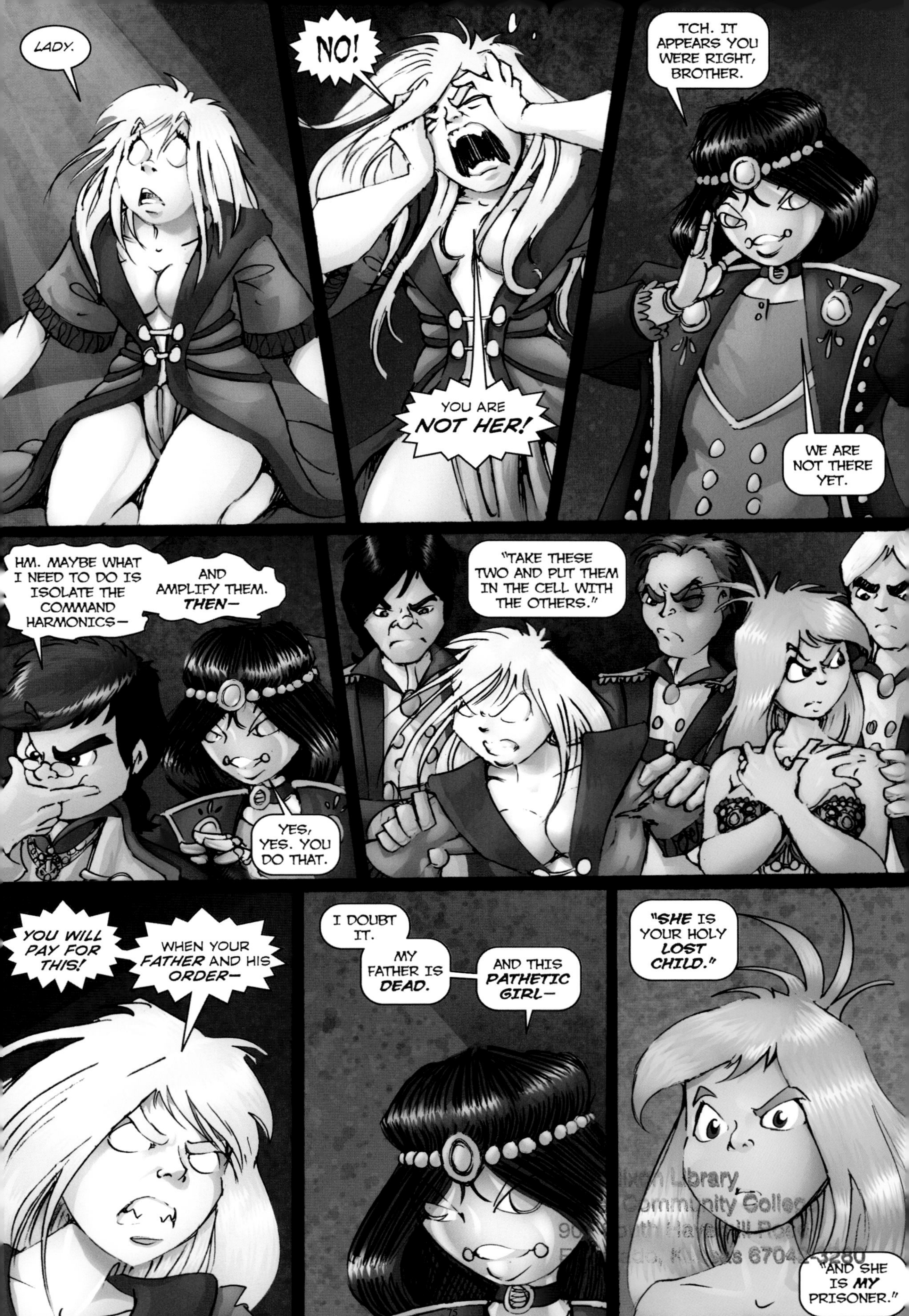
LADY.
NO!
YOU ARE NOT HER!
TCH. IT APPEARS YOU WERE RIGHT, BROTHER.
WE ARE NOT THERE YET.
HM. MAYBE WHAT I NEED TO DO IS ISOLATE THE COMMAND HARMONICS—
AND AMPLIFY THEM. THEN—
YES, YES. YOU DO THAT.
"TAKE THESE TWO AND PUT THEM IN THE CELL WITH THE OTHERS."
YOU WILL PAY FOR THIS!
WHEN YOUR FATHER AND HIS ORDER—
I DOUBT IT.
MY FATHER IS DEAD.
AND THIS PATHETIC GIRL—
"SHE IS YOUR HOLY LOST CHILD."
"AND SHE IS MY PRISONER."

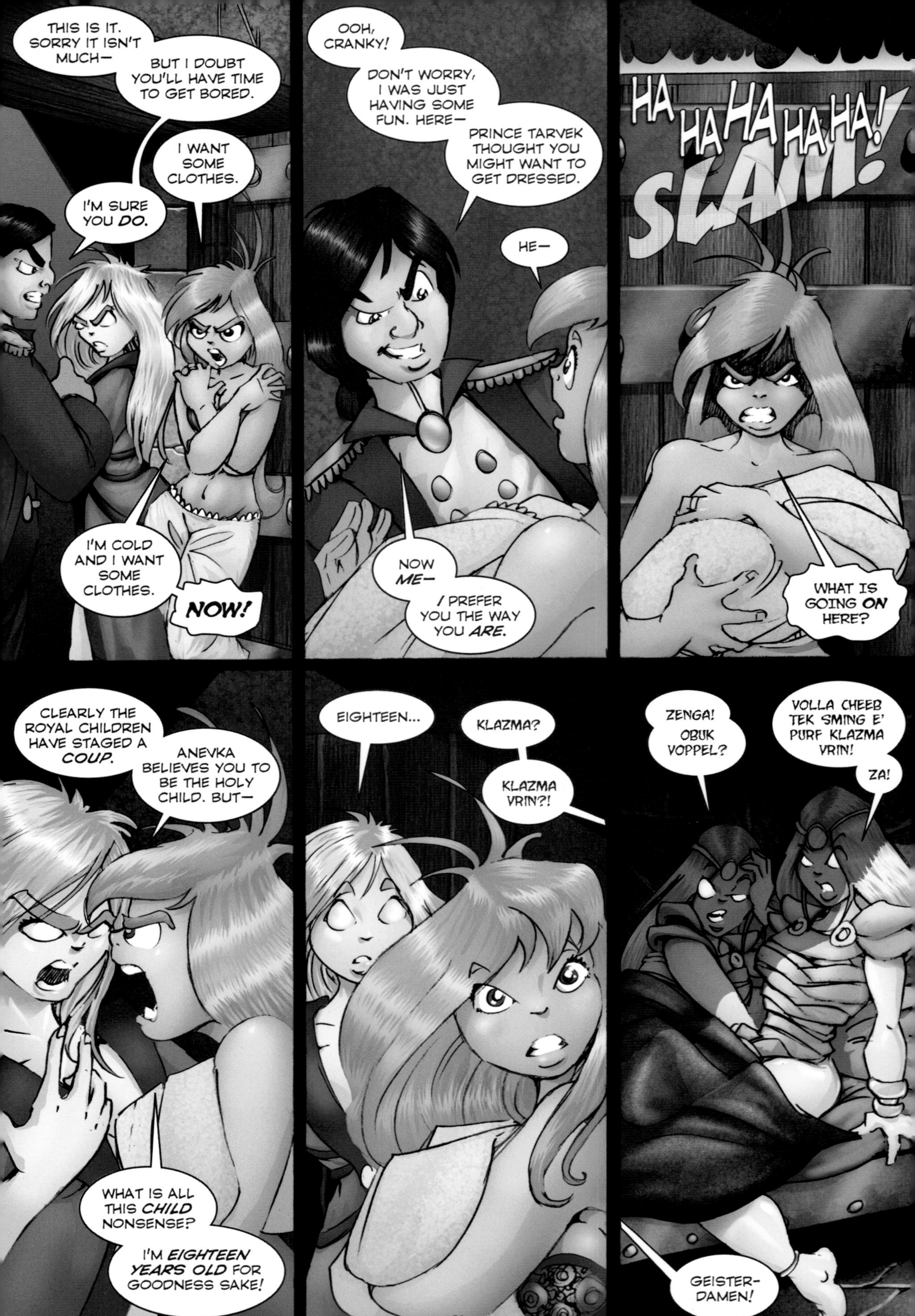
THIS IS IT. SORRY IT ISN'T MUCH—
BUT I DOUBT YOU'LL HAVE TIME TO GET BORED.
I WANT SOME CLOTHES.
I'M SURE YOU *DO.*
I'M COLD AND I WANT SOME CLOTHES.
NOW!
OOH, CRANKY!
DON'T WORRY, I WAS JUST HAVING SOME FUN. HERE—
PRINCE TARVEK THOUGHT YOU MIGHT WANT TO GET DRESSED.
HE—
NOW *ME*—
I PREFER YOU THE WAY YOU *ARE.*
HA HA HA HA HA HA!
SLAM!
WHAT IS GOING *ON* HERE?
CLEARLY THE ROYAL CHILDREN HAVE STAGED A *COUP.*
ANEVKA BELIEVES YOU TO BE THE HOLY CHILD. BUT—
WHAT IS ALL THIS *CHILD* NONSENSE?
I'M *EIGHTEEN YEARS OLD* FOR GOODNESS SAKE!
EIGHTEEN...
KLAZMA?
KLAZMA VRIN?!
ZENGA! OBUK VOPPEL?
VOLLA CHEEB TEK SMING E' PURF KLAZMA VRIN!
ZA!
GEISTER-DAMEN!

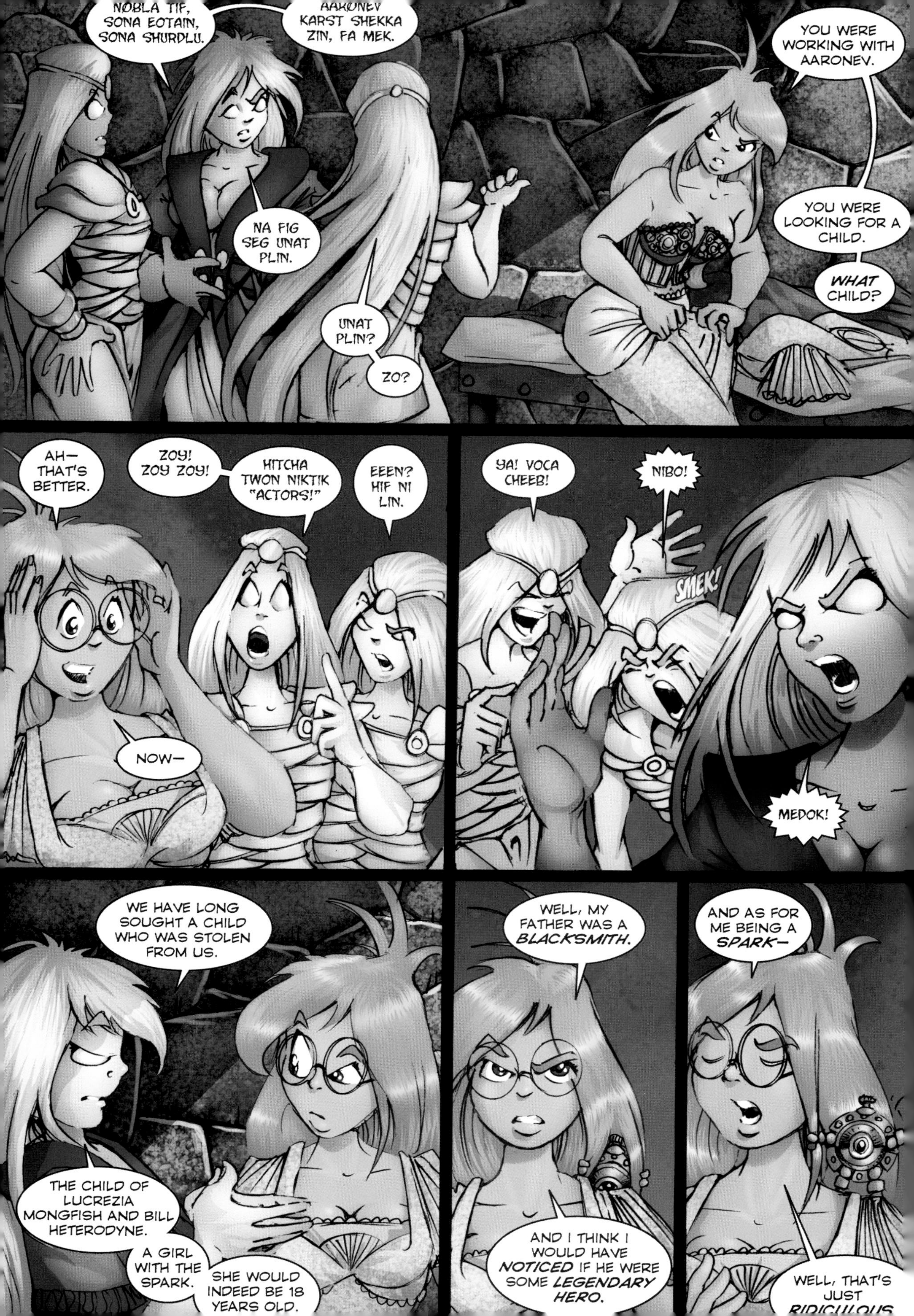
NOBLA TIF, SONA EOTAIN, SONA SHURDLU.
AARONEV KARST SHEKKA ZIN, FA MEK.
NA FIG SEG UNAT PLIN.
UNAT PLIN?
ZO?
YOU WERE WORKING WITH AARONEV.
YOU WERE LOOKING FOR A CHILD.
WHAT CHILD?
AH— THAT'S BETTER.
ZOY! ZOY ZOY!
HITCHA TWON NIKTIK "ACTORS!"
EEEN? HIF NI LIN.
NOW—
YA! VOCA CHEEB!
NIBO!
SMEK!
MEDOK!
WE HAVE LONG SOUGHT A CHILD WHO WAS STOLEN FROM US.
THE CHILD OF LUCREZIA MONGFISH AND BILL HETERODYNE.
A GIRL WITH THE SPARK.
SHE WOULD INDEED BE 18 YEARS OLD.
WELL, MY FATHER WAS A *BLACKSMITH*.
AND I THINK I WOULD HAVE *NOTICED* IF HE WERE SOME *LEGENDARY HERO*.
AND AS FOR ME BEING A *SPARK*—
WELL, THAT'S JUST *RIDICULOUS*.

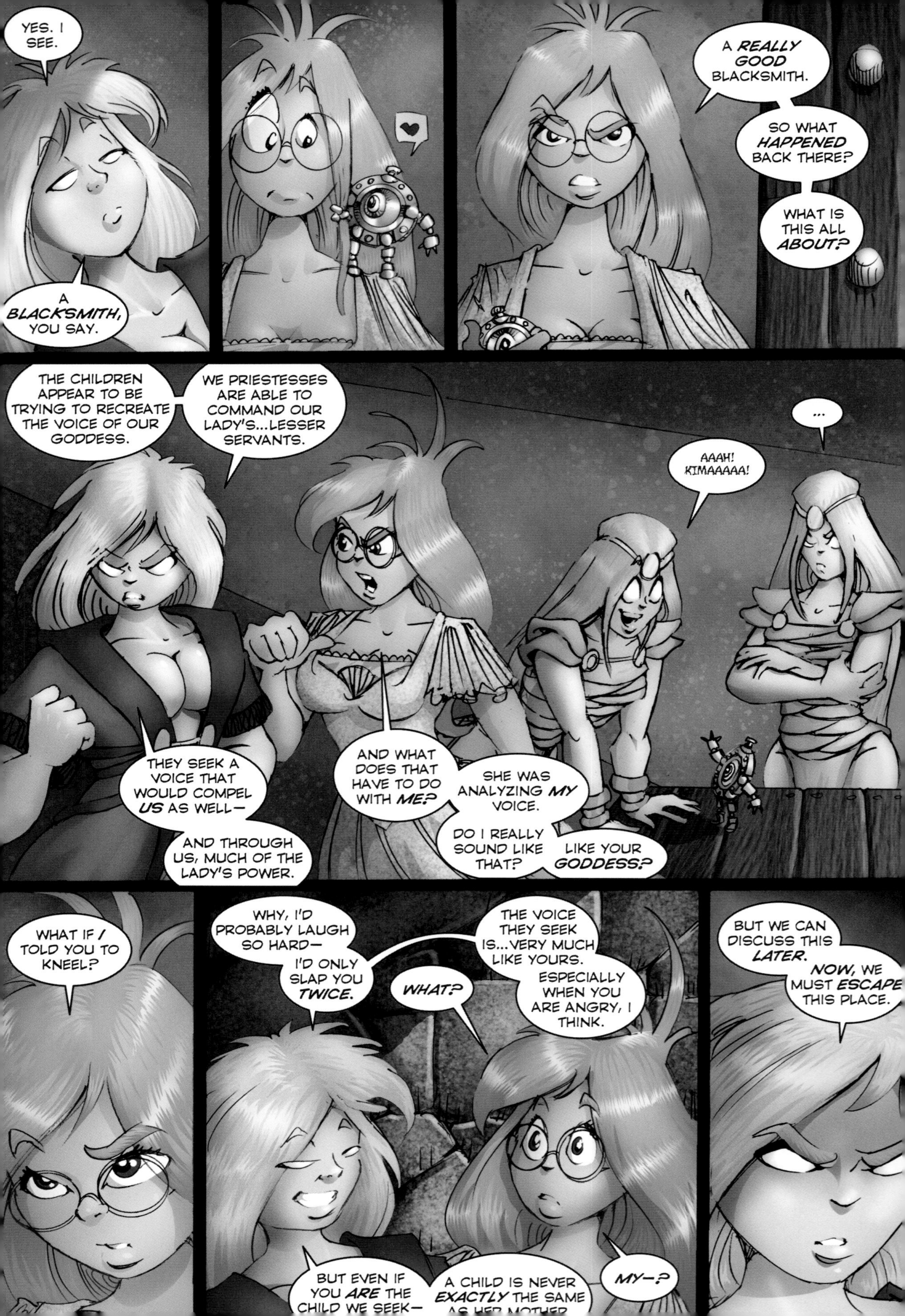
YES. I SEE.
A BLACKSMITH, YOU SAY.
A REALLY GOOD BLACKSMITH.
SO WHAT HAPPENED BACK THERE?
WHAT IS THIS ALL ABOUT?
THE CHILDREN APPEAR TO BE TRYING TO RECREATE THE VOICE OF OUR GODDESS.
WE PRIESTESSES ARE ABLE TO COMMAND OUR LADY'S...LESSER SERVANTS.
AAAH! KIMAAAAAA!
...
THEY SEEK A VOICE THAT WOULD COMPEL US AS WELL—
AND THROUGH US, MUCH OF THE LADY'S POWER.
AND WHAT DOES THAT HAVE TO DO WITH ME?
SHE WAS ANALYZING MY VOICE.
DO I REALLY SOUND LIKE THAT?
LIKE YOUR GODDESS?
WHAT IF I TOLD YOU TO KNEEL?
WHY, I'D PROBABLY LAUGH SO HARD—
I'D ONLY SLAP YOU TWICE.
THE VOICE THEY SEEK IS...VERY MUCH LIKE YOURS.
WHAT?
ESPECIALLY WHEN YOU ARE ANGRY, I THINK.
BUT WE CAN DISCUSS THIS LATER.
NOW, WE MUST ESCAPE THIS PLACE.
BUT EVEN IF YOU ARE THE CHILD WE SEEK—
A CHILD IS NEVER EXACTLY THE SAME
MY—?

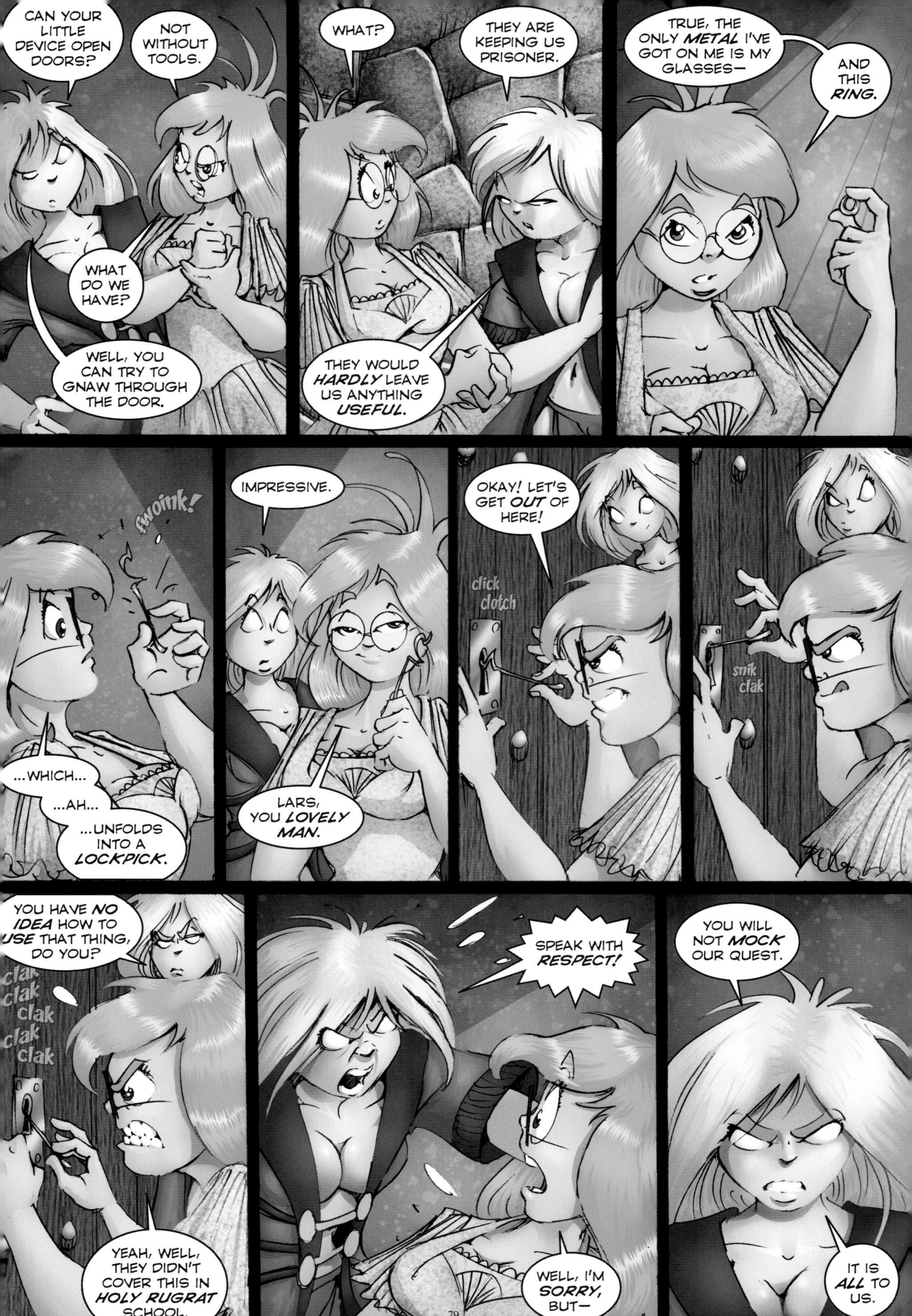
CAN YOUR LITTLE DEVICE OPEN DOORS?
NOT WITHOUT TOOLS.
WHAT DO WE HAVE?
WELL, YOU CAN TRY TO GNAW THROUGH THE DOOR.
WHAT?
THEY ARE KEEPING US PRISONER.
THEY WOULD HARDLY LEAVE US ANYTHING USEFUL.
TRUE, THE ONLY METAL I'VE GOT ON ME IS MY GLASSES—
AND THIS RING.
fwoink!
...WHICH...
...AH...
...UNFOLDS INTO A LOCKPICK.
IMPRESSIVE.
LARS, YOU LOVELY MAN.
OKAY! LET'S GET OUT OF HERE!
click clotch
snik clak
YOU HAVE NO IDEA HOW TO USE THAT THING, DO YOU?
clak clak clak clak clak
YEAH, WELL, THEY DIDN'T COVER THIS IN HOLY RUGRAT SCHOOL.
SPEAK WITH RESPECT!
WELL, I'M SORRY, BUT—
YOU WILL NOT MOCK OUR QUEST.
IT IS ALL TO US.

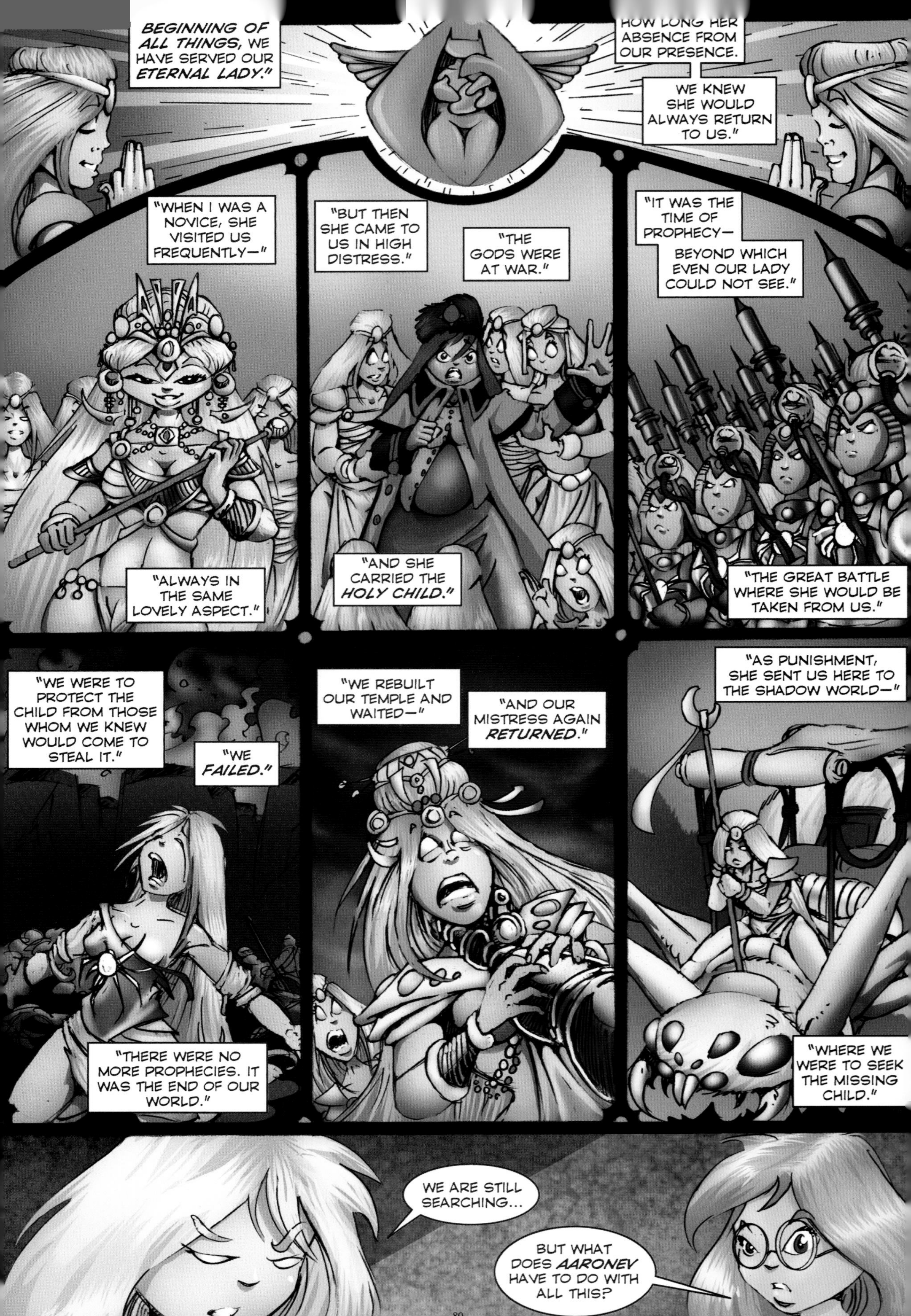

BEGINNING OF ALL THINGS, WE HAVE SERVED OUR ETERNAL LADY."
HOW LONG HER ABSENCE FROM OUR PRESENCE.
WE KNEW SHE WOULD ALWAYS RETURN TO US."
"WHEN I WAS A NOVICE, SHE VISITED US FREQUENTLY—"
"ALWAYS IN THE SAME LOVELY ASPECT."
"BUT THEN SHE CAME TO US IN HIGH DISTRESS."
"THE GODS WERE AT WAR."
"AND SHE CARRIED THE HOLY CHILD."
"IT WAS THE TIME OF PROPHECY—
BEYOND WHICH EVEN OUR LADY COULD NOT SEE."
"THE GREAT BATTLE WHERE SHE WOULD BE TAKEN FROM US."
"WE WERE TO PROTECT THE CHILD FROM THOSE WHOM WE KNEW WOULD COME TO STEAL IT."
"WE FAILED."
"THERE WERE NO MORE PROPHECIES. IT WAS THE END OF OUR WORLD."
"WE REBUILT OUR TEMPLE AND WAITED—"
"AND OUR MISTRESS AGAIN RETURNED."
"AS PUNISHMENT, SHE SENT US HERE TO THE SHADOW WORLD—"
"WHERE WE WERE TO SEEK THE MISSING CHILD."
WE ARE STILL SEARCHING...
BUT WHAT DOES AARONEV HAVE TO DO WITH ALL THIS?

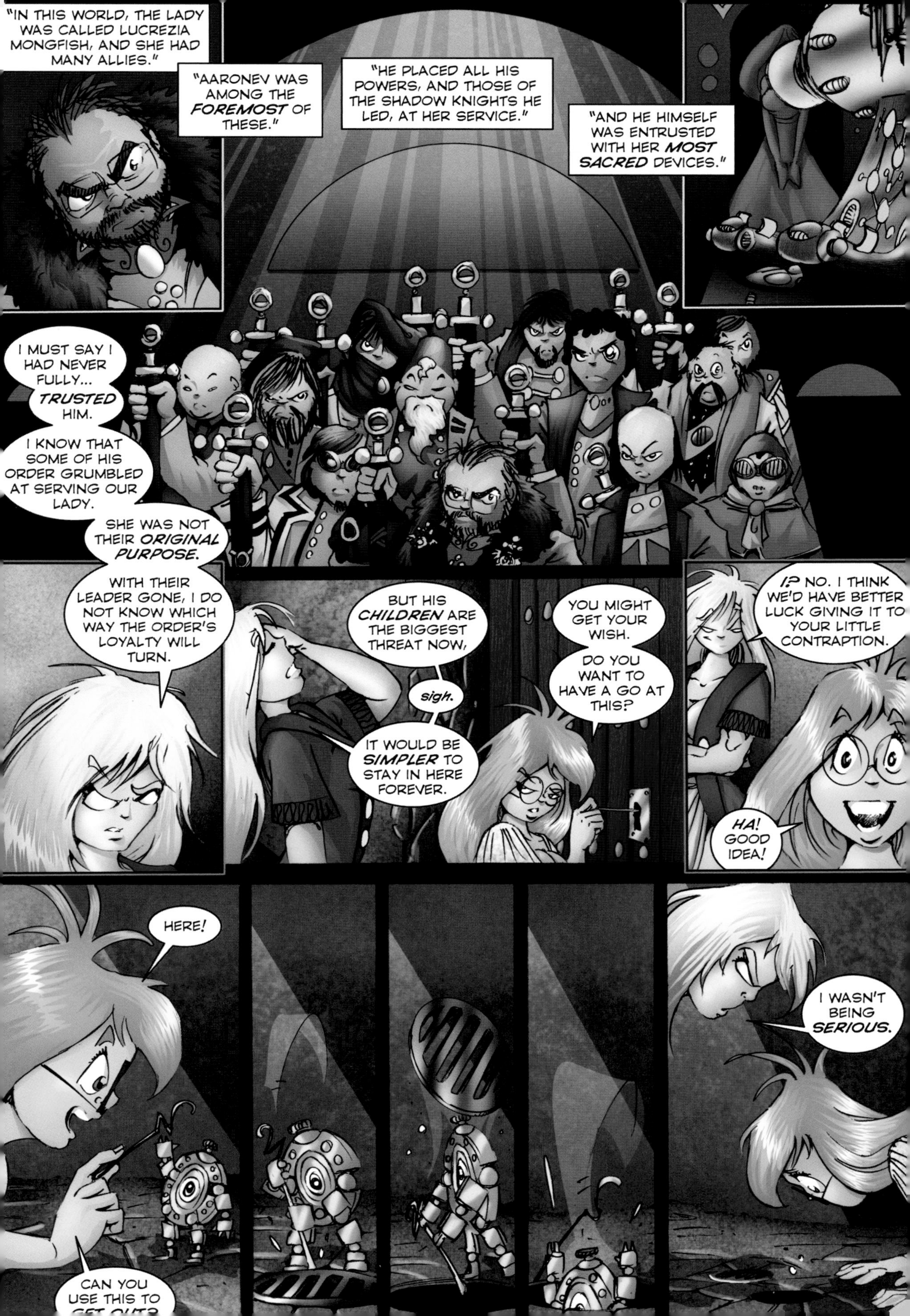

"IN THIS WORLD, THE LADY WAS CALLED LUCREZIA MONGFISH, AND SHE HAD MANY ALLIES."
"AARONEV WAS AMONG THE *FOREMOST* OF THESE."
"HE PLACED ALL HIS POWERS, AND THOSE OF THE SHADOW KNIGHTS HE LED, AT HER SERVICE."
"AND HE HIMSELF WAS ENTRUSTED WITH HER *MOST SACRED* DEVICES."
I MUST SAY I HAD NEVER FULLY... *TRUSTED* HIM.
I KNOW THAT SOME OF HIS ORDER GRUMBLED AT SERVING OUR LADY.
SHE WAS NOT THEIR *ORIGINAL PURPOSE.*
WITH THEIR LEADER GONE, I DO NOT KNOW WHICH WAY THE ORDER'S LOYALTY WILL TURN.
BUT HIS *CHILDREN* ARE THE BIGGEST THREAT NOW,
sigh.
IT WOULD BE *SIMPLER* TO STAY IN HERE FOREVER.
YOU MIGHT GET YOUR WISH.
DO YOU WANT TO HAVE A GO AT THIS?
I? NO. I THINK WE'D HAVE BETTER LUCK GIVING IT TO YOUR LITTLE CONTRAPTION.
HA! GOOD IDEA!
HERE!
CAN YOU USE THIS TO
I WASN'T BEING *SERIOUS.*

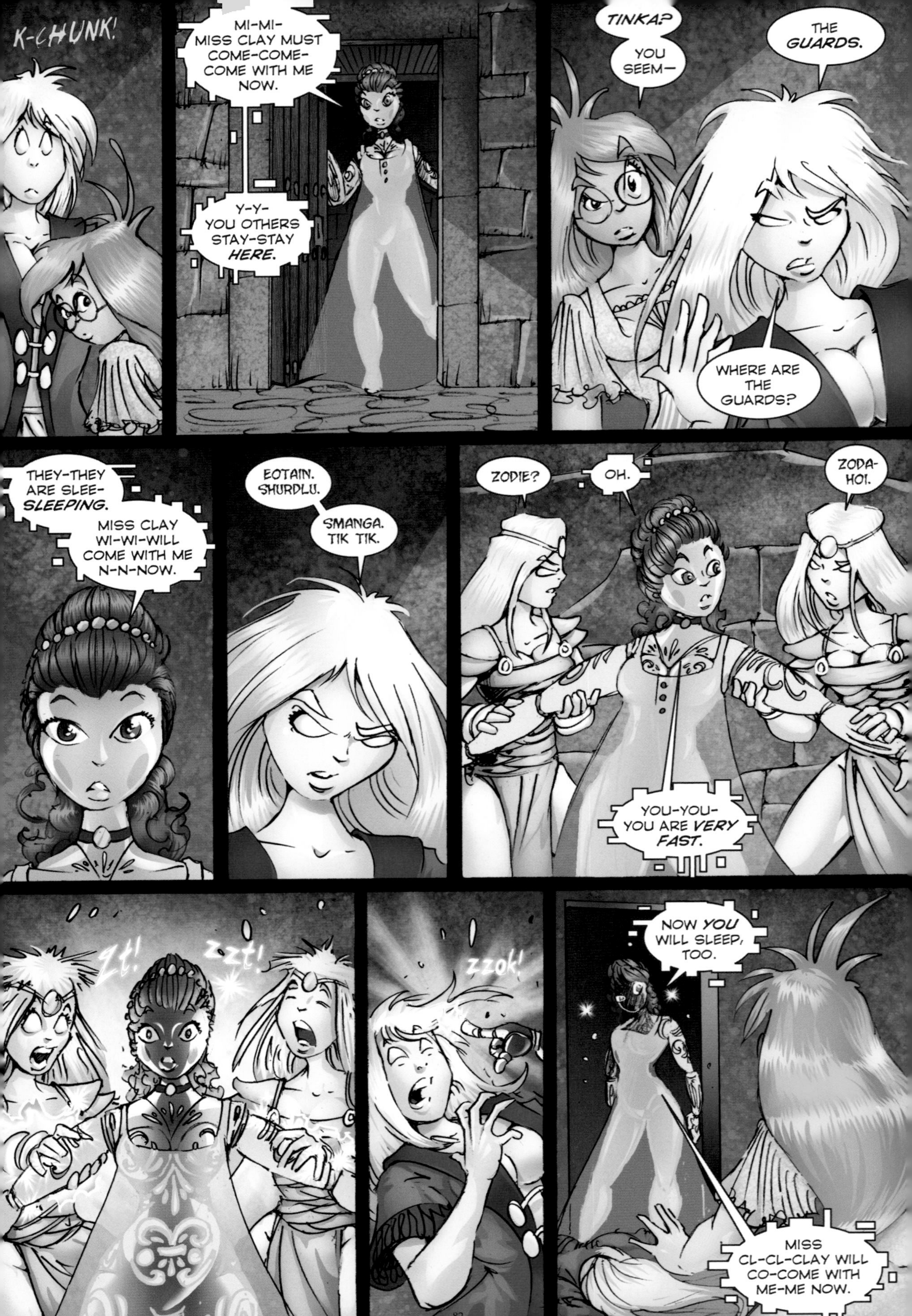
K-CHUNK!
MI-MI- MISS CLAY MUST COME-COME- COME WITH ME NOW.
Y-Y- YOU OTHERS STAY-STAY *HERE*.
TINKA?
YOU SEEM—
THE *GUARDS*.
WHERE ARE THE GUARDS?
THEY-THEY ARE SLEE- *SLEEPING*.
MISS CLAY WI-WI-WILL COME WITH ME N-N-NOW.
EOTAIN. SHURDLU.
SMANGA. TIK TIK.
ZODIE?
OH.
ZODA- HOI.
YOU-YOU- YOU ARE *VERY FAST*.
zt!
zzt!
zzok!
NOW *YOU* WILL SLEEP, TOO.
MISS CL-CL-CLAY WILL CO-COME WITH ME-ME NOW.

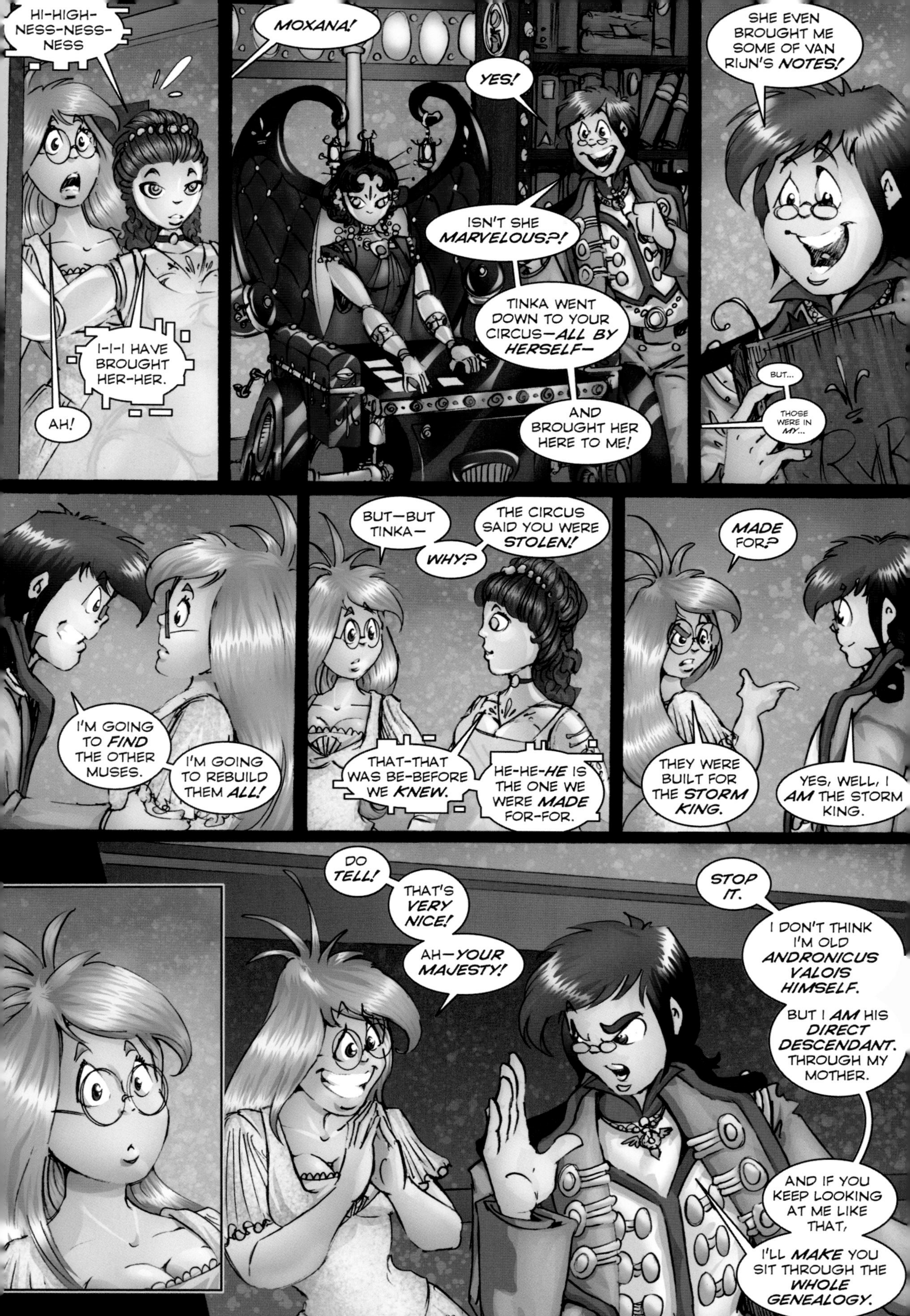
HI-HIGH-NESS-NESS-NESS
I-I-I HAVE BROUGHT HER-HER.
AH!
MOXANA!
YES!
ISN'T SHE MARVELOUS?!
TINKA WENT DOWN TO YOUR CIRCUS—ALL BY HERSELF—
AND BROUGHT HER HERE TO ME!
SHE EVEN BROUGHT ME SOME OF VAN RIJN'S NOTES!
BUT...
THOSE WERE IN MY...
I'M GOING TO FIND THE OTHER MUSES.
I'M GOING TO REBUILD THEM ALL!
BUT—BUT TINKA—
WHY?
THE CIRCUS SAID YOU WERE STOLEN!
THAT-THAT WAS BE-BEFORE WE KNEW.
HE-HE-HE IS THE ONE WE WERE MADE FOR-FOR.
MADE FOR?
THEY WERE BUILT FOR THE STORM KING.
YES, WELL, I AM THE STORM KING.
DO TELL!
THAT'S VERY NICE!
AH—YOUR MAJESTY!
STOP IT.
I DON'T THINK I'M OLD ANDRONICUS VALOIS HIMSELF.
BUT I AM HIS DIRECT DESCENDANT. THROUGH MY MOTHER.
AND IF YOU KEEP LOOKING AT ME LIKE THAT,
I'LL MAKE YOU SIT THROUGH THE WHOLE GENEALOGY.

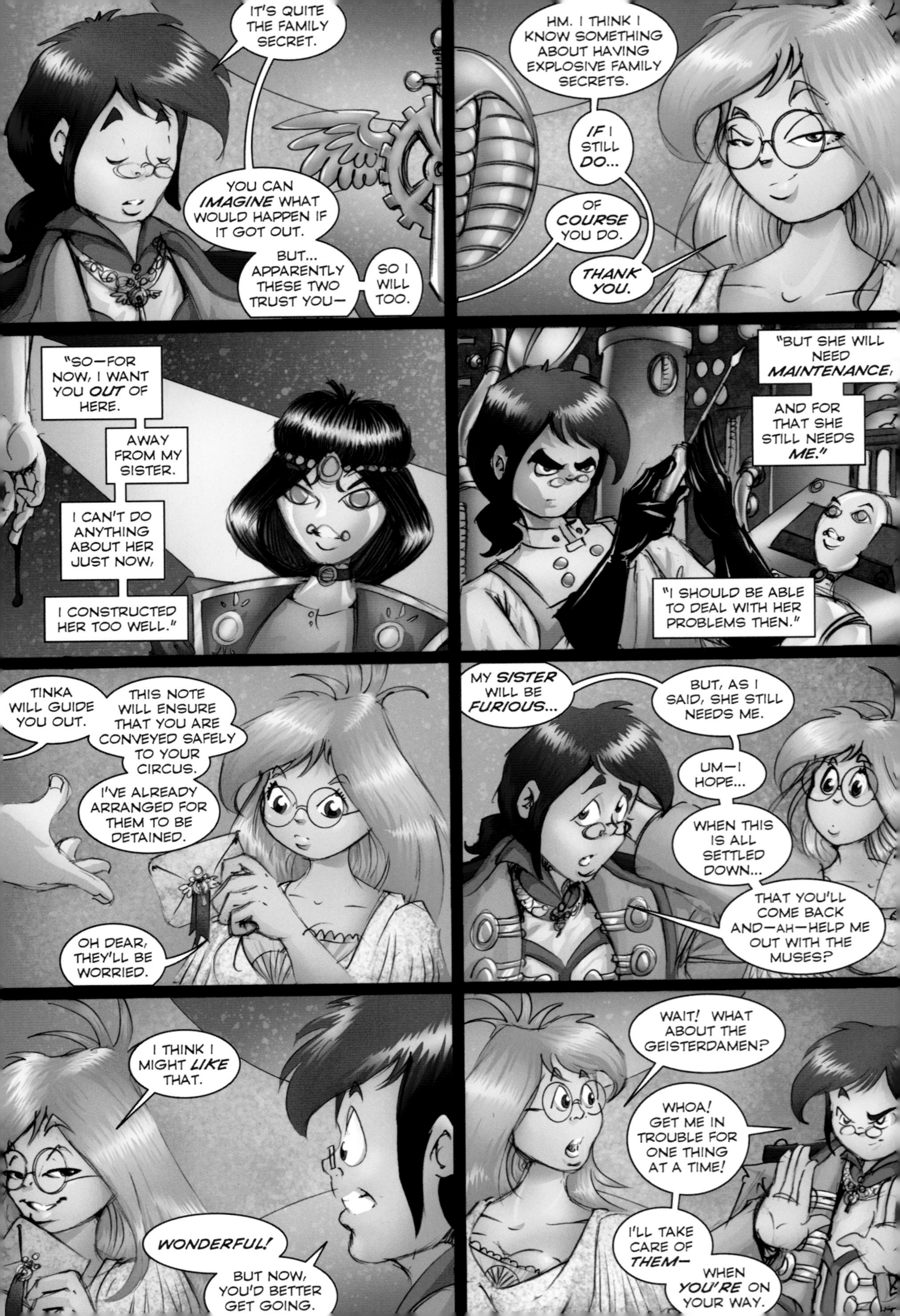
IT'S QUITE THE FAMILY SECRET.
YOU CAN *IMAGINE* WHAT WOULD HAPPEN IF IT GOT OUT.
BUT... APPARENTLY THESE TWO TRUST YOU—
SO I WILL TOO.
HM. I THINK I KNOW SOMETHING ABOUT HAVING EXPLOSIVE FAMILY SECRETS.
IF I STILL *DO*...
OF *COURSE* YOU DO.
THANK YOU.
"SO—FOR NOW, I WANT YOU *OUT* OF HERE.
AWAY FROM MY SISTER.
I CAN'T DO ANYTHING ABOUT HER JUST NOW,
I CONSTRUCTED HER TOO WELL."
"BUT SHE WILL NEED *MAINTENANCE*,
AND FOR THAT SHE STILL NEEDS *ME*."
"I SHOULD BE ABLE TO DEAL WITH HER PROBLEMS THEN."
TINKA WILL GUIDE YOU OUT.
THIS NOTE WILL ENSURE THAT YOU ARE CONVEYED SAFELY TO YOUR CIRCUS.
I'VE ALREADY ARRANGED FOR THEM TO BE DETAINED.
OH DEAR, THEY'LL BE WORRIED.
MY *SISTER* WILL BE *FURIOUS*...
BUT, AS I SAID, SHE STILL NEEDS ME.
UM—I HOPE...
WHEN THIS IS ALL SETTLED DOWN...
THAT YOU'LL COME BACK AND—AH—HELP ME OUT WITH THE MUSES?
I THINK I MIGHT *LIKE* THAT.
WONDERFUL!
BUT NOW, YOU'D BETTER GET GOING.
WAIT! WHAT ABOUT THE GEISTERDAMEN?
WHOA! GET ME IN TROUBLE FOR ONE THING AT A TIME!
I'LL TAKE CARE OF *THEM*—
WHEN *YOU'RE* ON YOUR WAY.

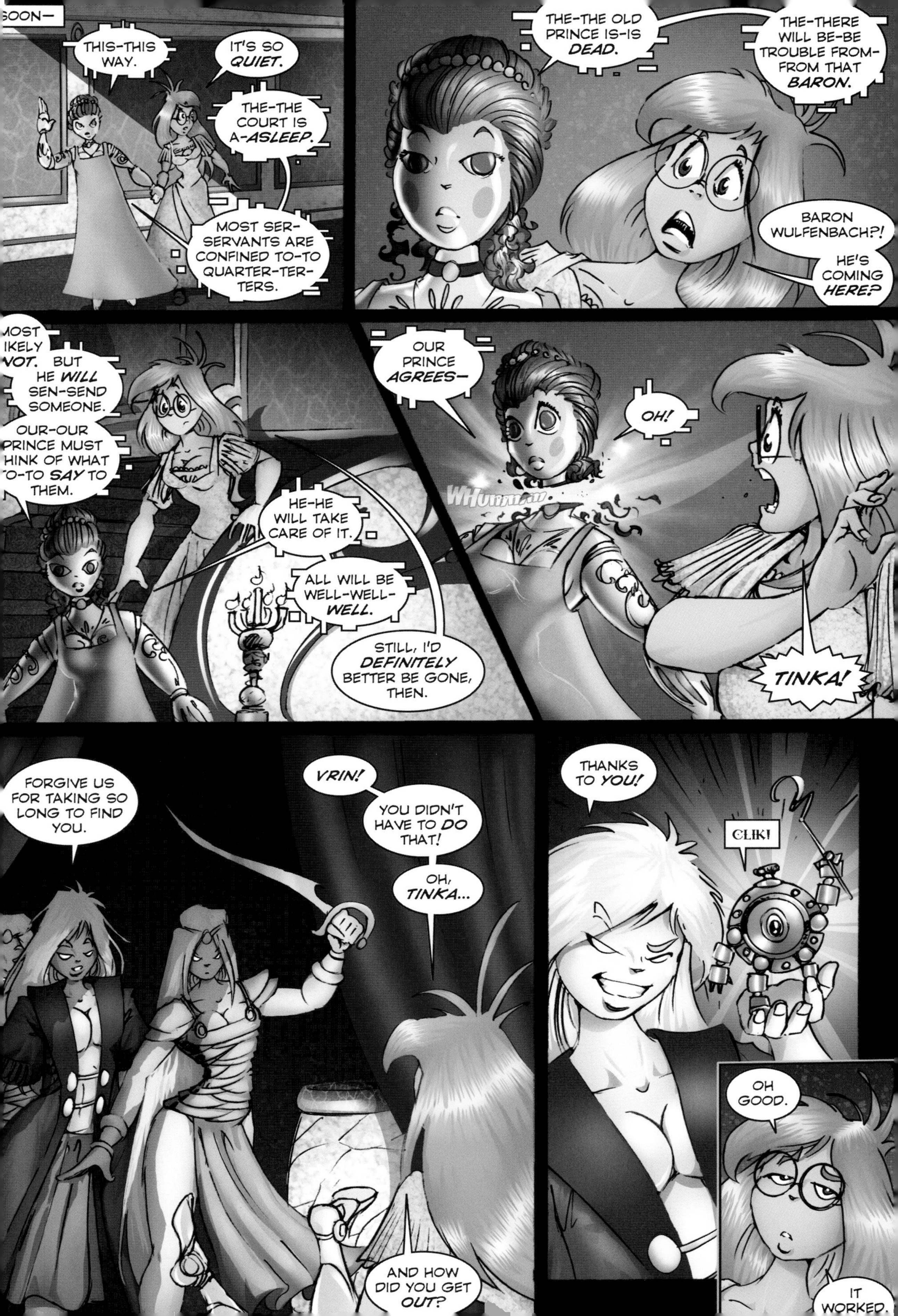
SOON—
THIS-THIS WAY.
IT'S SO QUIET.
THE-THE COURT IS A-ASLEEP.
MOST SER-SERVANTS ARE CONFINED TO-TO QUARTER-TER-TERS.
THE-THE OLD PRINCE IS-IS DEAD.
THE-THERE WILL BE-BE TROUBLE FROM-FROM THAT BARON.
BARON WULFENBACH?!
HE'S COMING HERE?
MOST LIKELY NOT. BUT HE WILL SEN-SEND SOMEONE.
OUR-OUR PRINCE MUST THINK OF WHAT TO-TO SAY TO THEM.
HE-HE WILL TAKE CARE OF IT.
ALL WILL BE WELL-WELL-WELL.
STILL, I'D DEFINITELY BETTER BE GONE, THEN.
OUR PRINCE AGREES—
OH!
TINKA!
FORGIVE US FOR TAKING SO LONG TO FIND YOU.
VRIN!
YOU DIDN'T HAVE TO DO THAT!
OH, TINKA...
AND HOW DID YOU GET OUT?
THANKS TO YOU!
CLIK!
OH GOOD.
IT WORKED.

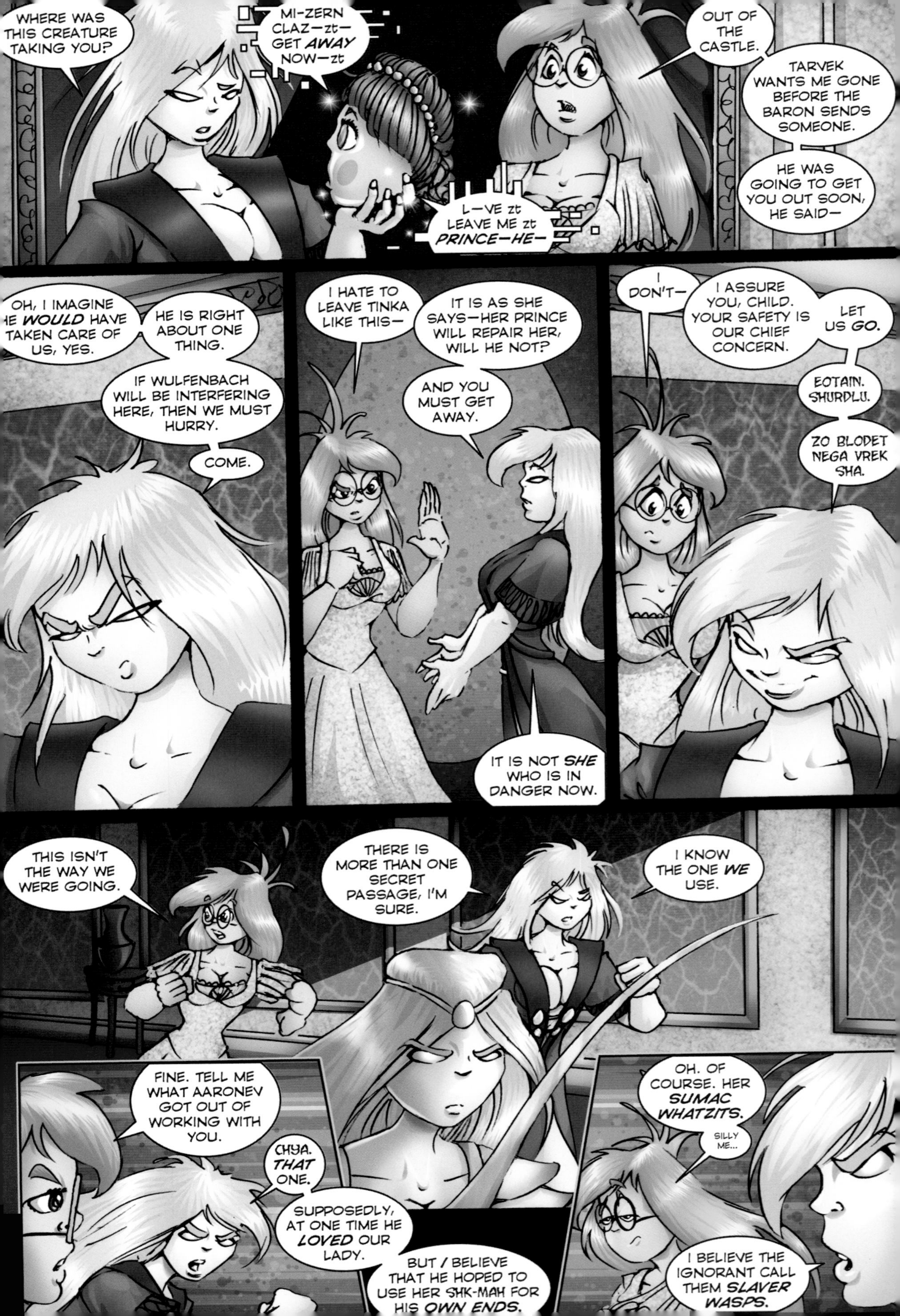
WHERE WAS THIS CREATURE TAKING YOU?
MI-ZERN CLAZ—zt— GET AWAY NOW—zt
OUT OF THE CASTLE.
TARVEK WANTS ME GONE BEFORE THE BARON SENDS SOMEONE.
HE WAS GOING TO GET YOU OUT SOON, HE SAID—
L—VE zt LEAVE ME zt PRINCE—HE—
OH, I IMAGINE HE WOULD HAVE TAKEN CARE OF US, YES.
HE IS RIGHT ABOUT ONE THING.
IF WULFENBACH WILL BE INTERFERING HERE, THEN WE MUST HURRY.
COME.
I HATE TO LEAVE TINKA LIKE THIS—
IT IS AS SHE SAYS—HER PRINCE WILL REPAIR HER, WILL HE NOT?
AND YOU MUST GET AWAY.
IT IS NOT SHE WHO IS IN DANGER NOW.
I DON'T—
I ASSURE YOU, CHILD. YOUR SAFETY IS OUR CHIEF CONCERN.
LET US GO.
EOTAIN. SHURDLU.
ZO BLODET NEGA VREK SHA.
THIS ISN'T THE WAY WE WERE GOING.
THERE IS MORE THAN ONE SECRET PASSAGE, I'M SURE.
I KNOW THE ONE WE USE.
FINE. TELL ME WHAT AARONEV GOT OUT OF WORKING WITH YOU.
CHYA. THAT ONE.
SUPPOSEDLY, AT ONE TIME HE LOVED OUR LADY.
BUT I BELIEVE THAT HE HOPED TO USE HER SHK-MAH FOR HIS OWN ENDS.
OH. OF COURSE. HER SUMAC WHATZITS.
SILLY ME...
I BELIEVE THE IGNORANT CALL THEM SLAVER WASPS.

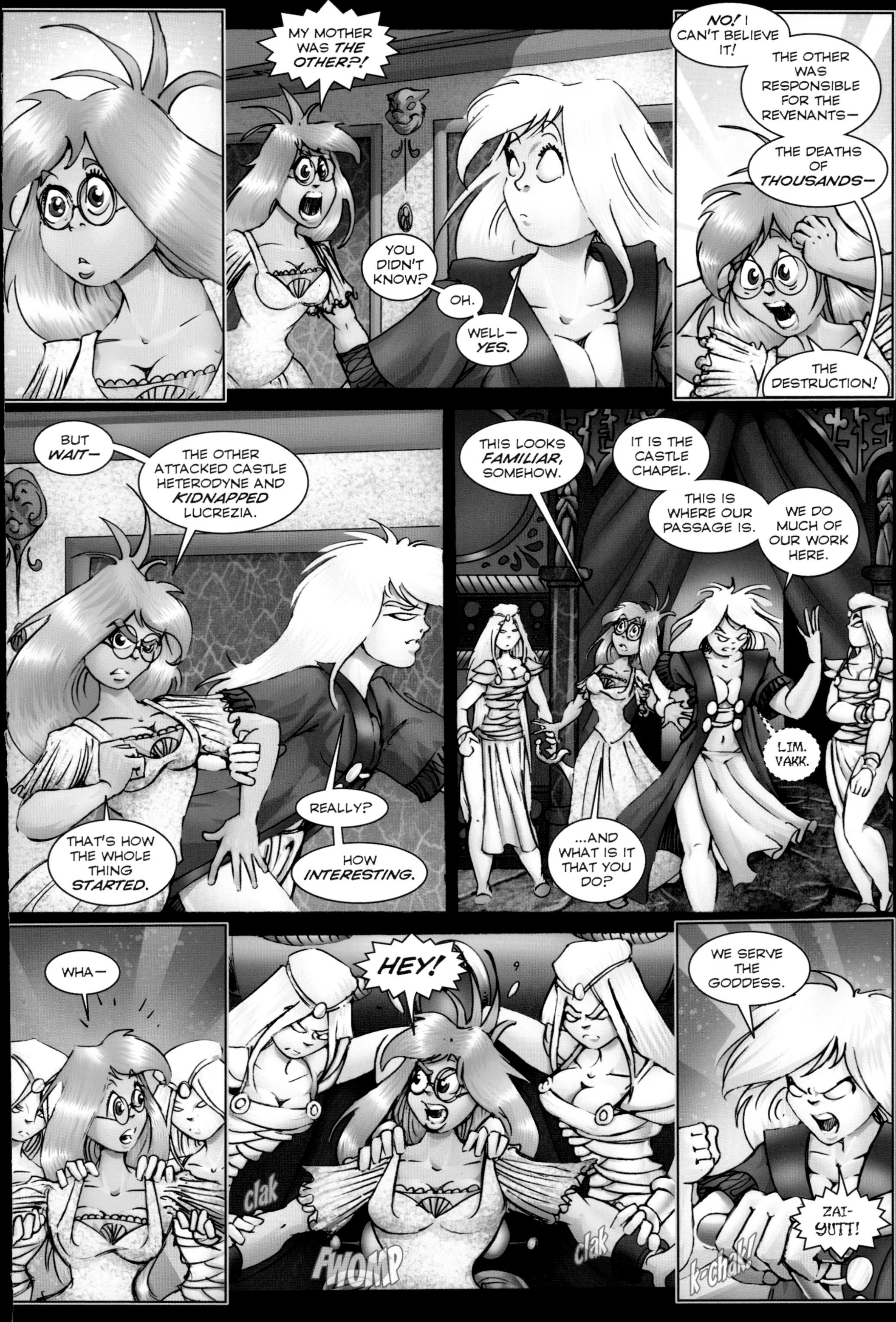
MY MOTHER WAS THE OTHER?!
YOU DIDN'T KNOW?
OH.
WELL— YES.
NO! I CAN'T BELIEVE IT!
THE OTHER WAS RESPONSIBLE FOR THE REVENANTS—
THE DEATHS OF THOUSANDS—
THE DESTRUCTION!
BUT WAIT—
THE OTHER ATTACKED CASTLE HETERODYNE AND KIDNAPPED LUCREZIA.
THAT'S HOW THE WHOLE THING STARTED.
REALLY?
HOW INTERESTING.
THIS LOOKS FAMILIAR, SOMEHOW.
IT IS THE CASTLE CHAPEL.
THIS IS WHERE OUR PASSAGE IS.
WE DO MUCH OF OUR WORK HERE.
LIM. VAKK.
...AND WHAT IS IT THAT YOU DO?
WHA—
HEY!
clak
FWOMP
clak
WE SERVE THE GODDESS.
ZAI-YUTT!
k-chak!

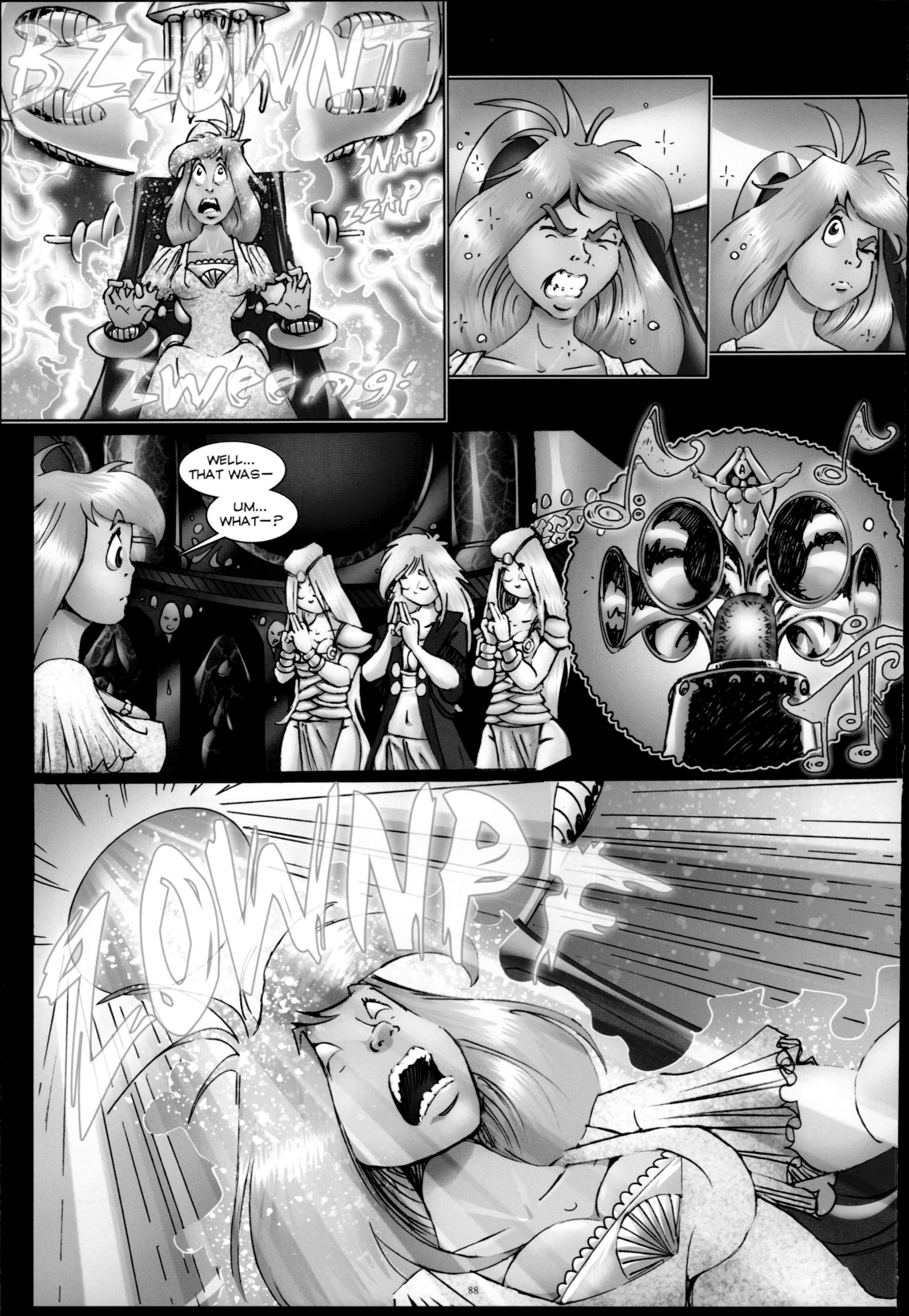
BZZOWNT
SNAP
ZAP
ZZAP
ZWEENG!
WELL... THAT WAS—
UM... WHAT—?
ZOWNP!

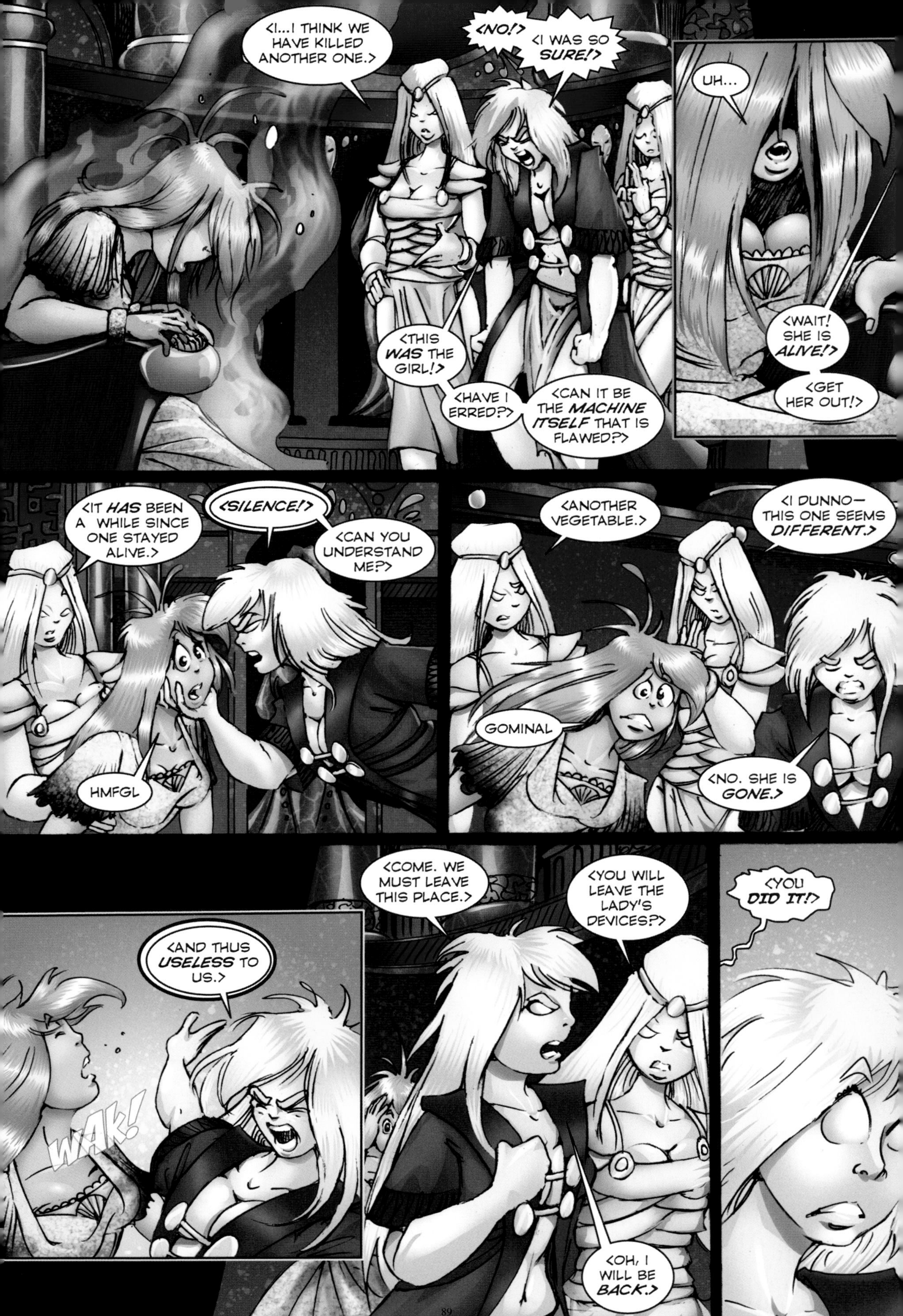
<I...I THINK WE HAVE KILLED ANOTHER ONE.>
<NO!>
<I WAS SO SURE!>
<THIS WAS THE GIRL!>
<HAVE I ERRED?>
<CAN IT BE THE MACHINE ITSELF THAT IS FLAWED?>
UH...
<WAIT! SHE IS ALIVE!>
<GET HER OUT!>
<IT HAS BEEN A WHILE SINCE ONE STAYED ALIVE.>
<SILENCE!>
<CAN YOU UNDERSTAND ME?>
HMFGL
<ANOTHER VEGETABLE.>
<I DUNNO— THIS ONE SEEMS DIFFERENT.>
GOMINAL
<NO. SHE IS GONE.>
<AND THUS USELESS TO US.>
WAK!
<COME. WE MUST LEAVE THIS PLACE.>
<YOU WILL LEAVE THE LADY'S DEVICES?>
<OH, I WILL BE BACK.>
<YOU DID IT!>

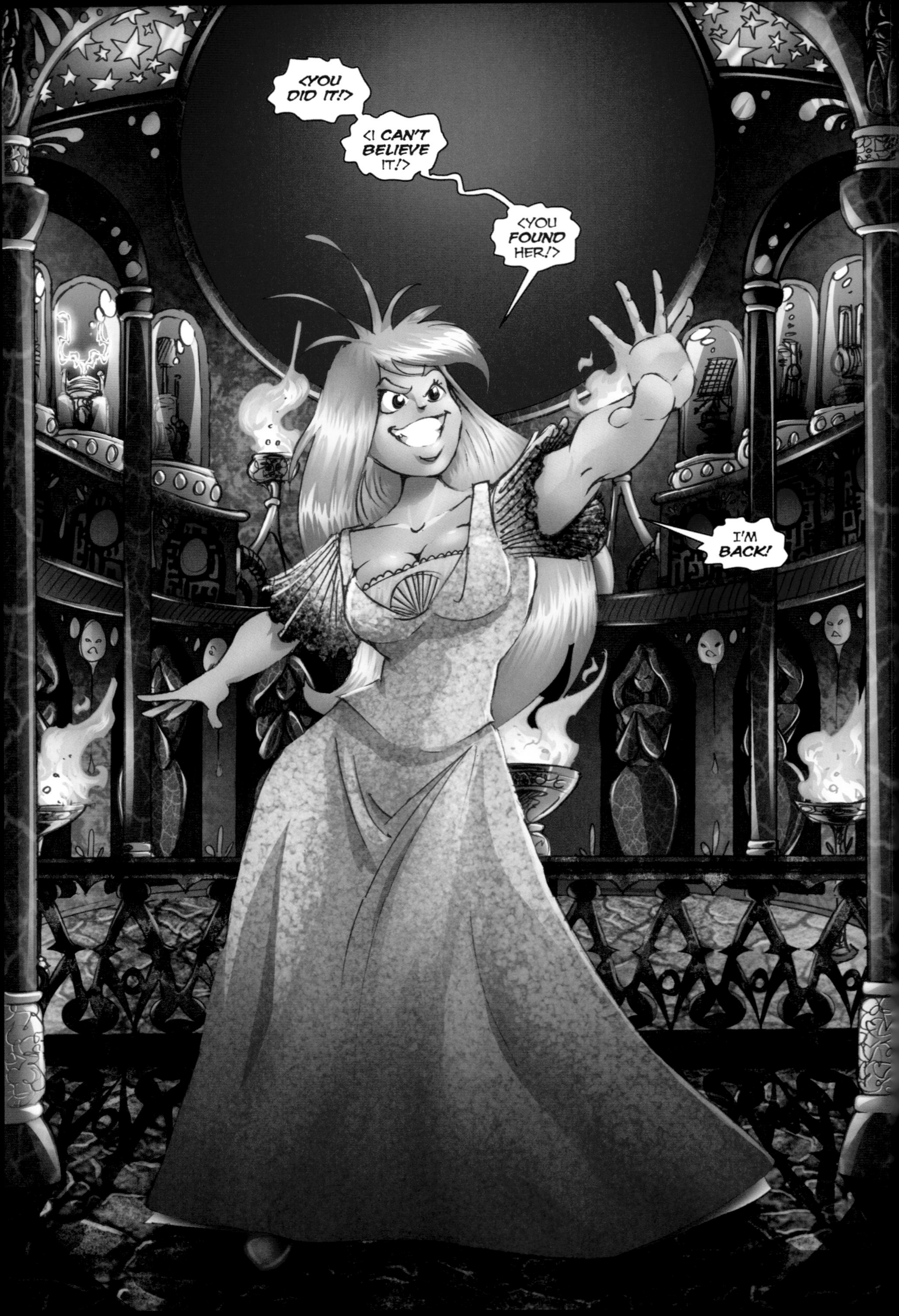
<YOU DID IT!>
<I CAN'T BELIEVE IT!>
<YOU FOUND HER!>
I'M BACK!

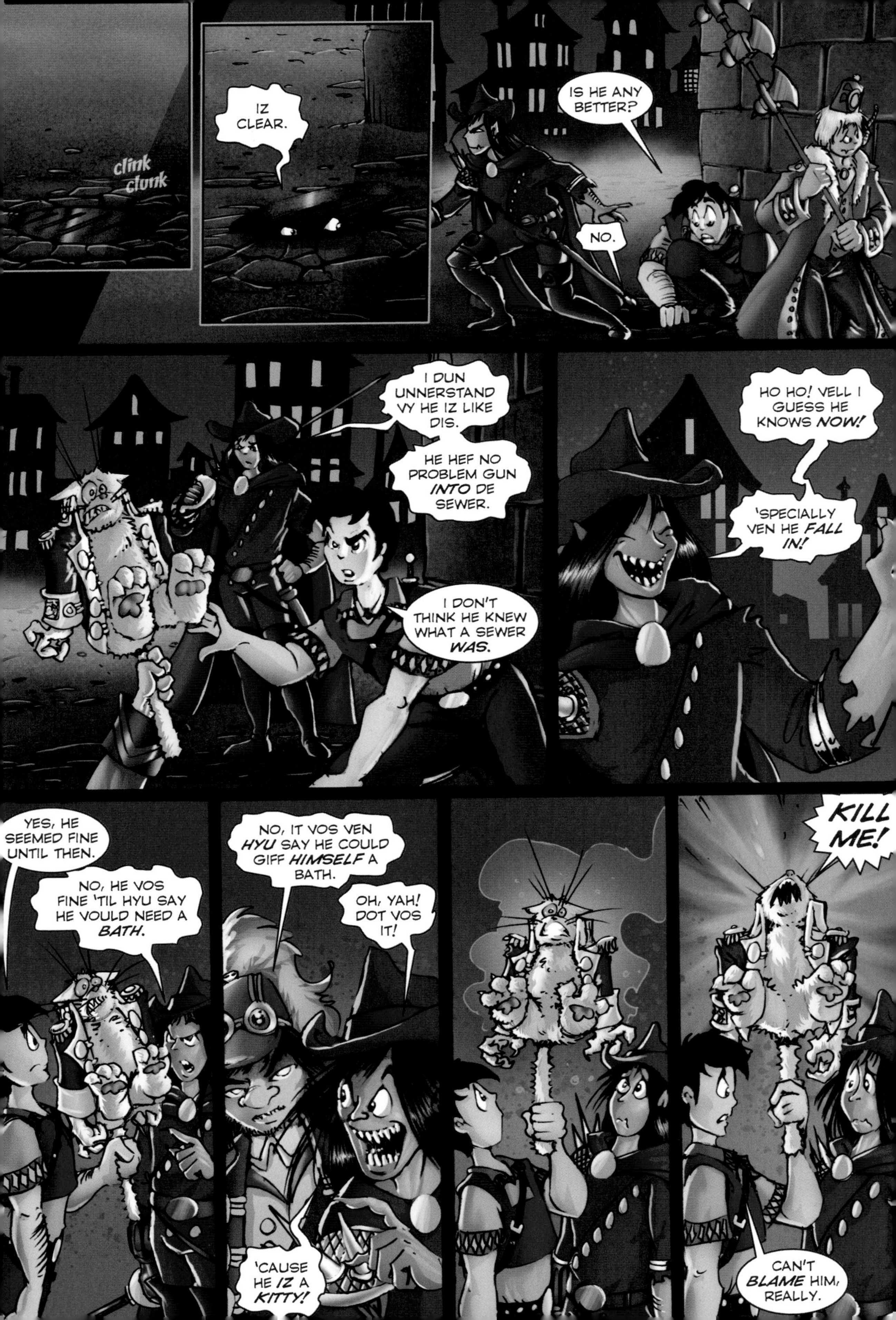
clink
clunk
IZ CLEAR.
IS HE ANY BETTER?
NO.
I DUN UNNERSTAND VY HE IZ LIKE DIS.
HE HEF NO PROBLEM GUN INTO DE SEWER.
I DON'T THINK HE KNEW WHAT A SEWER WAS.
HO HO! VELL I GUESS HE KNOWS NOW!
'SPECIALLY VEN HE FALL IN!
YES, HE SEEMED FINE UNTIL THEN.
NO, HE VOS FINE 'TIL HYU SAY HE VOULD NEED A BATH.
NO, IT VOS VEN HYU SAY HE COULD GIFF HIMSELF A BATH.
OH, YAH! DOT VOS IT!
'CAUSE HE IZ A KITTY!
KILL ME!
CAN'T BLAME HIM, REALLY.

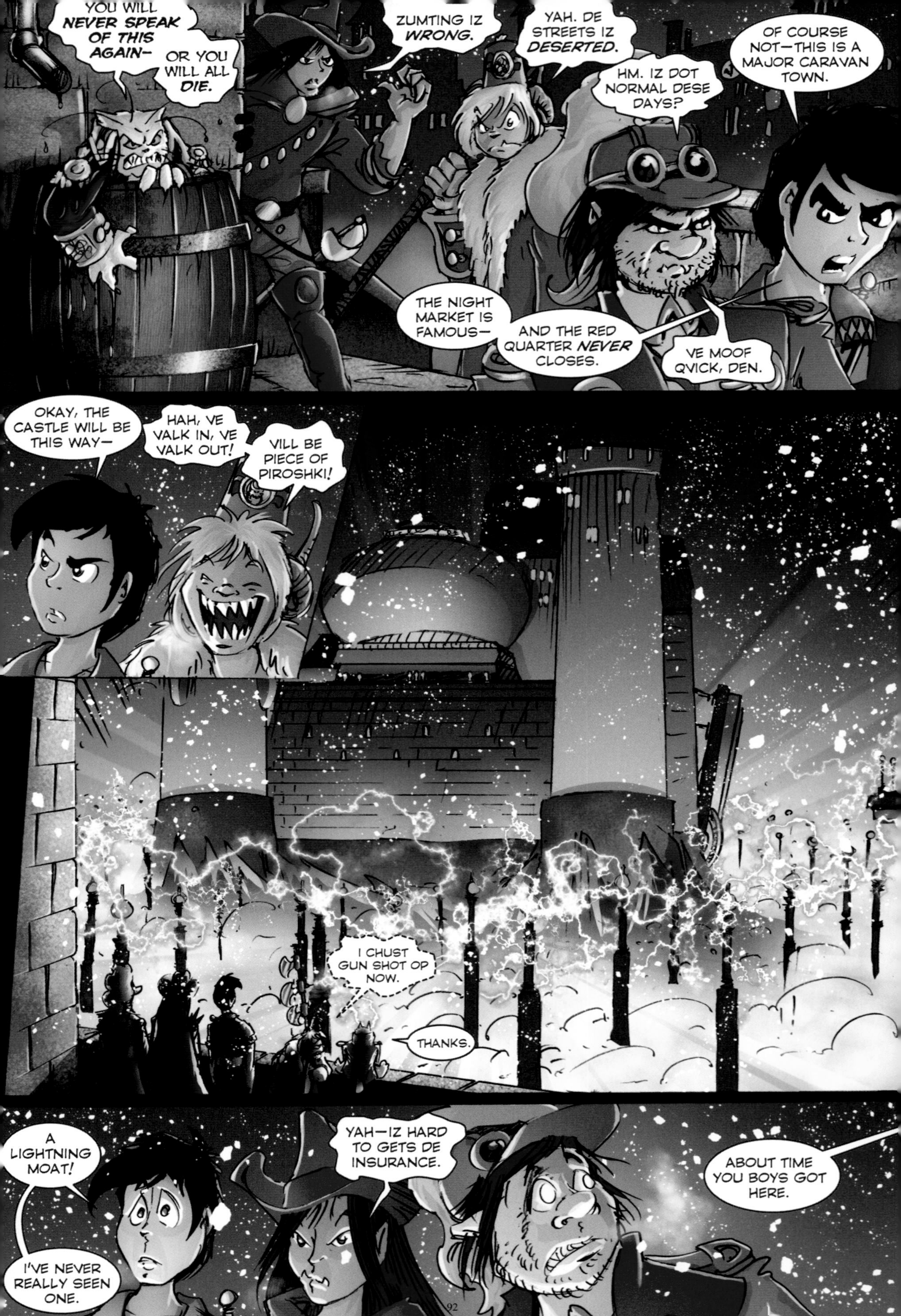
YOU WILL NEVER SPEAK OF THIS AGAIN—
OR YOU WILL ALL DIE.
ZUMTING IZ WRONG.
YAH. DE STREETS IZ DESERTED.
HM. IZ DOT NORMAL DESE DAYS?
OF COURSE NOT—THIS IS A MAJOR CARAVAN TOWN.
THE NIGHT MARKET IS FAMOUS—
AND THE RED QUARTER NEVER CLOSES.
VE MOOF QVICK, DEN.
OKAY, THE CASTLE WILL BE THIS WAY—
HAH, VE VALK IN, VE VALK OUT!
VILL BE PIECE OF PIROSHKI!
I CHUST GUN SHOT OP NOW.
THANKS.
A LIGHTNING MOAT!
I'VE NEVER REALLY SEEN ONE.
YAH—IZ HARD TO GETS DE INSURANCE.
ABOUT TIME YOU BOYS GOT HERE.

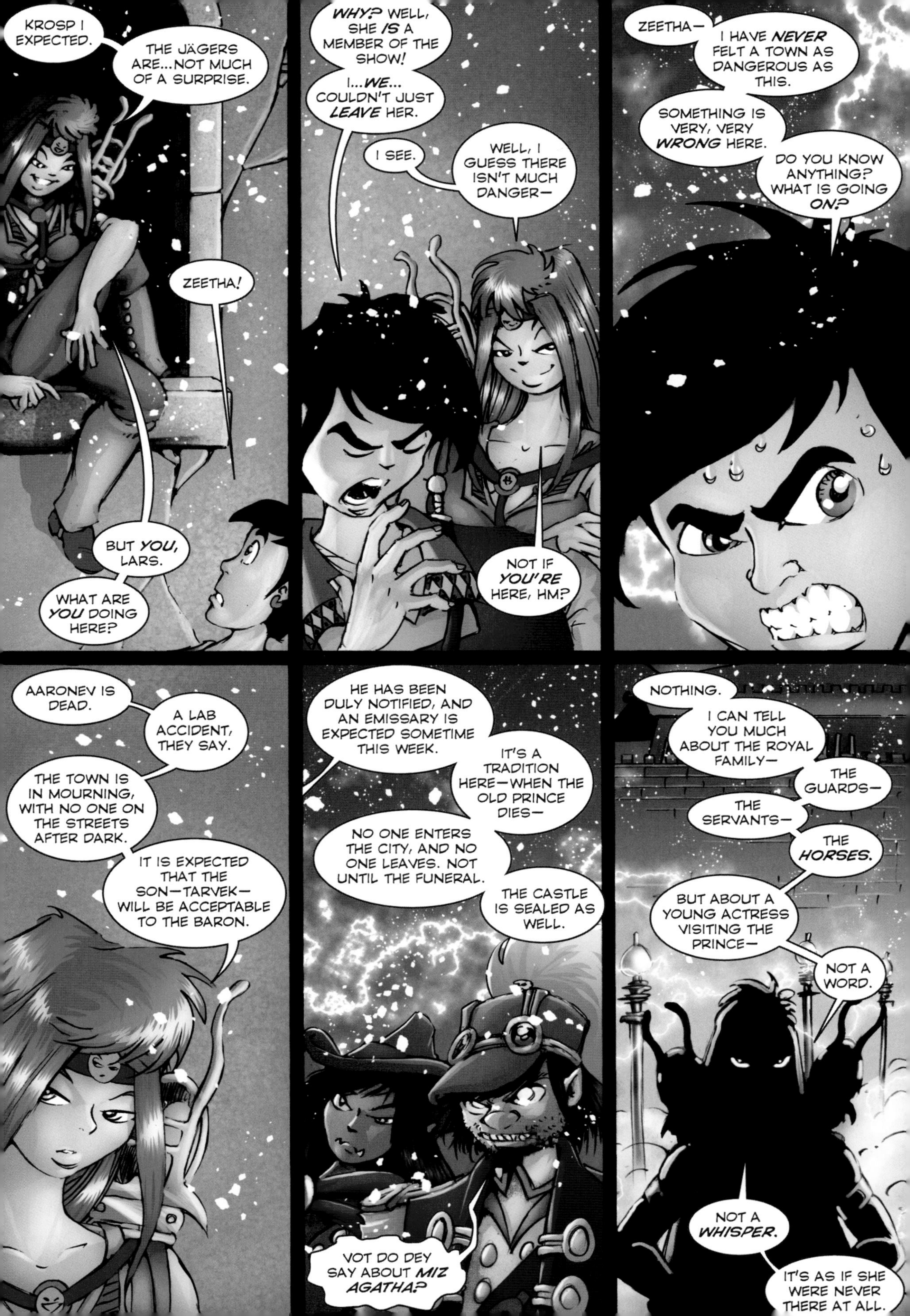
KROSP I EXPECTED.
THE JÄGERS ARE...NOT MUCH OF A SURPRISE.
ZEETHA!
BUT YOU, LARS.
WHAT ARE YOU DOING HERE?
WHY? WELL, SHE IS A MEMBER OF THE SHOW!
I...WE... COULDN'T JUST LEAVE HER.
I SEE.
WELL, I GUESS THERE ISN'T MUCH DANGER—
NOT IF YOU'RE HERE, HM?
ZEETHA—
I HAVE NEVER FELT A TOWN AS DANGEROUS AS THIS.
SOMETHING IS VERY, VERY WRONG HERE.
DO YOU KNOW ANYTHING? WHAT IS GOING ON?
AARONEV IS DEAD.
A LAB ACCIDENT, THEY SAY.
THE TOWN IS IN MOURNING, WITH NO ONE ON THE STREETS AFTER DARK.
IT IS EXPECTED THAT THE SON—TARVEK— WILL BE ACCEPTABLE TO THE BARON.
HE HAS BEEN DULY NOTIFIED, AND AN EMISSARY IS EXPECTED SOMETIME THIS WEEK.
IT'S A TRADITION HERE—WHEN THE OLD PRINCE DIES—
NO ONE ENTERS THE CITY, AND NO ONE LEAVES. NOT UNTIL THE FUNERAL.
THE CASTLE IS SEALED AS WELL.
VOT DO DEY SAY ABOUT MIZ AGATHA?
NOTHING.
I CAN TELL YOU MUCH ABOUT THE ROYAL FAMILY—
THE GUARDS—
THE SERVANTS—
THE HORSES.
BUT ABOUT A YOUNG ACTRESS VISITING THE PRINCE—
NOT A WORD.
NOT A WHISPER.
IT'S AS IF SHE WERE NEVER THERE AT ALL.

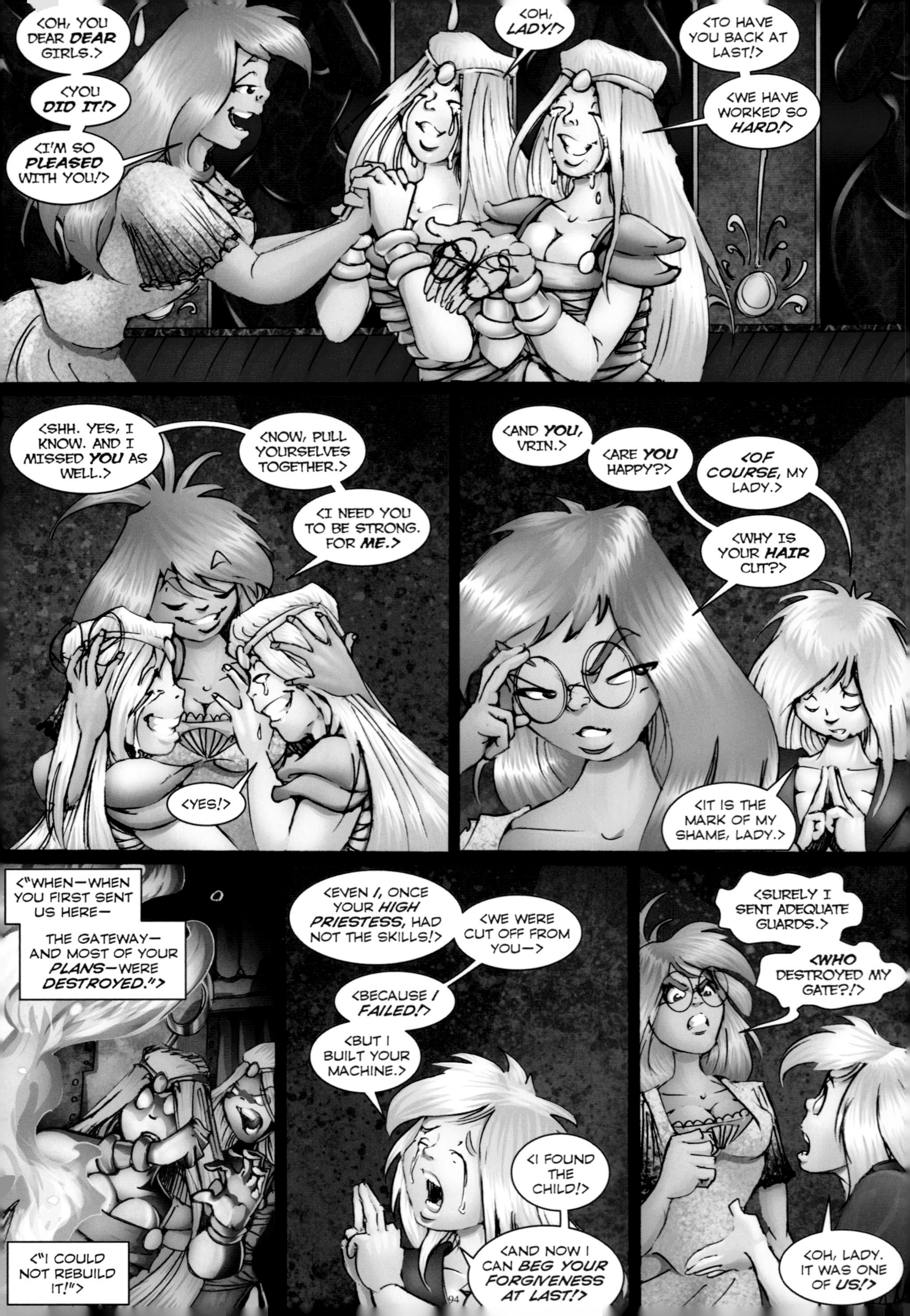

<OH, YOU DEAR DEAR GIRLS.>
<YOU DID IT!>
<I'M SO PLEASED WITH YOU!>
<OH, LADY!>
<TO HAVE YOU BACK AT LAST!>
<WE HAVE WORKED SO HARD!>
<SHH. YES, I KNOW. AND I MISSED YOU AS WELL.>
<NOW, PULL YOURSELVES TOGETHER.>
<I NEED YOU TO BE STRONG. FOR ME.>
<YES!>
<AND YOU, VRIN.>
<ARE YOU HAPPY?>
<OF COURSE, MY LADY.>
<WHY IS YOUR HAIR CUT?>
<IT IS THE MARK OF MY SHAME, LADY.>
<"WHEN—WHEN YOU FIRST SENT US HERE—
THE GATEWAY—AND MOST OF YOUR PLANS—WERE DESTROYED.">
<"I COULD NOT REBUILD IT!">
<EVEN I, ONCE YOUR HIGH PRIESTESS, HAD NOT THE SKILLS!>
<WE WERE CUT OFF FROM YOU—>
<BECAUSE I FAILED!>
<BUT I BUILT YOUR MACHINE.>
<I FOUND THE CHILD!>
<AND NOW I CAN BEG YOUR FORGIVENESS AT LAST!>
<SURELY I SENT ADEQUATE GUARDS.>
<WHO DESTROYED MY GATE?!>
<OH, LADY. IT WAS ONE OF US!>

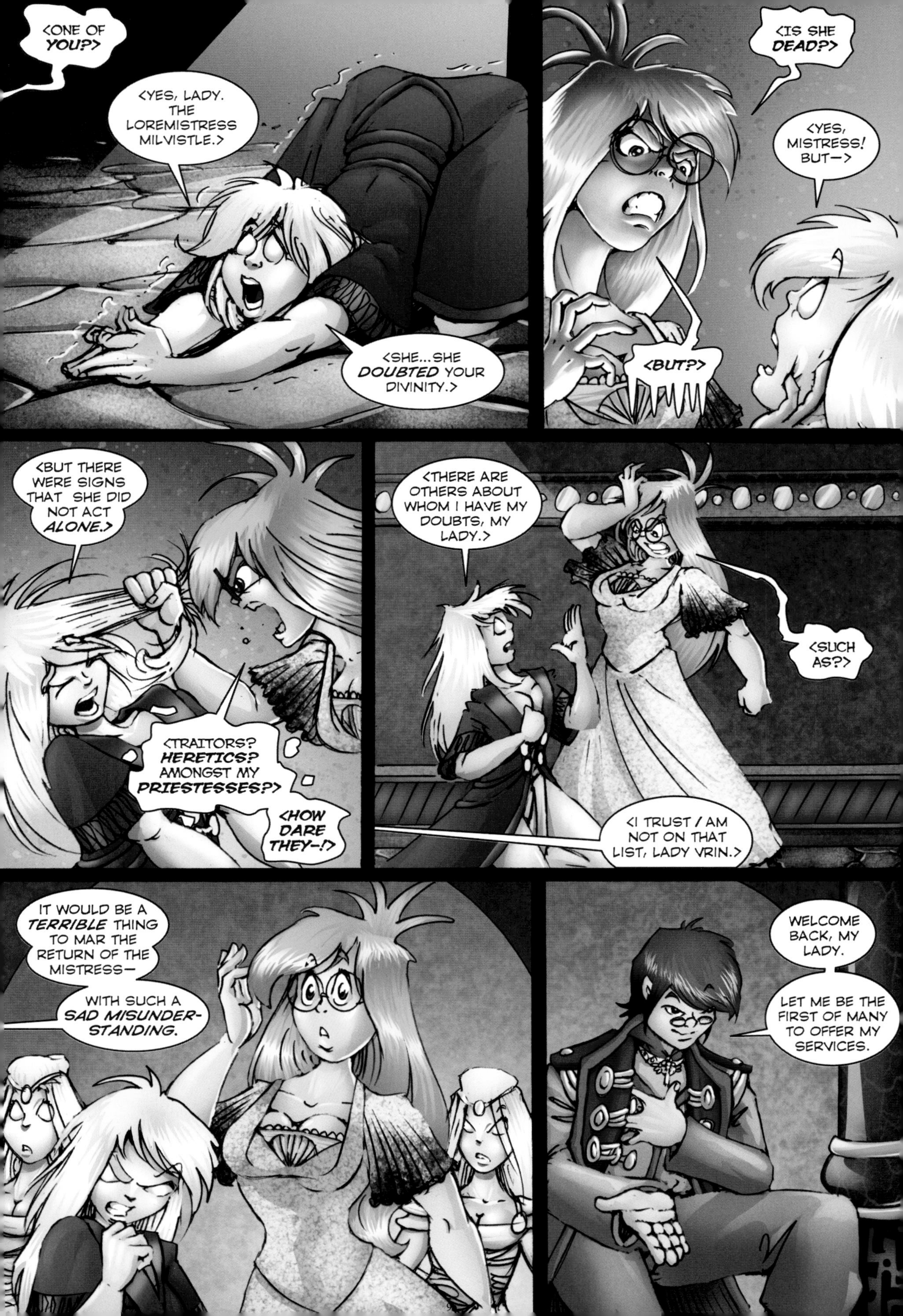
<ONE OF YOU?>
<YES, LADY. THE LOREMISTRESS MILVISTLE.>
<SHE...SHE DOUBTED YOUR DIVINITY.>
<IS SHE DEAD?>
<YES, MISTRESS! BUT—>
<BUT?>
<BUT THERE WERE SIGNS THAT SHE DID NOT ACT ALONE.>
<TRAITORS? HERETICS? AMONGST MY PRIESTESSES?>
<HOW DARE THEY–!>
<THERE ARE OTHERS ABOUT WHOM I HAVE MY DOUBTS, MY LADY.>
<SUCH AS?>
<I TRUST I AM NOT ON THAT LIST, LADY VRIN.>
IT WOULD BE A TERRIBLE THING TO MAR THE RETURN OF THE MISTRESS—
WITH SUCH A SAD MISUNDER-STANDING.
WELCOME BACK, MY LADY.
LET ME BE THE FIRST OF MANY TO OFFER MY SERVICES.

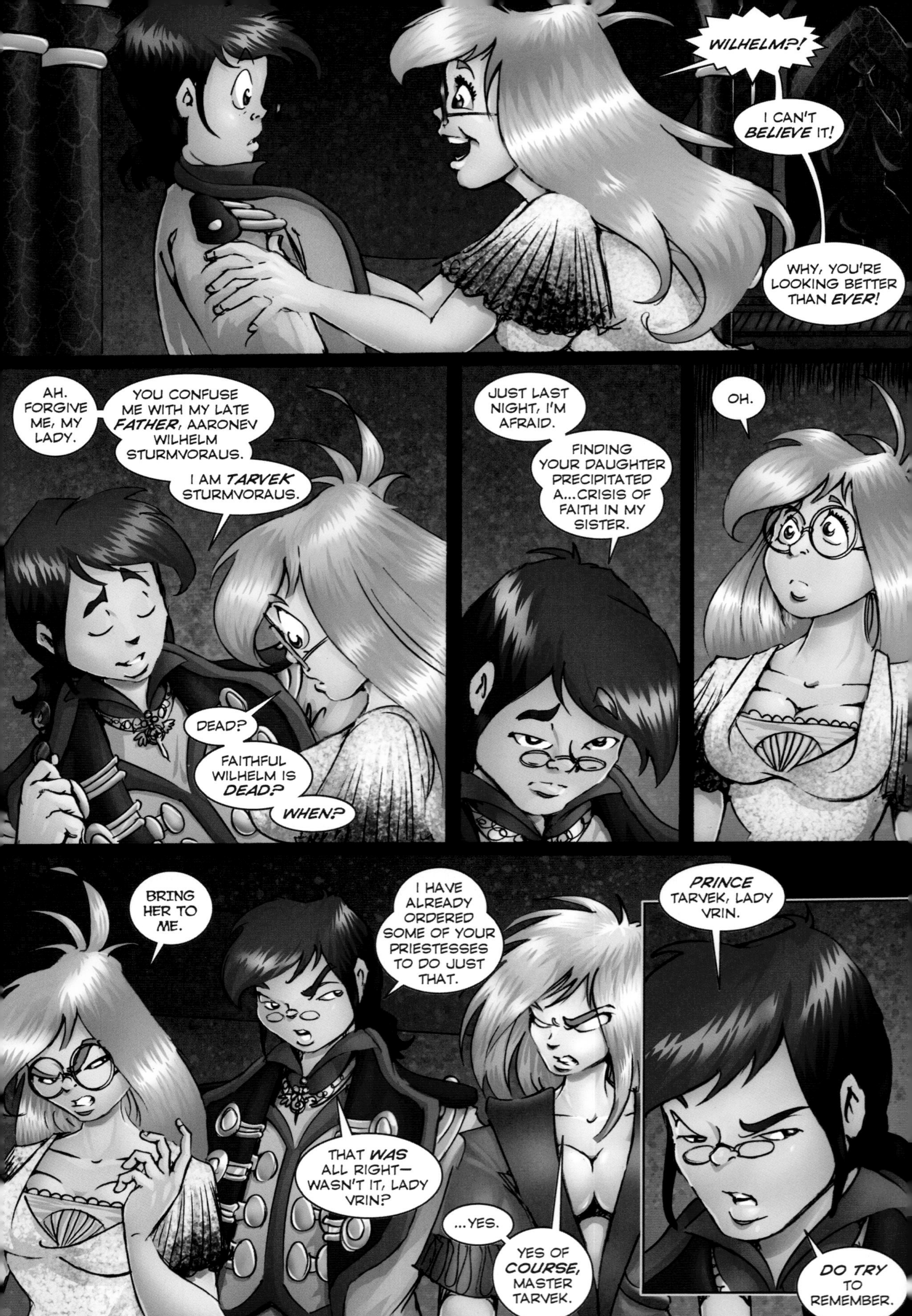
WILHELM?!
I CAN'T BELIEVE IT!
WHY, YOU'RE LOOKING BETTER THAN EVER!
AH. FORGIVE ME, MY LADY.
YOU CONFUSE ME WITH MY LATE FATHER, AARONEV WILHELM STURMVORAUS.
I AM TARVEK STURMVORAUS.
DEAD?
FAITHFUL WILHELM IS DEAD?
WHEN?
JUST LAST NIGHT, I'M AFRAID.
FINDING YOUR DAUGHTER PRECIPITATED A...CRISIS OF FAITH IN MY SISTER.
OH.
BRING HER TO ME.
I HAVE ALREADY ORDERED SOME OF YOUR PRIESTESSES TO DO JUST THAT.
THAT WAS ALL RIGHT— WASN'T IT, LADY VRIN?
...YES.
YES OF COURSE, MASTER TARVEK.
PRINCE TARVEK, LADY VRIN.
DO TRY TO REMEMBER.

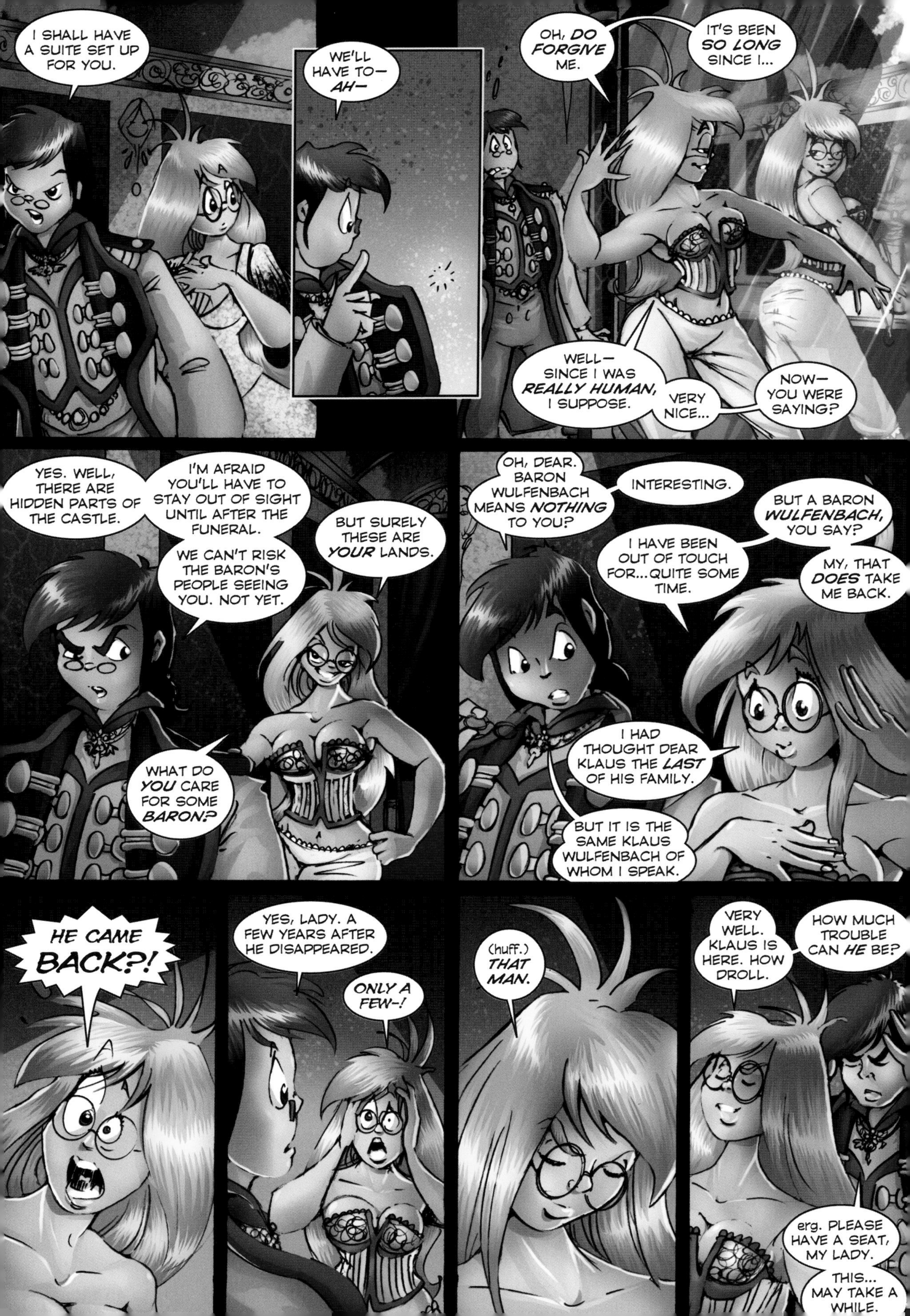

I SHALL HAVE A SUITE SET UP FOR YOU.
WE'LL HAVE TO— AH—
OH, DO FORGIVE ME.
IT'S BEEN SO LONG SINCE I...
WELL— SINCE I WAS REALLY HUMAN, I SUPPOSE.
VERY NICE...
NOW— YOU WERE SAYING?
YES. WELL, THERE ARE HIDDEN PARTS OF THE CASTLE.
I'M AFRAID YOU'LL HAVE TO STAY OUT OF SIGHT UNTIL AFTER THE FUNERAL.
WE CAN'T RISK THE BARON'S PEOPLE SEEING YOU. NOT YET.
BUT SURELY THESE ARE YOUR LANDS.
WHAT DO YOU CARE FOR SOME BARON?
OH, DEAR. BARON WULFENBACH MEANS NOTHING TO YOU?
INTERESTING.
BUT A BARON WULFENBACH, YOU SAY?
I HAVE BEEN OUT OF TOUCH FOR...QUITE SOME TIME.
MY, THAT DOES TAKE ME BACK.
I HAD THOUGHT DEAR KLAUS THE LAST OF HIS FAMILY.
BUT IT IS THE SAME KLAUS WULFENBACH OF WHOM I SPEAK.
HE CAME BACK?!
YES, LADY. A FEW YEARS AFTER HE DISAPPEARED.
ONLY A FEW-!
(huff.) THAT MAN.
VERY WELL. KLAUS IS HERE. HOW DROLL.
HOW MUCH TROUBLE CAN HE BE?
erg. PLEASE HAVE A SEAT, MY LADY.
THIS... MAY TAKE A WHILE.

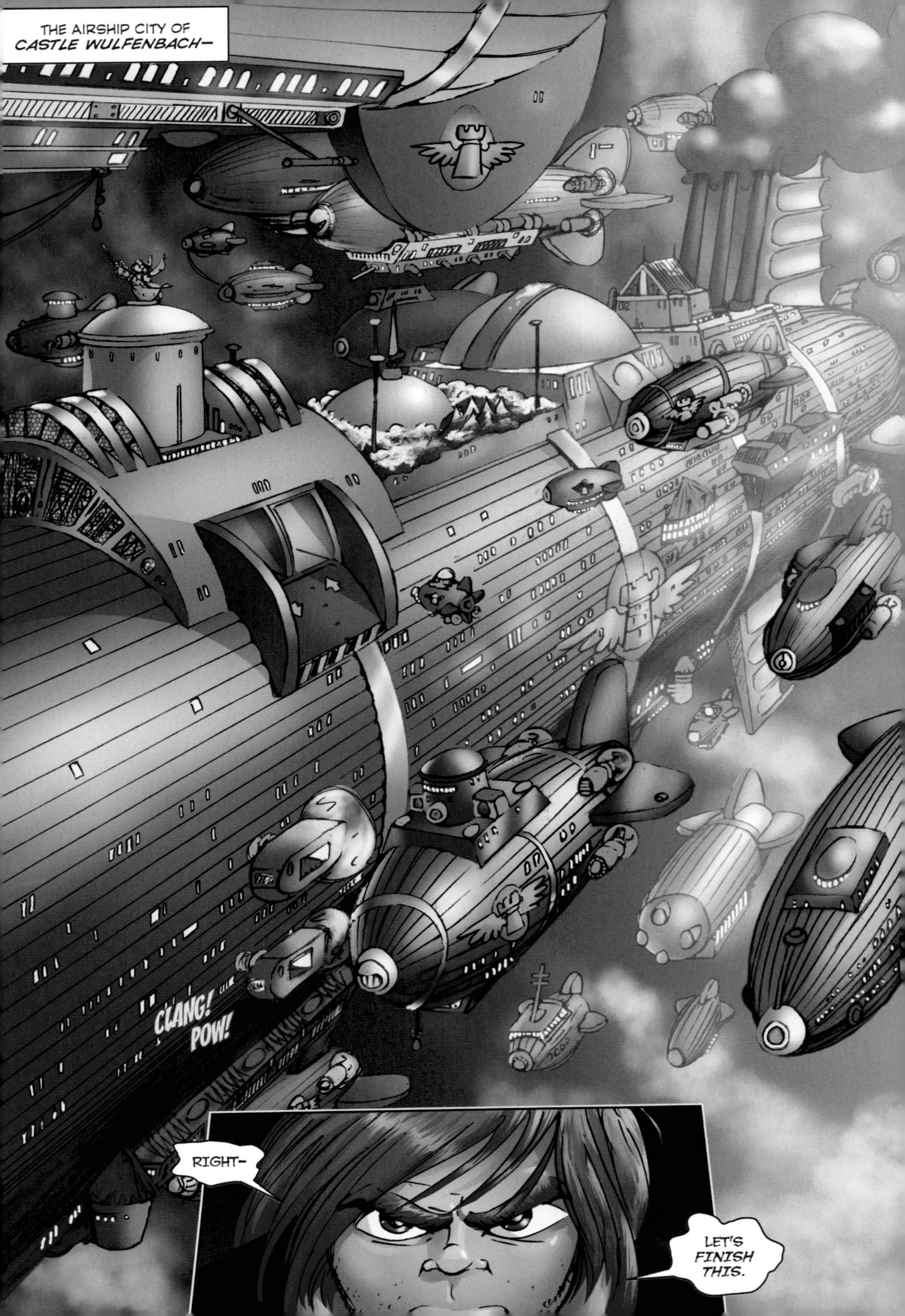
THE AIRSHIP CITY OF
CASTLE WULFENBACH—
CLANG!
POW!
RIGHT—
LET'S FINISH THIS.

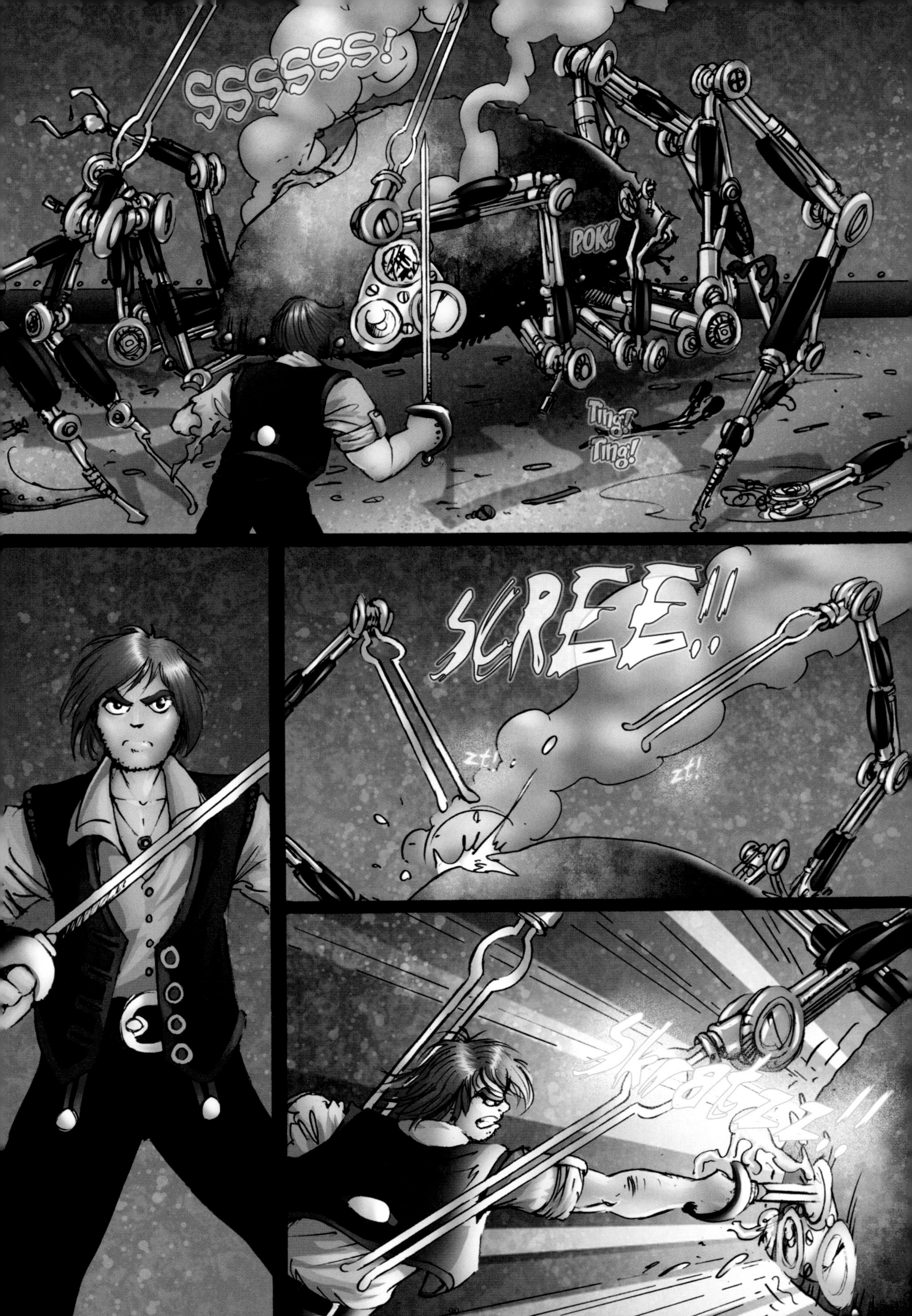
SSSSSS!
POK!
Ting!
Ting!
SCREE!!
zt!
zt!
SKRATZZ!!

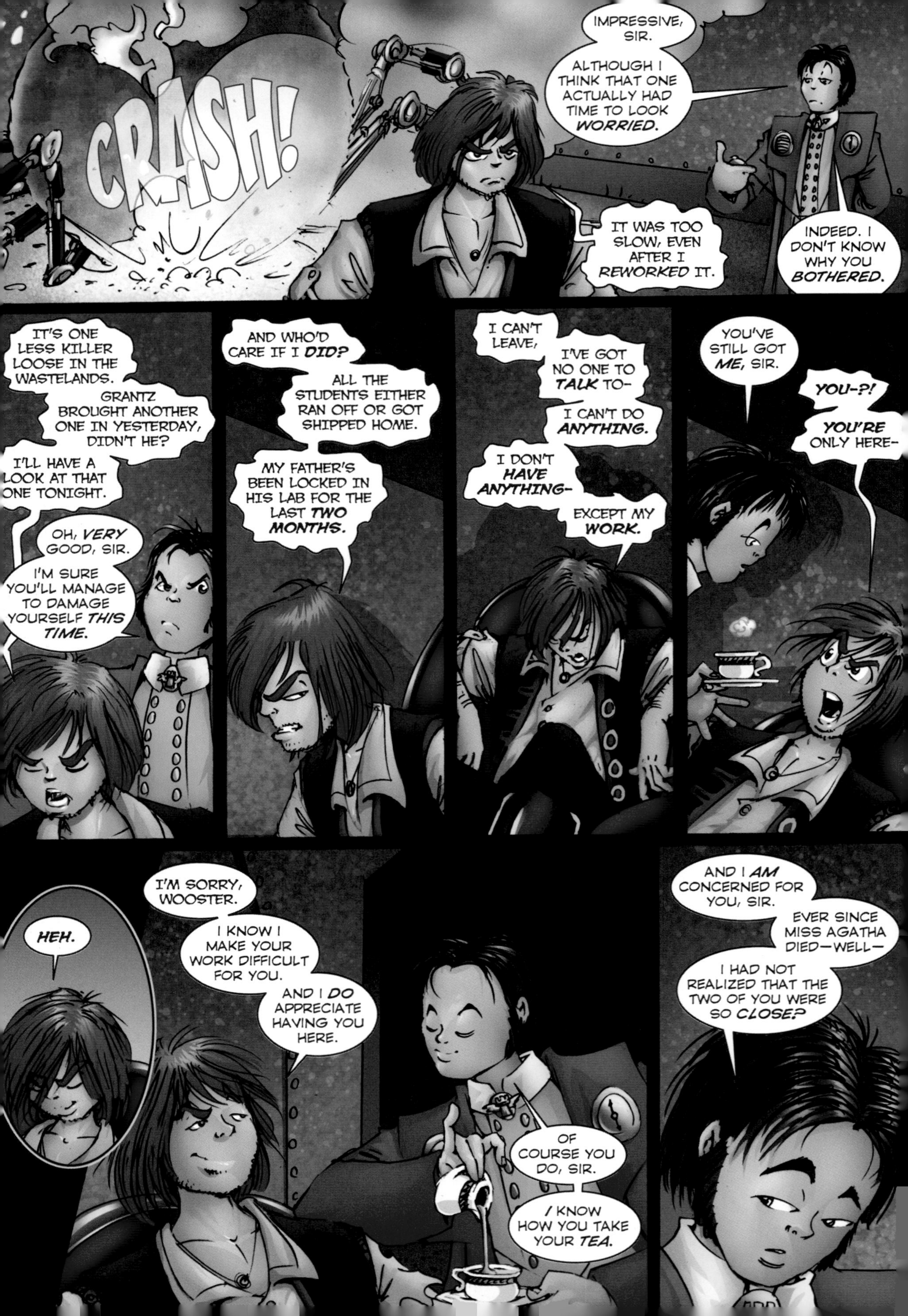
CRASH!
IMPRESSIVE, SIR.
ALTHOUGH I THINK THAT ONE ACTUALLY HAD TIME TO LOOK WORRIED.
IT WAS TOO SLOW, EVEN AFTER I REWORKED IT.
INDEED. I DON'T KNOW WHY YOU BOTHERED.
IT'S ONE LESS KILLER LOOSE IN THE WASTELANDS.
GRANTZ BROUGHT ANOTHER ONE IN YESTERDAY, DIDN'T HE?
I'LL HAVE A LOOK AT THAT ONE TONIGHT.
OH, VERY GOOD, SIR.
I'M SURE YOU'LL MANAGE TO DAMAGE YOURSELF THIS TIME.
AND WHO'D CARE IF I DID?
ALL THE STUDENTS EITHER RAN OFF OR GOT SHIPPED HOME.
MY FATHER'S BEEN LOCKED IN HIS LAB FOR THE LAST TWO MONTHS.
I CAN'T LEAVE,
I'VE GOT NO ONE TO TALK TO-
I CAN'T DO ANYTHING.
I DON'T HAVE ANYTHING-
EXCEPT MY WORK.
YOU'VE STILL GOT ME, SIR.
YOU-?!
YOU'RE ONLY HERE-
HEH.
I'M SORRY, WOOSTER.
I KNOW I MAKE YOUR WORK DIFFICULT FOR YOU.
AND I DO APPRECIATE HAVING YOU HERE.
OF COURSE YOU DO, SIR.
I KNOW HOW YOU TAKE YOUR TEA.
AND I AM CONCERNED FOR YOU, SIR.
EVER SINCE MISS AGATHA DIED—WELL—
I HAD NOT REALIZED THAT THE TWO OF YOU WERE SO CLOSE?

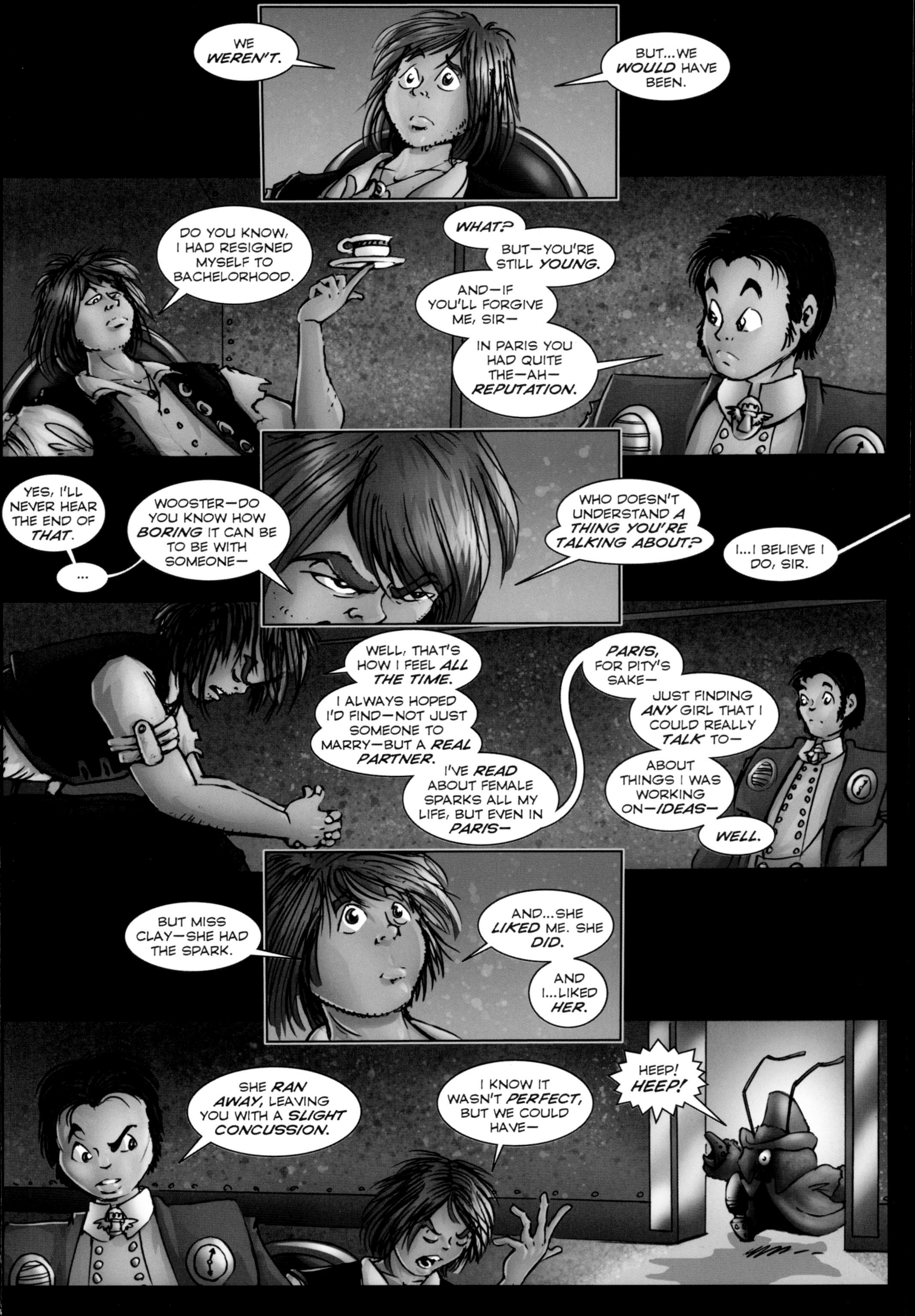
WE *WEREN'T.*
BUT...WE *WOULD* HAVE BEEN.
DO YOU KNOW, I HAD RESIGNED MYSELF TO BACHELORHOOD.
WHAT?
BUT—YOU'RE STILL *YOUNG.*
AND—IF YOU'LL FORGIVE ME, SIR—
IN PARIS YOU HAD QUITE THE—AH—*REPUTATION.*
YES, I'LL NEVER HEAR THE END OF *THAT*.
...
WOOSTER—DO YOU KNOW HOW *BORING* IT CAN BE TO BE WITH SOMEONE—
WHO DOESN'T UNDERSTAND *A THING YOU'RE TALKING ABOUT?*
I...I BELIEVE I DO, SIR.
WELL, THAT'S HOW I FEEL *ALL THE TIME.*
I ALWAYS HOPED I'D FIND—NOT JUST SOMEONE TO MARRY—BUT A *REAL PARTNER.*
I'VE *READ* ABOUT FEMALE SPARKS ALL MY LIFE, BUT EVEN IN *PARIS*—
PARIS, FOR PITY'S SAKE—
JUST FINDING *ANY* GIRL THAT I COULD REALLY *TALK* TO—
ABOUT THINGS I WAS WORKING ON—*IDEAS*—
WELL.
BUT MISS CLAY—SHE HAD THE SPARK.
AND...SHE *LIKED* ME. SHE *DID.*
AND I...LIKED *HER.*
SHE *RAN AWAY,* LEAVING YOU WITH A *SLIGHT CONCUSSION.*
I KNOW IT WASN'T *PERFECT,* BUT WE COULD HAVE—
HEEP! *HEEP!*

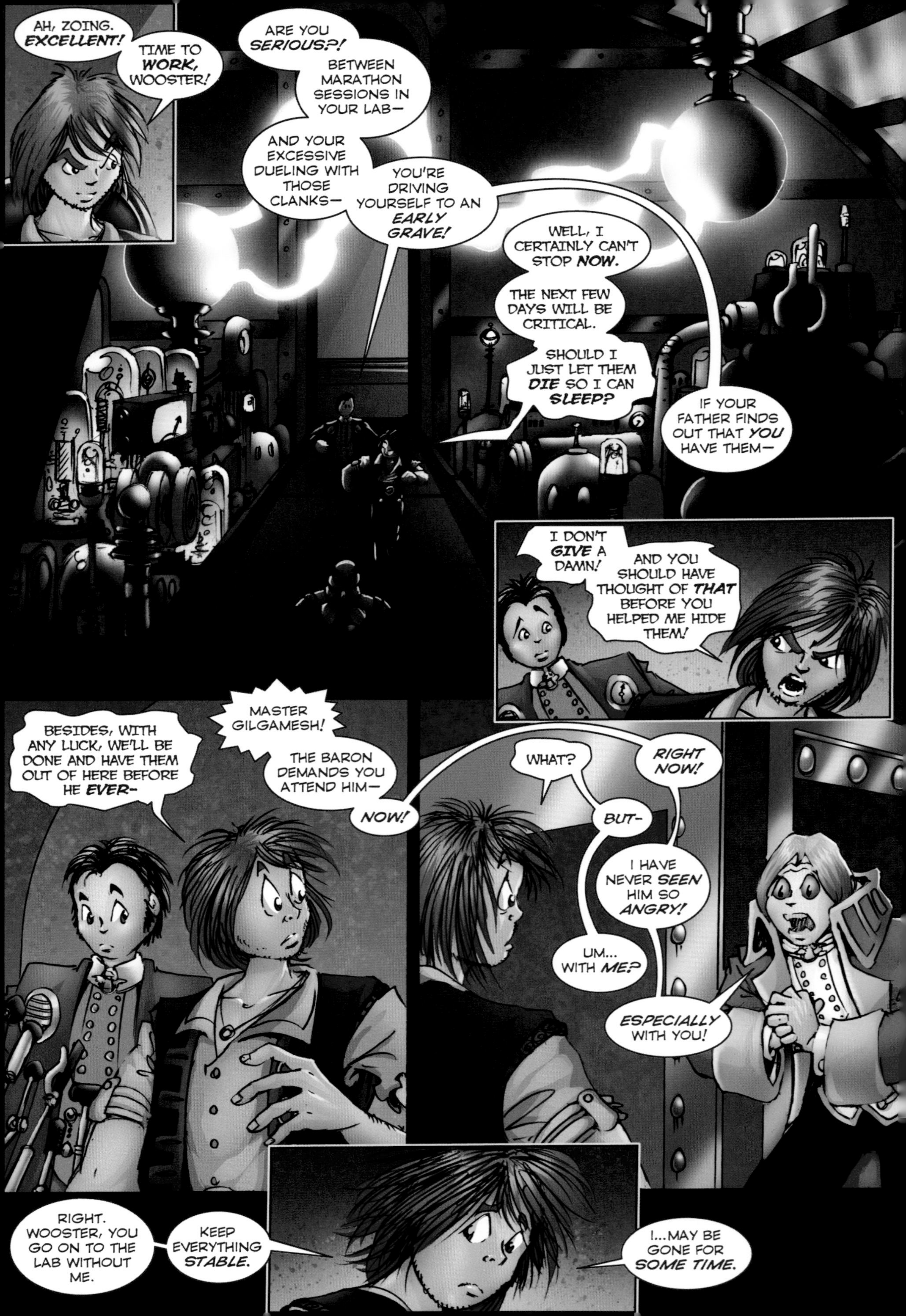
AH, ZOING. EXCELLENT!
TIME TO WORK, WOOSTER!
ARE YOU SERIOUS?!
BETWEEN MARATHON SESSIONS IN YOUR LAB—
AND YOUR EXCESSIVE DUELING WITH THOSE CLANKS—
YOU'RE DRIVING YOURSELF TO AN EARLY GRAVE!
WELL, I CERTAINLY CAN'T STOP NOW.
THE NEXT FEW DAYS WILL BE CRITICAL.
SHOULD I JUST LET THEM DIE SO I CAN SLEEP?
IF YOUR FATHER FINDS OUT THAT YOU HAVE THEM—
I DON'T GIVE A DAMN!
AND YOU SHOULD HAVE THOUGHT OF THAT BEFORE YOU HELPED ME HIDE THEM!
BESIDES, WITH ANY LUCK, WE'LL BE DONE AND HAVE THEM OUT OF HERE BEFORE HE EVER-
MASTER GILGAMESH!
THE BARON DEMANDS YOU ATTEND HIM—
NOW!
WHAT?
RIGHT NOW!
BUT-
I HAVE NEVER SEEN HIM SO ANGRY!
UM... WITH ME?
ESPECIALLY WITH YOU!
RIGHT. WOOSTER, YOU GO ON TO THE LAB WITHOUT ME.
KEEP EVERYTHING STABLE.
I...MAY BE GONE FOR SOME TIME.

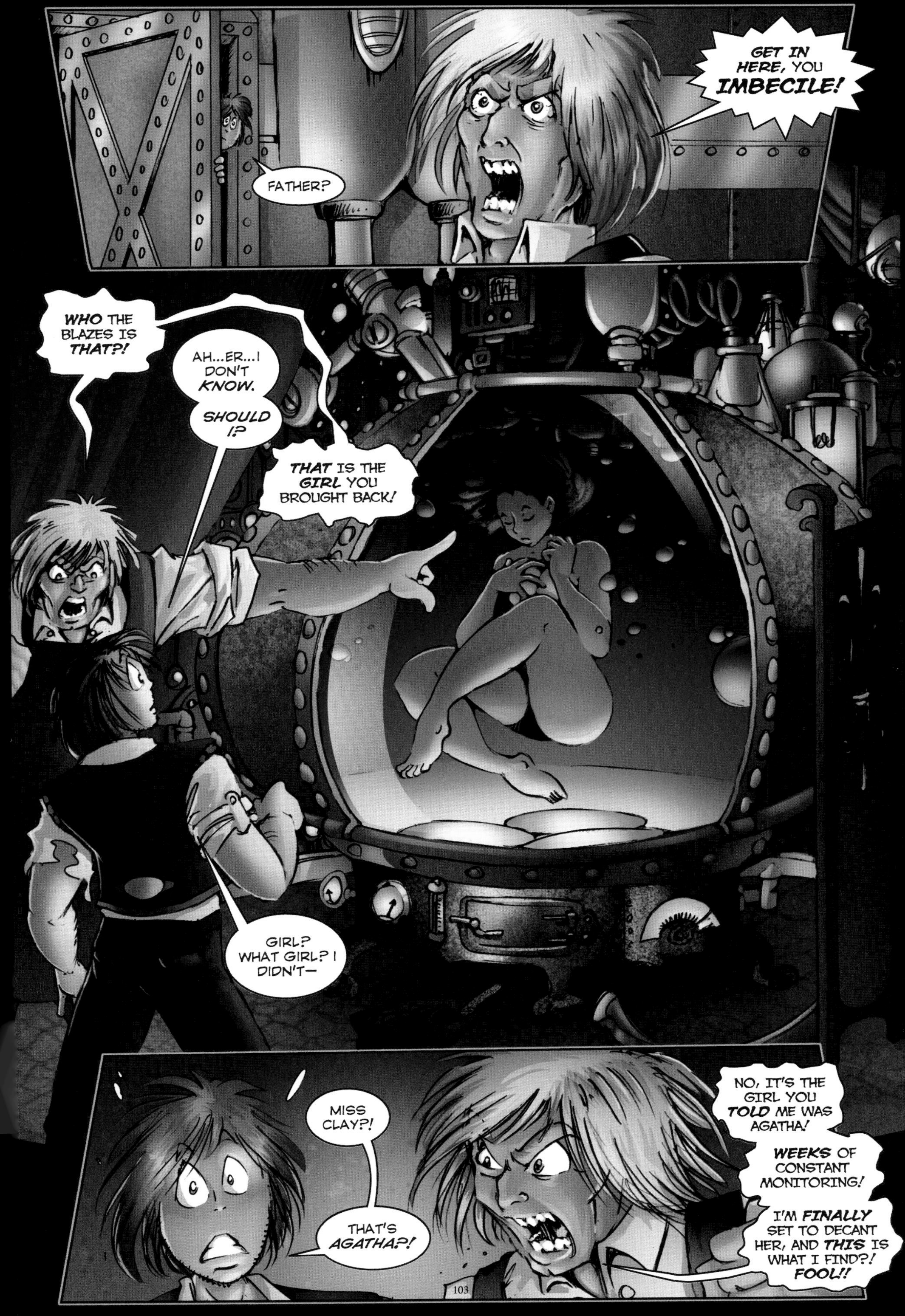
FATHER?
GET IN HERE, YOU IMBECILE!
WHO THE BLAZES IS THAT?!
AH...ER...I DON'T KNOW.
SHOULD I?
THAT IS THE GIRL YOU BROUGHT BACK!
GIRL? WHAT GIRL? I DIDN'T—
MISS CLAY?!
THAT'S AGATHA?!
NO, IT'S THE GIRL YOU TOLD ME WAS AGATHA!
WEEKS OF CONSTANT MONITORING!
I'M FINALLY SET TO DECANT HER, AND THIS IS WHAT I FIND?! FOOL!!

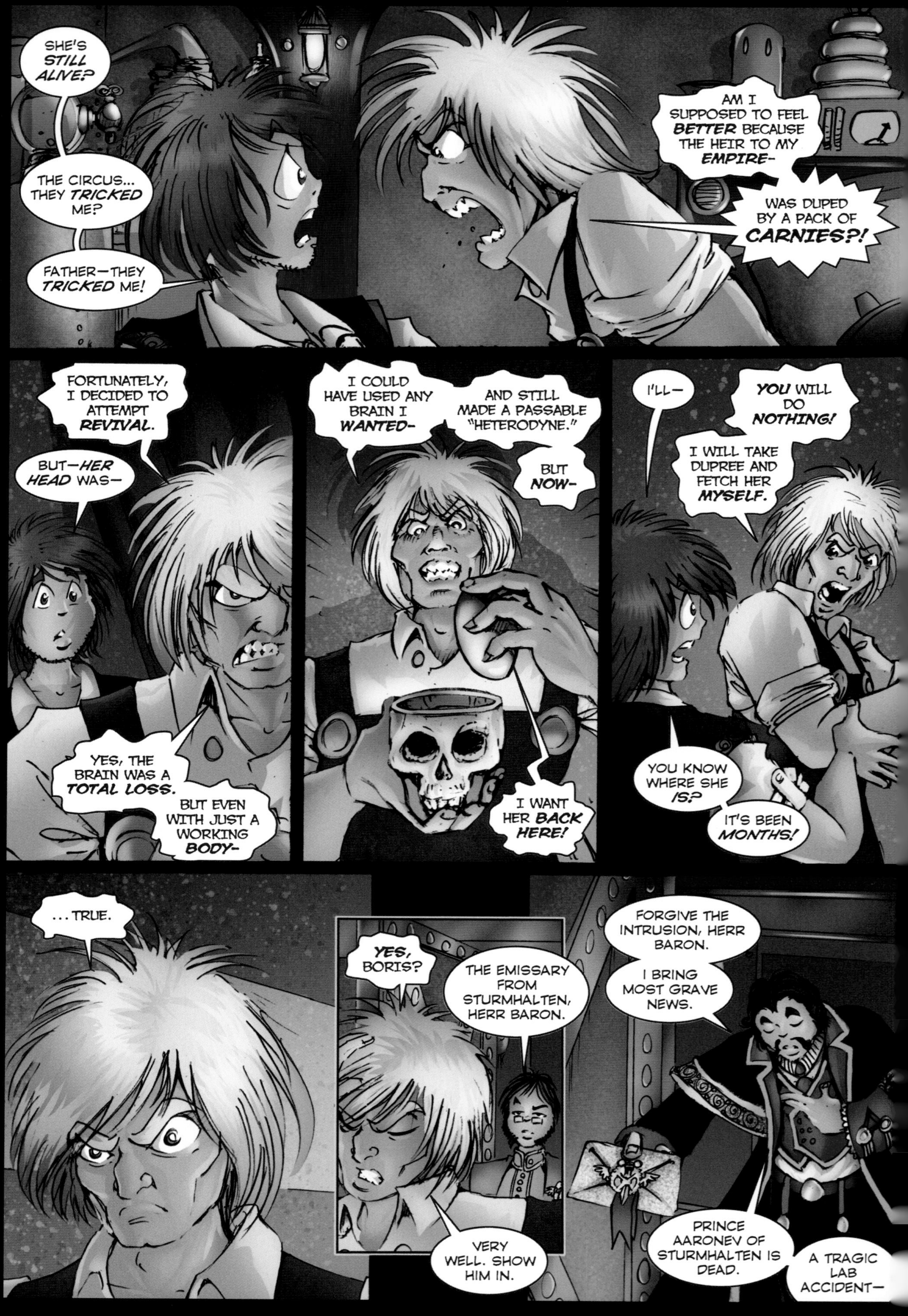
SHE'S STILL ALIVE?
THE CIRCUS... THEY TRICKED ME?
FATHER—THEY TRICKED ME!
AM I SUPPOSED TO FEEL BETTER BECAUSE THE HEIR TO MY EMPIRE-
WAS DUPED BY A PACK OF CARNIES?!
FORTUNATELY, I DECIDED TO ATTEMPT REVIVAL.
BUT—HER HEAD WAS—
YES, THE BRAIN WAS A TOTAL LOSS.
BUT EVEN WITH JUST A WORKING BODY-
I COULD HAVE USED ANY BRAIN I WANTED-
AND STILL MADE A PASSABLE "HETERODYNE."
BUT NOW-
I WANT HER BACK HERE!
I'LL—
YOU WILL DO NOTHING!
I WILL TAKE DUPREE AND FETCH HER MYSELF.
YOU KNOW WHERE SHE IS?
IT'S BEEN MONTHS!
. . . TRUE.
YES, BORIS?
THE EMISSARY FROM STURMHALTEN, HERR BARON.
VERY WELL. SHOW HIM IN.
FORGIVE THE INTRUSION, HERR BARON.
I BRING MOST GRAVE NEWS.
PRINCE AARONEV OF STURMHALTEN IS DEAD.
A TRAGIC LAB ACCIDENT—

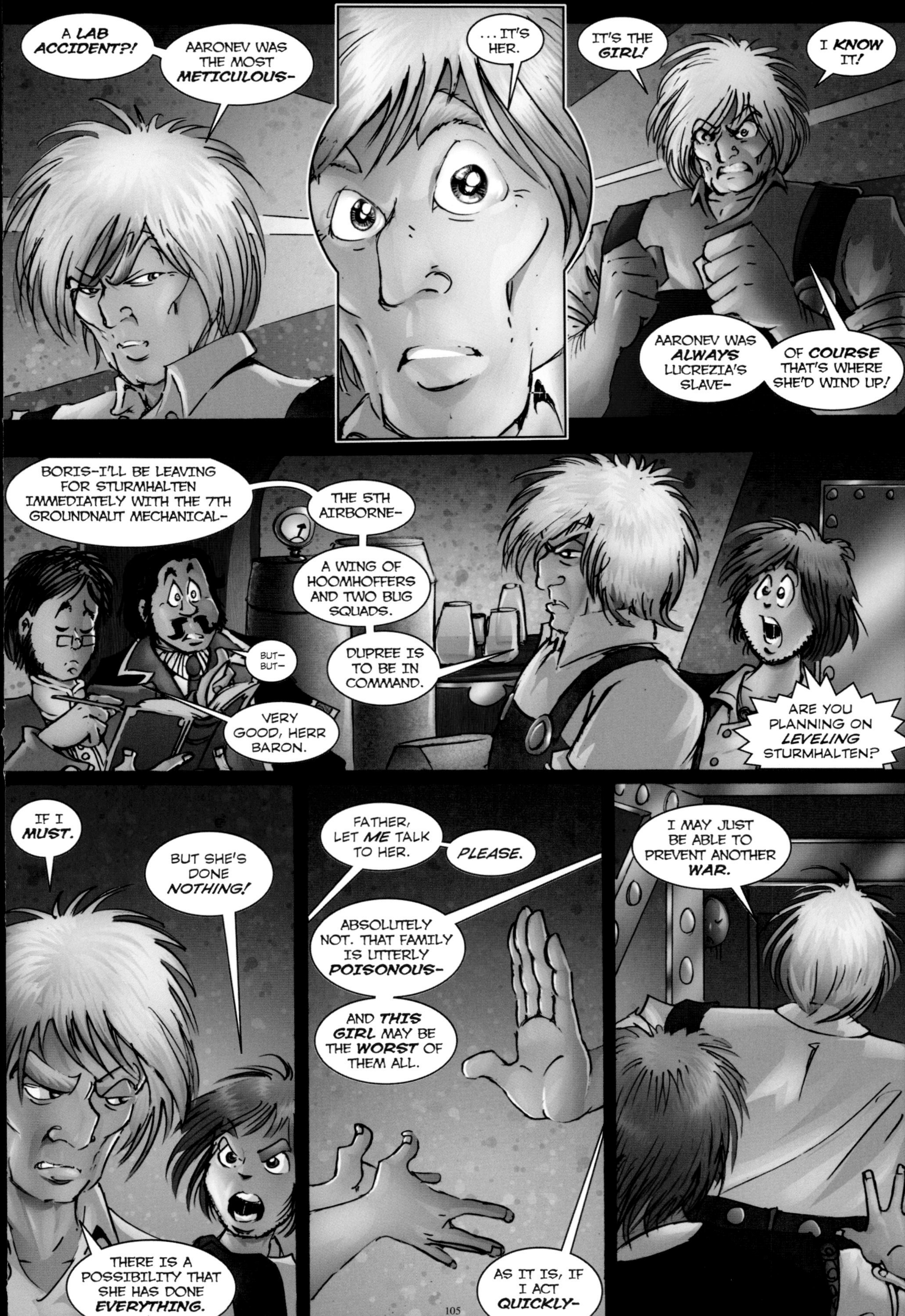
A LAB ACCIDENT?!
AARONEV WAS THE MOST METICULOUS-
...IT'S HER.
IT'S THE GIRL!
I KNOW IT!
AARONEV WAS ALWAYS LUCREZIA'S SLAVE-
OF COURSE THAT'S WHERE SHE'D WIND UP!
BORIS-I'LL BE LEAVING FOR STURMHALTEN IMMEDIATELY WITH THE 7TH GROUNDNAUT MECHANICAL-
THE 5TH AIRBORNE-
A WING OF HOOMHOFFERS AND TWO BUG SQUADS.
BUT- BUT-
DUPREE IS TO BE IN COMMAND.
VERY GOOD, HERR BARON.
ARE YOU PLANNING ON LEVELING STURMHALTEN?
IF I MUST.
BUT SHE'S DONE NOTHING!
THERE IS A POSSIBILITY THAT SHE HAS DONE EVERYTHING.
FATHER, LET ME TALK TO HER.
PLEASE.
ABSOLUTELY NOT. THAT FAMILY IS UTTERLY POISONOUS-
AND THIS GIRL MAY BE THE WORST OF THEM ALL.
AS IT IS, IF I ACT QUICKLY-
I MAY JUST BE ABLE TO PREVENT ANOTHER WAR.

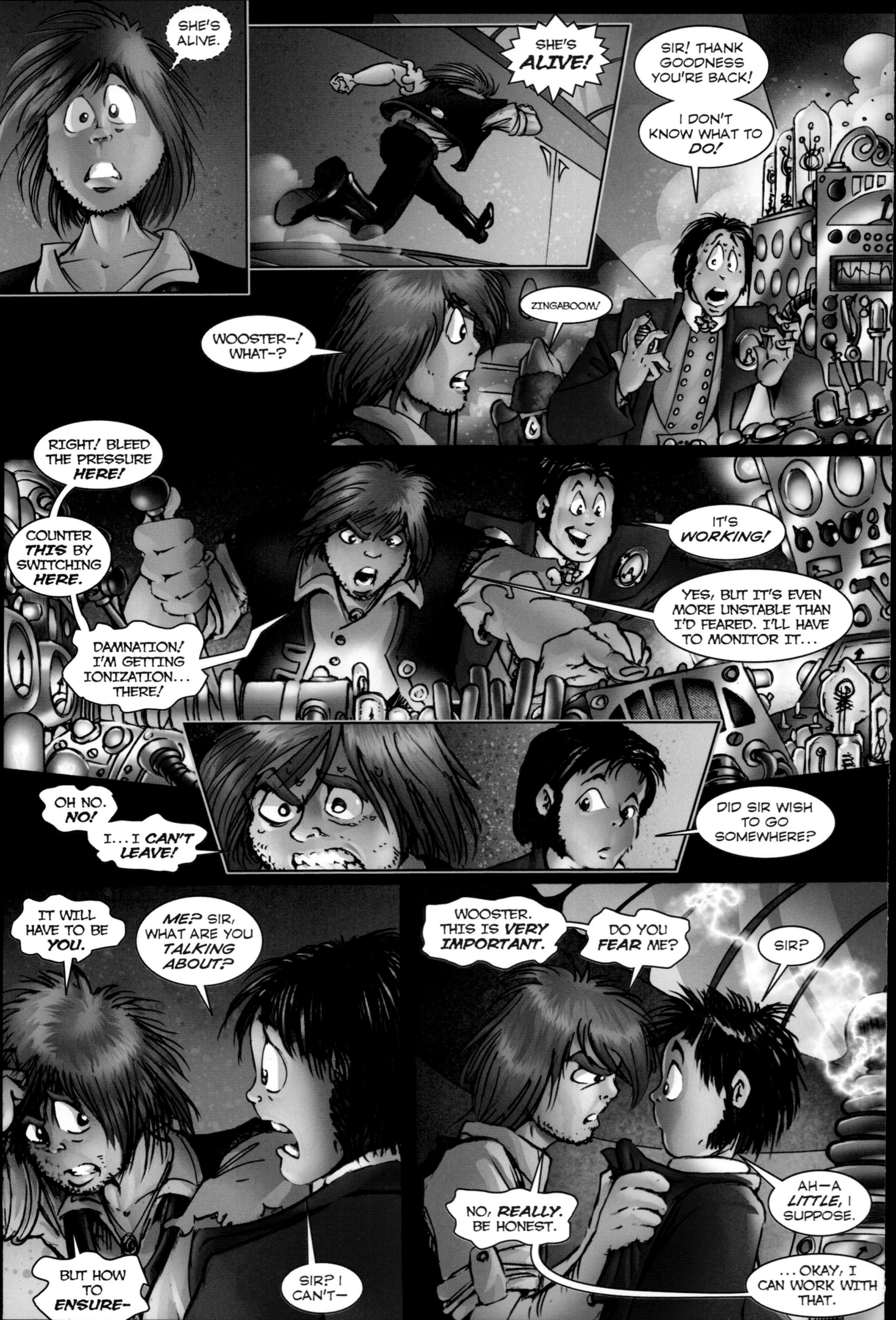
SHE'S ALIVE.
SHE'S **ALIVE!**
SIR! THANK GOODNESS YOU'RE BACK!
I DON'T KNOW WHAT TO **DO!**
WOOSTER-! WHAT-?
ZINGABOOM!
RIGHT! BLEED THE PRESSURE **HERE!**
COUNTER **THIS** BY SWITCHING **HERE.**
IT'S **WORKING!**
YES, BUT IT'S EVEN MORE UNSTABLE THAN I'D FEARED. I'LL HAVE TO MONITOR IT...
DAMNATION! I'M GETTING IONIZATION... THERE!
OH NO. **NO!**
I... I **CAN'T LEAVE!**
DID SIR WISH TO GO SOMEWHERE?
IT WILL HAVE TO BE **YOU.**
ME? SIR, WHAT ARE YOU **TALKING ABOUT?**
BUT HOW TO **ENSURE-**
SIR? I CAN'T—
WOOSTER. THIS IS **VERY IMPORTANT.**
DO YOU **FEAR** ME?
SIR?
AH—A **LITTLE,** I SUPPOSE.
NO, **REALLY.** BE HONEST.
...OKAY, I CAN WORK WITH THAT.

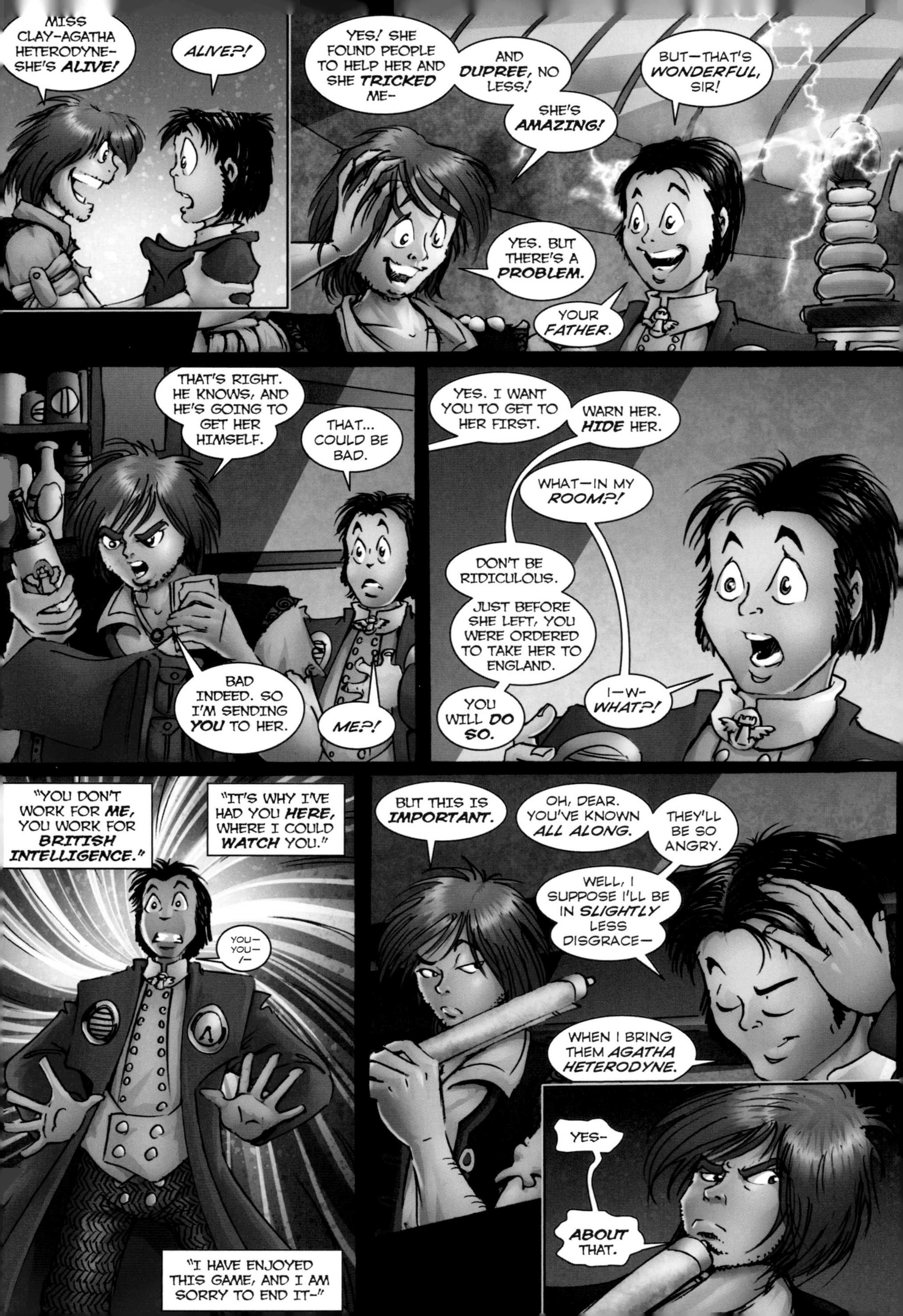
MISS CLAY—AGATHA HETERODYNE—SHE'S ALIVE!
ALIVE?!
YES! SHE FOUND PEOPLE TO HELP HER AND SHE TRICKED ME—
AND DUPREE, NO LESS!
SHE'S AMAZING!
BUT—THAT'S WONDERFUL, SIR!
YES. BUT THERE'S A PROBLEM.
YOUR FATHER.
THAT'S RIGHT. HE KNOWS, AND HE'S GOING TO GET HER HIMSELF.
THAT... COULD BE BAD.
BAD INDEED. SO I'M SENDING YOU TO HER.
ME?!
YES. I WANT YOU TO GET TO HER FIRST.
WARN HER. HIDE HER.
WHAT—IN MY ROOM?!
DON'T BE RIDICULOUS.
JUST BEFORE SHE LEFT, YOU WERE ORDERED TO TAKE HER TO ENGLAND.
YOU WILL DO SO.
I—W—WHAT?!
"YOU DON'T WORK FOR ME, YOU WORK FOR BRITISH INTELLIGENCE."
"IT'S WHY I'VE HAD YOU HERE, WHERE I COULD WATCH YOU."
YOU—YOU—I—
"I HAVE ENJOYED THIS GAME, AND I AM SORRY TO END IT—"
BUT THIS IS IMPORTANT.
OH, DEAR. YOU'VE KNOWN ALL ALONG.
THEY'LL BE SO ANGRY.
WELL, I SUPPOSE I'LL BE IN SLIGHTLY LESS DISGRACE—
WHEN I BRING THEM AGATHA HETERODYNE.
YES—
ABOUT THAT.

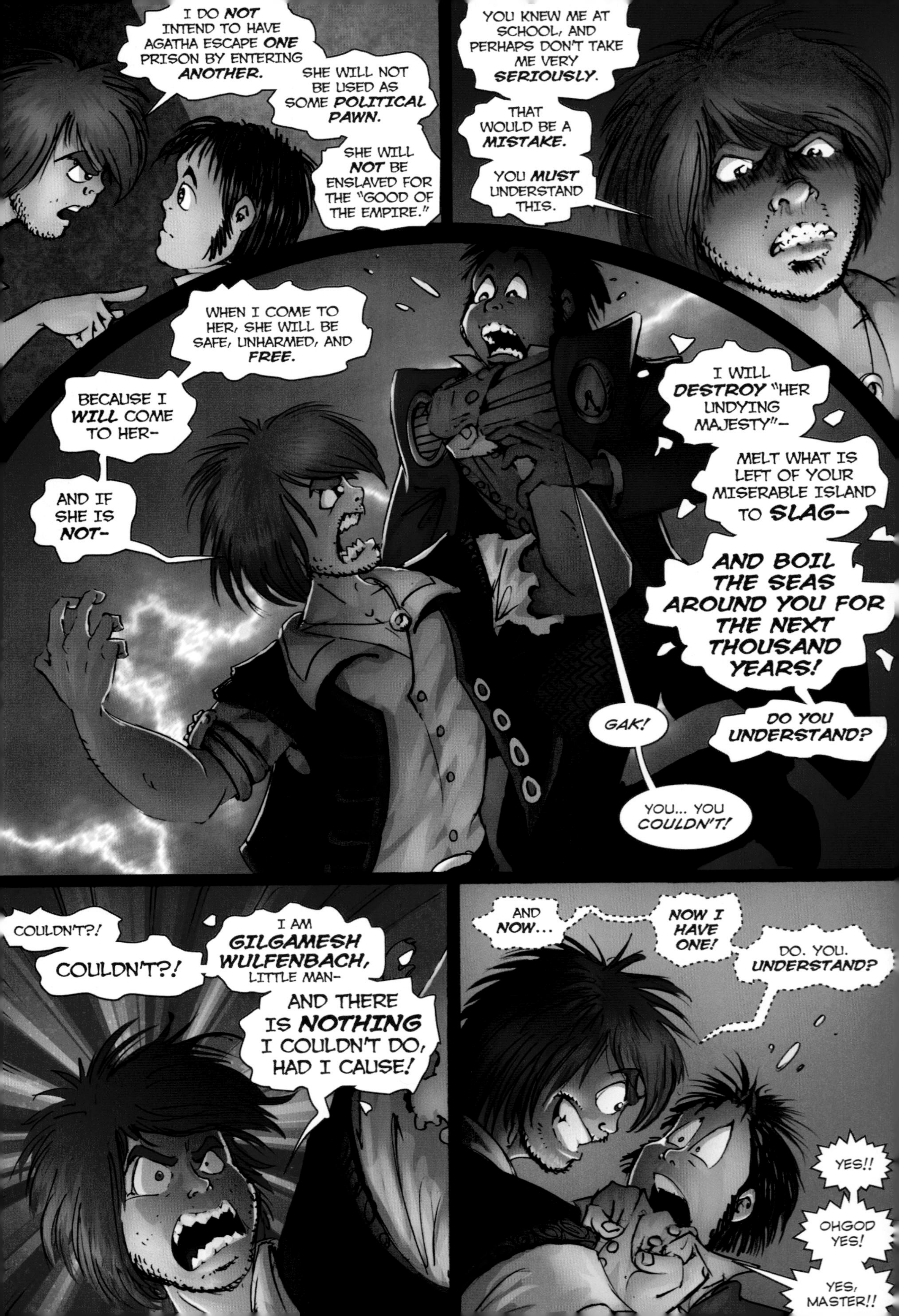
I DO NOT INTEND TO HAVE AGATHA ESCAPE ONE PRISON BY ENTERING ANOTHER.
SHE WILL NOT BE USED AS SOME POLITICAL PAWN.
SHE WILL NOT BE ENSLAVED FOR THE "GOOD OF THE EMPIRE."
YOU KNEW ME AT SCHOOL, AND PERHAPS DON'T TAKE ME VERY SERIOUSLY.
THAT WOULD BE A MISTAKE.
YOU MUST UNDERSTAND THIS.
WHEN I COME TO HER, SHE WILL BE SAFE, UNHARMED, AND FREE.
BECAUSE I WILL COME TO HER-
AND IF SHE IS NOT-
I WILL DESTROY "HER UNDYING MAJESTY"-
MELT WHAT IS LEFT OF YOUR MISERABLE ISLAND TO SLAG-
AND BOIL THE SEAS AROUND YOU FOR THE NEXT THOUSAND YEARS!
DO YOU UNDERSTAND?
GAK!
YOU... YOU COULDN'T!
COULDN'T?!
COULDN'T?!
I AM GILGAMESH WULFENBACH, LITTLE MAN-
AND THERE IS NOTHING I COULDN'T DO, HAD I CAUSE!
AND NOW...
NOW I HAVE ONE!
DO. YOU. UNDERSTAND?
YES!!
OHGOD YES!
YES, MASTER!!

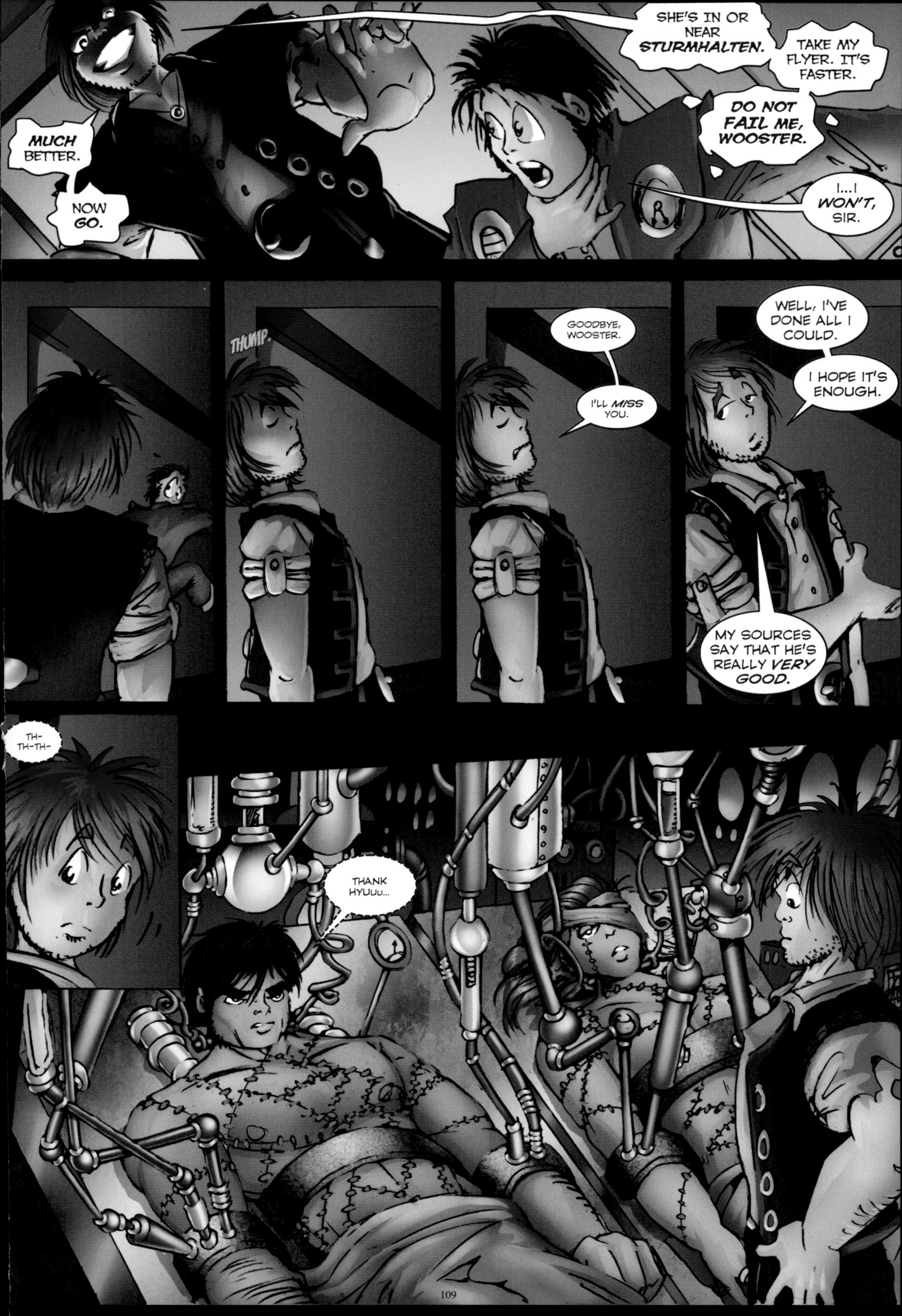
SHE'S IN OR NEAR STURMHALTEN.
TAKE MY FLYER. IT'S FASTER.
DO NOT FAIL ME, WOOSTER.
MUCH BETTER.
NOW GO.
I...I WON'T, SIR.
THUMP.
GOODBYE, WOOSTER.
I'LL MISS YOU.
WELL, I'VE DONE ALL I COULD.
I HOPE IT'S ENOUGH.
MY SOURCES SAY THAT HE'S REALLY VERY GOOD.
TH- TH-TH-
THANK HYUUU...

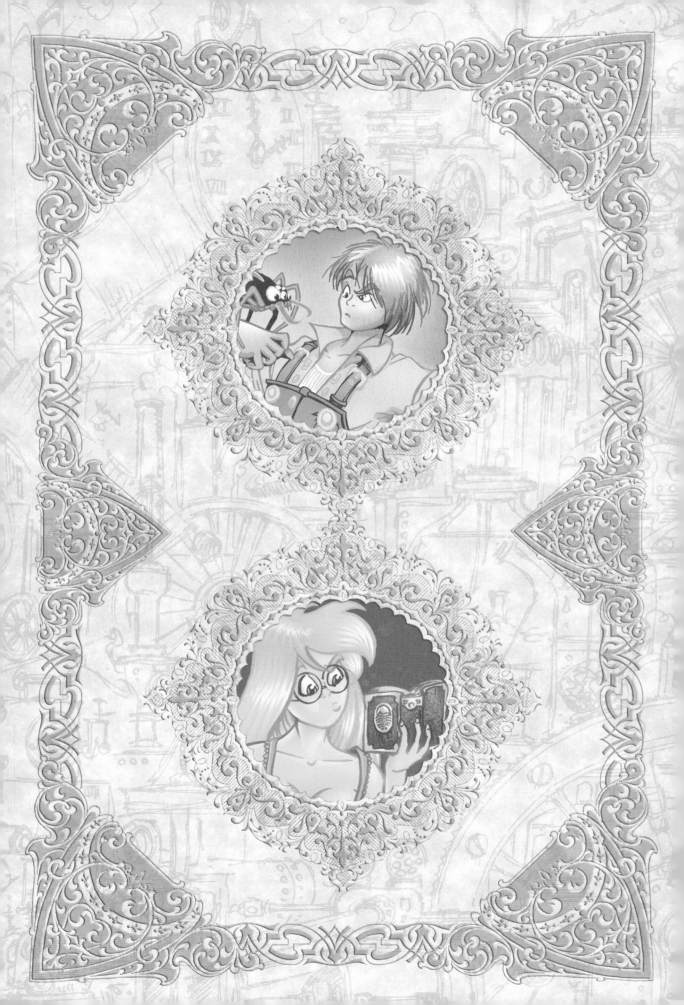

TO BE CONTINUED IN: GIRL GENIUS® Book SIX:

AGATHA HETERODYNE & THE GOLDEN TRILOBITE

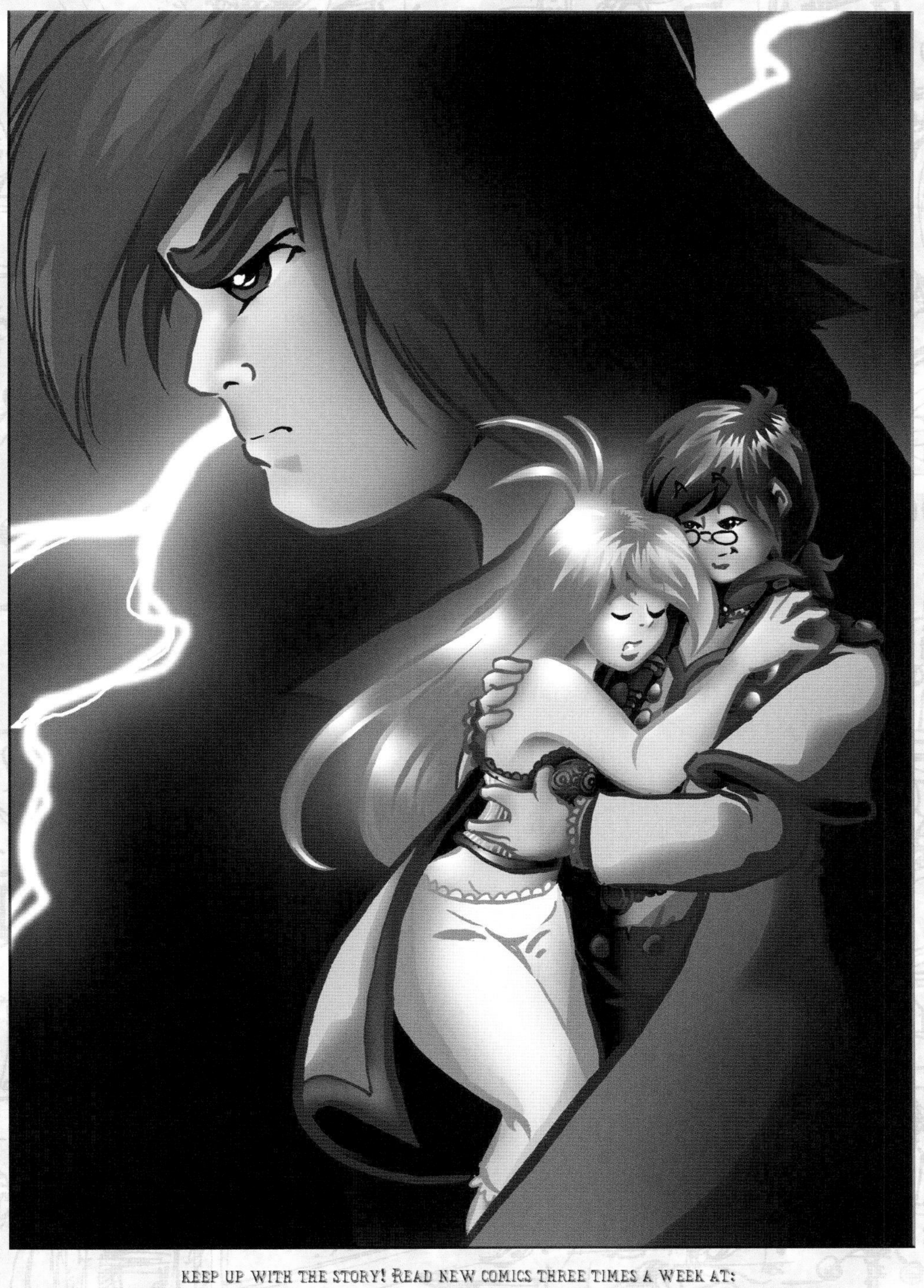

KEEP UP WITH THE STORY! READ NEW COMICS THREE TIMES A WEEK AT:

WWW.GIRLGENIUS.NET